D1488696

Leonard Nelson.

1926

SOCRATIC METHOD
AND
CRITICAL PHILOSOPHY

Selected Essays

BY

LEONARD NELSON

TRANSLATED BY THOMAS K. BROWN III

FOREWORD BY BRAND BLANSHARD

INTRODUCTION BY JULIUS KRAFT

NEW YORK
DOVER PUBLICATIONS, INC.

This Dover edition, first published in 1965, is an unabridged and unaltered republication of the work first published by Yale University Press in 1949.

This edition is published by special arrangement with The Leonard Nelson Foundation, Inc.

Library of Congress Catalog Card Number: 65-20486

Manufactured in the United States of America

Dover Publications, Inc.
180 Varick Street
New York, N. Y. 10014

CONTENTS

ACKNOWLEDGMENTS

"The Socratic Method" was originally translated by Hugh Jedell and "The World-View of Ethics and Religion" by W. Lansdell. Thomas K. Brown III has revised both translations and brought their terminology and style into harmony with the other essays. These and the other essays have been edited by Marion Kuhn. L. H. Grunebaum planned the translation of this collection of essays and is responsible for the addition of the starred footnotes and of the excerpts from Plato's *Theætetus*.

FOREWORD

LEONARD NELSON, that remarkable German philosopher with the the very English name, is practically unknown in this country, even to the philosophic community. I knew nothing about him myself until one of his former pupils, Dr. Julius Kraft, sent me some of the essays contained in this book and asked whether I thought they merited publication. I had no hesitation in saying that they did. Leonard Nelson should be better known. He was an arresting personality; by all accounts he was a strikingly original teacher; and he was a philosopher whose words have a special importance in our own time.

As for Nelson personally, what impresses one first is the variety of achievements he crowded into a life that was far too short. He died at forty-five, leaving behind him a three-volume work on the foundations of ethics and politics; substantial books on jurisprudence and on the theory of knowledge; a treatise, still unpublished, on the history of metaphysics; and a great many essays on mathematics, epistemology, and educational theory. So far he sounds like many another sedulous German professor. But he was more than that. He was moulded of the stuff of which reformers are made. In accordance with the principles of an exacting ethics, he lived with Spartan simplicity and Stoic self-discipline. He practiced as well as preached new methods of teaching, and in order to carry out more freely his educational and social principles, he founded the Walkemühle School near Cassel. One of its chief aims was to train its pupils in enlightened and liberal citizenship. Not unnaturally it fell under the ban of Hitler and had to be transferred first to Denmark and later to England.

Nelson was an ardent internationalist, an outspoken opponent of power politics, and an eloquent advocate of the sort of law, domestic and international, that is based on a common reason. On July 31, 1914, the day before the outbreak of the First World War, he ended his long cycle of lectures on the philosophy of politics with a plan and a plea for a League of Nations. "The glory of a nation," he said, "like that of an individual, does not consist in things which one can grasp with one's hands or of which one can deprive another, but consists only in the innate spirit of justice." The lecture could not at the time appear in print, but Nelson did succeed in publishing in the midst of the war a fearless book on *Jurisprudence without Justice*, in which he indicted all legal systems that contribute to the cult of power. Though he did not live into the Hitler regime, his influence definitely did. One of his students writes: "All Nelson's pupils who remained in Germany were engaged, as long as they were not imprisoned, in underground or other illegal work against Nazism." His courage as well as his philosophy left its mark.

Secondly, Nelson developed in his own classrooms a method of teaching philosophy that seems to have been extraordinarily effective. He believed it to be derived from the nature of the subject itself. What is philosophy essentially? It is not a body of historical fact to be transmitted, nor of established scientific law to be painstakingly mastered. It is a special kind of mental activity directed toward a special end. If we can agree about this end, we can perhaps also agree about the activity, and about the best means by which one mind may induce it in others. Leonard Nelson belonged to the Kantian tradition and believed that the business of philosophy was criticism, the bringing to light of the fundamental presuppositions of our thinking, the ultimate standards—logical, ethical, esthetic—that are implicit in our ordinary judgments. Nobody can tell us from the outside what these presuppositions are, since nobody but ourselves can know what we really think; we must see these things for ourselves; we must arrive at them through a process of self-examination and self-criticism. The function of the teacher is to help this process forward.

Now this is precisely the conception of Socrates. Philosophy in his hands *was* self-examination. Since the unexamined life seemed to him hardly worth living, he set himself up as the midwife to men's minds, helping them to bring to birth in clear understanding the ideas that would make possible for them an ordered and reasonable life. What do we really mean when we use the tremendous little words, "good," "right," "cause," "true," "I," "free," "know"? Philosophy, for Leonard Nelson, meant the arduous process of getting clear about such things; and in the Socratic method he found a technique for achieving such clarity which he believed had never been surpassed. To the defense of this belief he devotes what is perhaps the most interesting essay in this volume.

But there is a still more important reason why Nelson merits a hearing: he has something to say which, at the present time, has peculiar force and pertinence. One of the most striking characteristics of our time on the intellectual side is its loss of confidence in reason. Psychological analysts tell us that our subterranean minds are nests of irrational complexes constantly pulling us unawares out of the rational course; indeed, the desire to be rational is itself one of these complexes and not the least dangerous of them. Analysts in logic tell us that the only certainties left to us are tautologies in which we make clear to ourselves our own meanings; certainty about anything in nature—rational knowledge of anything outside our own meanings—is set down as illusion. Analysts of ethical judgment tell us that there are no rational insights in ethics, for an ethical judgment is only the expression of feeling. Analysts in the social sciences remind us that in view of the variety of human mores, to speak any longer of *the* reasonable action or of a single standard of rightness is the mark of provincialism.

Leonard Nelson was not unaware of these tendencies; they had all begun to show themselves before he laid down his pen. But he would have none of them. His attitude toward the nominalists and relativists was a little like that of Kant toward Hume: he felt sure they were mistaken and set himself, as we have seen, to elicit from experience and place in a clear light those principles that were beyond rational questioning. For him these principles were incapable of proof in the sense of being derived from anything else; they were not tautologies; they were not empirical generalizations; they were not postulates, accepted merely because experience confirmed them. They were synthetic a priori insights. If Nelson had been writing today, he would have used different and more guarded language, and it is not unlikely that some of the principles he gives as examples of such insight would need to be re-examined. Nor is the reader always happy, even where he agrees with Nelson, about the involved way in which simple things are sometimes said. But in urging that a self-critical reason can lay hold of principles that are more than tautologies, principles that yield important truth about values and about the nature of things, I believe that Nelson was on the right road. That road should be further explored. In view of the developments since his death, its exploration is needed all the more urgently. It is to be hoped that these essays will convey some sense of the man and his thought to readers in lands not his own, and perhaps prompt some other mind to continue an inquiry so ably begun and so prematurely closed.

BRAND BLANSHARD

Yale University,
December 1, 1948.

INTRODUCTION

THIS first American publication of selected philosophical essays by Leonard Nelson (1882–1927) marks the beginning of a comprehensive effort to bring to the attention of the English-speaking world the work of a creative German philosopher which, up to now, has been generally unknown, and the significance of which is almost entirely unrecognized. This lack of international attention is all the more noteworthy since Nelson's philosophical work is characterized by a rare clarity and timeliness, and his life, which was devoted to thinking and teaching and to the educational and political renewal of human civilization, was the life of a citizen of the world.

The breadth and quality of Nelson's writing can be measured by the fact that it embraces almost all branches of philosophy, and that in both its critical and its constructive aspects it is concerned with problems of the first order. Nelson did not hesitate to challenge the entire structure of such epochal doctrines as Cohen's and Natorp's neo-Kantianism, Mach's empiricism, and Spengler's historical mysticism; he developed a fully documented and penetratingly executed reinterpretation of the history of metaphysics since Hume; and he accomplished the imposing task of erecting a complete system of ethics together with its epistemological foundation. In like manner Nelson's practical work was concerned with the root difficulties of social, political, and educational conditions, never with their surface problems. As a philosophical teacher Nelson demanded of his students the keenest clarity of understanding, and himself adhered to unique standards of lucidity in instruction, making him a modern Socratean [1] in deed and not merely in word. It was characteristic of him not only inside, but outside the university as well, that he translated his teachings into action. Not satisfied merely with contemplation and writing, with lecturing and discussing in the old and distinguished University of Göttingen, he founded his own Philosophical-Political Academy (at Melsungen near Cassel) for the education of responsible political leaders. [2]

1. Nelson's lecture, "The Socratic Method" (see this volume, p. 1), gives a vivid account of the method of philosophical exercises practiced by him at the University of Göttingen for eighteen years (1909–27).
2. A future political history of Germany will have to record how, out of this Academy and the youth groups connected with it, came a number of heroic men and women who fought against the National Socialist regime and who, since the

Whatever may be the lasting value of Nelson's theoretical and practical work, its scope and level entitled it to serious consideration. How is it that his work, and especially his philosophical writings, failed to attract more general attention? The answer is very simple: Nelson was a philosophical heretic of the twentieth century, and his heresies were of such an outspoken and universal character that they earned him the sworn enmity of the dominant philosophical schools in Germany and brought him into conflict with her whole cultural atmosphere. Public indifference to Nelson in Germany, however, was bound to have the most adverse consequences for the international recognition of his work, and so it had.

Nelson's fundamental heresy was his conviction that there is one, and only one, philosophical truth, and that it is attainable by thinking.[3] This conviction, inspiring his whole life, was squarely opposed to the spirit of his time, which, for the first one or two decades of the century, was characterized by skepticism, and then turned more and more in the direction of mysticism, developments that were climaxed by the imposition on the German people of National Socialism as the obligatory world-view—just five years after Nelson's premature death. This unexampled cultural breakdown may be viewed as a dramatic historical commentary on the practical import of warnings Nelson had uttered time and again. He had always contended that the rejection of rational philosophical truth by his contemporaries could result only in subjection to an invented irrational "truth." The intense awareness of this danger gives to Nelson's critical and constructive writings a uniquely passionate tone. He is never indifferent; he always takes a determined stand. But it is the stand of a thoroughly prepared case. Even the severest critic will not find in Nelson's writings that "dim magnificence" which, as Macaulay says, "if it is admitted into a demonstration . . . is very much worse than absolute nonsense."

Nelson's philosophical work—the most mature parts of which are the *Lectures on the Foundations of Ethics* [4] and the yet unpublished

---

fall of that regime, have borne with equal courage their share in the struggle for a new and better order in Germany.

3. A nontechnical account of this guiding conviction may be found in the essay, "The Art of Philosophizing" (see this volume, p. 83).

4. *Vorlesungen über die Grundlagen der Ethik*, Vol. I, *Kritik der praktischen Vernunft (Critique of Practical Reason)* (1917); Vol. II, *System der philosophischen Ethik und Pädagogik (System of Philosophical Ethics and Pedagogics)* (1932, posthumously); Vol. III, *System der philosophischen Rechtslehre und Politik (System of the Philosophy of Law and Politics)* (1924).

"Lectures on the History of Metaphysics" [5]—is the achievement of
a superior power of abstraction and of an iron will, both of them
formed and purified by theoretical and practical influences of great
significance. The most momentous of them is a philosophical rediscovery that Nelson made when only a high-school student. Just as
Felix Mendelssohn-Bartholdy (to whom Nelson was related through
his mother's family) rediscovered Bach's forgotten masterpiece,
"The Passion According to St. Matthew," so Nelson rediscovered
the forgotten writing of a forgotten philosopher, J. F. Fries (1773–
1843), whose work had fallen into oblivion by a coincidence of adverse cultural and political circumstances, namely, the crushing effect of post-Kantian philosophical mysticism—as cultivated by
Fichte, Hegel, Schelling—and the police state of Metternich.

The rediscovery of Fries's *New or Anthropological Critique of
Reason* (2d ed., 1828; reprinted in 1935), his *System of Metaphysics*
(1824), *The History of Philosophy Set Forth in Accordance with
the Progress of Its Scientific Development* (1837–40),[6] and of numerous other books and essays by him and his pupils (particularly
E. F. Apelt) was the spark that kindled the flame of devotion to a
rebirth of critical philosophy, which burned all through Nelson's
life. Nelson's study of Fries convinced him that the Fichte-Hegel-
Schelling school was mistaken in arrogating to itself the role of carrying on the work of Kant, and that, therefore, the failure of its
speculations did not imply the failure of critical philosophy. The
study of Fries convinced him further that the cultivation of critical
philosophy excludes the blind acceptance of the Kantian letter. Continuing and extending the penetrating critical analysis applied by
Maimon (1754–1800) to Kant's transcendental proofs (which
Maimon demonstrated to be circular), Fries subjected Kant's whole
system to rigorous criticism. The result was to eliminate metaphysical agnosticism and epistemological subjectivism from the structure
of critical philosophy.[7]

5. "Vorlesungen über die Geschichte der Metaphysik," Pt. I, "Fortschritte der
Metaphysik, insbesondere bei Hume und Kant" ("Advances in Metaphysics Particularly in Hume and Kant"); Pt. II, "Rückschritte der Metaphysik seit Kant"
("Regress in Metaphysics since Kant"); Pt. III, "Fortschritte der Metaphysik seit
Kant" ("Advances in Metaphysics since Kant").
6. *Neue oder anthropologische Kritik der Vernunft; System der Metaphysik;
Die Geschichte der Philosophie dargestellt nach den Fortschritten ihrer wissen-
schaftlichen Entwicklung.*
7. Fries's central technical procedure is a reconsideration of the relation between metaphysics, epistemology, and psychology of knowledge, a highly important methodological subject taken up again in one of Nelson's first essays,

This structure is determined by the requirement that philosophy be established within the limitations of human knowledge. Trivial though it may seem, this requirement is nevertheless a most fruitful principle, the disregard of which has largely characterized the history of philosophy. Though it obliges us neither to assert that space, time, causality, the moral law, or even God is inherent in a "universal consciousness," nor to advocate a demolition of metaphysics, it does demand of us that we give an account of the elements of knowledge out of which it is possible for the human mind to construct metaphysics. Fries undertook to show how the method of the critique of reason had to be modified if it was to apply to the foundation of the theoretical sciences, and to ethics, art, and religion. Without falling into epistemological subjectivism or metaphysical agnosticism, he demonstrated how this revised critique supported the fundamental finding of Kant about Leibniz' logicism and Hume's empiricism, namely, that both collapse under the impact of the theory of the synthetic a priori propositions. He went on to show that Kant was also right as against Aristotle, whose realism breaks down before the distinction between the phenomenal and the noumenal aspects of the universe.

His lifelong association with critical philosophy, although the most significant, was not the only formative theoretical influence on Nelson's intellectual development. There were at least two others, mathematics and social science. His mathematical studies under Hessenberg, and under Hilbert whose friendship and high intellectual esteem he enjoyed, gave him a thorough acquaintance with mathematical methods and sharpened his logical tools. His friendship with Franz Oppenheimer [8] introduced him to the sociology of the state and to economic theory, and exposed him to an honest criticism of Marxism. As a consequence, all his life he was opposed to the dogma-

---

"The Critical Method and the Relation of Psychology to Philosophy" (see this volume, p. 105). This essay is the best introduction to the delineation of Kant's transcendental and Fries's psychological method of the critique of reason and of the related distinction between the analysis ("exposition") and the validation ("deduction") of philosophical principles.

8. The names of both Hessenberg and Oppenheimer appear as co-editors of the *Abhandlungen der Fries'schen Schule. Neue Folge,* established by Nelson in 1904. The first *Abhandlungen der Fries'schen Schule* was established in 1847 by Apelt (author of a comprehensive textbook on critical philosophy in its Friesian version, *Metaphysik* [1857], re-edited by R. Otto [1910]), Schleiden (the biologist), Schlömilch (the mathematician), and H. Schmid (a Fries pupil who made important contributions to the philosophy and psychology of religion and published very stimulating *Lectures on the Nature of Philosophy* [*Vorlesungen über das Wesen der Philosophie* (1836)], re-edited by R. Otto [1911, 1948]).

tism of historical materialism, and when, after the First World War, he made a trip to Russia, he did not hesitate to speak out against what he considered to be the errors of this doctrine. Nelson's ethical system, however, with its insistence on a realistic approach to human society, bears witness to the fruitfulness of his acquaintance with social science.

Even more important proved to be his contacts with social reality, which largely determined the direction of his philosophical work, that is, its gravitation toward ethics. Nelson was reared in a highly cultured Berlin family, his father a distinguished lawyer of idealistic outlook, his mother a woman with considerable talent for drawing, which her son inherited. Young Nelson did not find high school or university very congenial; he looked back with horror to his later high-school years. His concern with philosophical scrutiny, which developed very early, suffered under the dogmatism that pervaded the teaching methods of even one of the best high schools in Berlin, and his keen sense of personal dignity and independence made him hate the traditional methods of school discipline. Nelson's university studies at Berlin, Heidelberg, and Göttingen gave him a solid grasp of mathematics and the natural sciences, including psychology, and of their methods. Yet in none of these universities did he find satisfaction for his philosophical longings. His technical philosophical education, therefore, was acquired almost entirely through self-study guided by his rediscovery of Fries.[9]

The field to which the tools thus acquired were to be mainly applied was largely determined by the historical events of the time: the First World War, the social and cultural tensions of the Weimar Republic, and the international political crisis stemming from the Russian Revolution. Nelson lived through these events not as a passive philosophic bystander but as a man who increasingly felt the responsibility to contribute his gifts of clear thought and unswerving purpose to the struggle to free mankind from the recurrent torment of political "destinies." Nelson's zeal for a higher form of social existence than can be found in a world torn by wars, class conflicts, and cultural disintegration made it imperative for him to devote his thought to a study and appraisal of all serious movements in the furtherance of peace, social justice, and cultural progress. Practical con-

9. Nelson's philosophical dissertation, "Jakob Friedrich Fries und seine jüngsten Kritiker" ("Jacob Friedrich Fries and His Most Recent Critics"), *Abhandlungen der Fries'schen Schule. Neue Folge* I (1904), analyzes, reformulates, and defends Fries's transformation of Kant's transcendental critique into a psychological one against Kuno Fischer, Hermann Cohen, Windelband, Scheler, and others.

siderations, then, and not theoretical preferences, determined Nelson's preoccupation with ethics, and the logical rigor of his ethical system is the expression not of an intellectualistic motivation but of an intellectually refined conscience.

Nelson was a person of fearless directness who never equivocated, his work even showing evidence of a certain intellectual and practical obstinacy. He pursued the ideal of the acting philosopher in the Platonic sense of the word, yet in certain phases of his educational and political activity there is a tendency to fanatical activism, and his philosophizing was not entirely free of overemphasis on the finality of results and on the exclusiveness of specific approaches to complex problems. Correspondingly, there were traces of harshness in his personality. But his self-sacrificing devotion to truth and justice was such a powerful force in his life and in his work that his limitations may be said to be merely what Goethe called the "*Erdenrest zu tragen peinlich.*"

Notwithstanding Nelson's preoccupation with ethics, he made great contributions to theoretical philosophy, witness his papers on general epistemology and the methodology of science, and his unpublished history of metaphysics, a historical systematic introduction to the entire field of critical metaphysics. Nelson's most exhaustive work in general epistemology, his *On the So-called "Problem of Knowledge"* (1908),[10] has to be viewed in the light of the fact that the prevailing trend in Continental philosophy during at least the first decade of the century was almost exclusively toward preoccupation with *Erkenntnistheorie*. This *Erkenntnistheorie* is, of course, an echo of Kant's critique of reason, though only a very remote one, indeed. The neo-Kantians, the empiricists, and the phenomenologists had substituted for the basic problem of an analysis of knowledge the problem of finding a criterion for the validity of knowledge in general. This problem admits only of circular "solutions" and is therefore fictitious. The elimination of this problem, however, was by no means intended to discredit epistemology and metaphysics. On the contrary, the critical review of the post-Kantian epistemology in *On the So-called "Problem of Knowledge"* shows how powerful were the tools supplied by Fries's epistemological methods for the foundation of rational metaphysics.

Whereas this essay departs in important points from Kant's procedures (though not from his systematic intentions), Nelson's con-

10. *Über das sogenannte Erkenntnis-Problem.*

tributions to the methodology of mathematics and the empirical sciences are chiefly concerned with the reformulation and defense of some of the basic theories of the *Critique of Pure Reason*. Kant asserts that both mathematics and empirical science stand or fall on the assumption of synthetic propositions a priori. Nelson very early recognized the crucial character of this assumption, and never lost sight of it. This is evident in the "Remarks on Non-Euclidean Geometry and the Basis of Mathematical Certainty" (1905–6), in "Is a Natural Science Free of Metaphysics Possible?" (1908), and in his lecture on "Critical Philosophy and Mathematical Axiomatics," [11] which he delivered in 1927 shortly before his death. All these essays have the character of preparatory studies testing the Kantian assertion regarding synthetic propositions a priori on scientific developments, such as non-Euclidean geometry and mathematical axiomatics, unknown to Kant, and on modern methodological theories, such as mathematical conventionalism and Mach's empiricism. The result is a strong vindication of Kant's fundamental discovery.

This outcome is, in a sense, less remote from the present state of methodological discussion than may appear at first glance. The nominalistic dissolution of science into man-made symbol systems— this newest phase in the evolution of empiricist methodology—entails the consequence that consistent empiricism is incompatible with the assumption that there is scientific knowledge. Contrariwise, adherence to this assumption compels the abandonment of an empiricist methodology. That such an abandonment cannot be carried out in the form of a new logicism is sufficiently established by the failure of logicistic undertakings from Leibniz to Russell.[12] The hour has come, therefore, to reconsider seriously the feasibility of a methodology of science that employs as one of its basic constructive tools the concept of the synthetic proposition a priori.[13] In the proc-

11. "Bemerkungen über die Nicht-Euklidische Geometrie und den Ursprung der mathematischen Gewissheit"; "Ist metaphysikfreie Naturwissenschaft möglich?"; "Kritische Philosophie und mathematische Axiomatik." "Critical Philosophy and Mathematical Axiomatics" appears in this volume, p. 158.

12. Nelson did not overlook the epistemological importance of logic proper. His "Remarks on the Paradoxes of Russell and Burali-Forti" ("Bemerkungen zu den Paradoxien von Russell und Burali-Forti [zusammen mit Kurt Grelling]"), written with Grelling, formulated for the first time the now familiar paradox of words being either autological or heterological. It should be noted further that two outstanding symbolic logicians, Bernays and Ackermann, owe their philosophical education to Nelson.

13. Another pupil of Nelson, Grete Hermann, subjected modern physics and its current positivistic interpretations to the scrutiny of a philosophical analysis guided by Nelson's methodological approach to science. Her carefully reasoned results

ess it will become apparent that such irreconcilable doctrines as mathematical conventionalism and mathematical intuitionism, physicalistic positivism and the mystical philosophy of physics of Eddington and others, all contain valid elements, which find their place in a philosophy of science whose cornerstone is the Kantian conception of the synthetic proposition a priori.

To the solidity of this cornerstone Nelson's *Lectures on the Foundations of Ethics* [14] testifies constructively. This may seem paradoxical in view of the formalistic character of Kant's own ethics, but here again the Kantian letter and the Kantian spirit are not alike. The systematic structure of critical philosophy by no means entails a categorical imperative without content. This Kantian doctrine, being a logicistic remnant in his system, is not required by critical ethics. Nelson demonstrated this thesis in a historical-logical analysis, *The Critical Ethics of Kant, Schiller, and Fries. A Revision of Their Principles* (1914),[15] in which he also systematically traced the development of nonformalistic critical ethics in the writings of these men.

Ethics, then, holds up as its fundamental concept the category of a task, without being forced into a formalistic doctrine of duties. Armed with this insight, Nelson undertook a further step in preparation of his practical philosophy: a devastating attack against the positivistic philosophy of law which, confusing the world of changing legal arrangements with the unchangeable norm of justice, ends up in political relativism and thus destroys a main condition of political progress, namely, the possibility of well-founded political ideas. The exposure of the positivistic theory of constitutional and international law and of legal relativism made in Nelson's *Jurisprudence without Justice* (1917) [16] is distinguished not only by its logical forcefulness and brilliance but also by its moral courage. Pub-

---

corroborate the necessity and specify the formulation of synthetic propositions a priori for physics. See Hermann-May-Vogel, *Die Bedeutung der modernen Physik für die Theorie der Erkenntnis* (1937) (*The Importance of Modern Physics for Epistemology*); G. Hermann, "Die naturphilosophischen Grundlagen der Quantenmechanik" ("The Philosophical Foundation of Quantum Mechanics"), *Abhandlungen der Fries'schen Schule. Neue Folge* VI (1935), No. 2; Hermann, "Über die Grundlagen physikalischer Aussagen in den älteren und den modernen Theorien" ("On the Foundations of Physical Statements in Old and Modern Theories"), *ibid.*, VI (1937), Nos. 3–4.

14. See note 4.
15. *Die kritische Ethik bei Kant, Schiller und Fries. Eine Revision ihrer Prinzipien.*
16. *Die Rechtswissenschaft ohne Recht.*

lished in the war year 1917, it contains at its conclusion a consideration of "Jurisprudence and the War" that minces no words in castigating the abuse of legal science engaged in a "dance around the Golden Calf of sovereignty." [17] Prior to this Nelson had asserted the necessity for the limitation of sovereignty when, at the outbreak of the war and in the face of militaristic hysteria, he had publicly defended at the University of Göttingen the ideal of international peace.

The year 1917 also saw the publication of another work of Nelson's, which is likely to be regarded as his greatest: the *Critique of Practical Reason*.[18] Nelson knew what he was about when he selected this Kantian title and dedicated his work to Hilbert. He took up again certain fundamental unsolved epistemological problems of ethics and approached the task of their solution with tools forged by Kant and Fries and refined by mathematical axiomatics. These are the tools employed in solving both the *quaestio facti* and the *quaestio juris* of ethics, that is, the *formulation* of the principles of ethics and their *validation*. If Nelson's *Critique of Practical Reason* contained no more than the formulation ("exposition") of the principles of ethics, it would still be a notable philosophical achievement. Its analysis of such concepts as "duty," "right," "justice," "equality," "retribution" is unparalleled for clarity and simplicity. One has only to compare these Nelsonian abstractions with the contemporaneous efforts of Scheler and N. Hartmann to "intuit" phenomenologically the essence of ethical values to realize the difference between philosophical discrimination and philosophical confusion. A particularly original outcome of Nelson's research in ethics is his exposition of "ideals" or "categorical optatives," whereby the Kantian restriction of ethics to a theory of duties is removed and the way is opened to an ethics which not merely forbids but also formulates positive goals worthy of human effort.

The validation of ethical principles is carried out through their psychological "deduction," i.e., by proof of the fact that our ethical

17. The combination of irresistible logical criticism and prophetic scorn characteristic of *Die Rechtswissenschaft ohne Recht* is again evident in a philosophical pamphlet entitled *Spuk. Einweihung in das Geheimnis der Wahrsagerkunst Oswald Spenglers* (*Spook. Initiation into the Secrets of the Prophetic Art of Oswald Spengler*), published not long after the end of the First World War. This time the immediate object of exposure was one book by one man, but indirectly he aimed at the spirit of a whole generation. The book is Spengler's *Decline of the West*, representative of a generation that had lost confidence in itself and was therefore only too willing to lend its ear to a prophet of impending doom.

18. See note 4.

xviii *Socratic Method and Critical Philosophy*

feelings, namely, our conscience and our ideal evaluations of human life, are of a qualitatively unique character. They cannot be broken down into sensual elements like fear or libido, yet they are capable of reduction to nonsensual elements that are not directly contained in our consciousness. These nonconscious elements of ethical feelings belong to what Fries called "immediate knowledge," and they are the nonintuitive but rational basis of ethics. It has often been asserted (from Kuno Fischer to Cassirer) that Fries's psychological "deduction" is a form of "psychologism" and therefore of empiricism. There is no better refutation of this statement than Nelson's psychological deduction of the principles of ethics, which he in no way derives logically from psychological principles, but the bases of which he ascertains psychologically in the qualitative characteristics of "practical reason." The "deduction" of ethical principles is, then, at the same time a vindication of the rational nature of man.

"Exposition" and "deduction" do not exhaust the content of the *Critique of Practical Reason.* It also contains a lucid methodology of ethics, an analysis of the idea of the free will, and finally an axiomatics of all possible ethical theories.

This is really, as Nelson felt it to be, an attempt to conquer a vast new territory for philosophy. Its fruits are apparent in the *System of Philosophical Ethics and Pedagogics* and in the *System of the Philosophy of Law and Politics.*[19] The term "system" in combination with ethics has long had a somewhat stuffy sound. Too many "systems" of ethics have broken down for us to regard new ones with anything but skepticism. Yet granted that philosophy has to deal with the problems of ethics, their exact treatment requires a systematic form. The recurring breakdown of ethical systems does not prove the fictitiousness of ethical systematization, but rather the necessity to improve radically the rigor of ethics. This is accomplished in Nelson's systematic treatment, which, guided by the postulate of mathematical axiomatics, seeks to derive the theorems of a system with a minimum of assumptions. Only a concentrated study of this ethics can give an adequate idea of the striking way in which the application of this postulate insures a richness of content entirely beyond the reach of system haters.

The present writer was privileged to attend several of Nelson's courses in ethics, where he underwent the stirring experience of coming into possession of new tools for solving old problems, an experience intensified by Nelson's superior art of philosophical teach-

19. See note 4.

ing. What was presented in those courses orally the reader will find in Nelson's *Systems*. He will discover how problems generally considered to be undecidable suddenly become decidable when they and the means available for their solution are rigorously formulated. It would serve no purpose to list at length those ethical problems of personal conduct, education, politics, and to report Nelson's answers to them. The innermost spirit of his *Ethics* forbids such a survey procedure. This spirit is a reassertion of an autonomous ethics, that is, of an ethical certainty that is subject to argument.

Nelson's system is a monumental protest against authoritarian certainties and nonauthoritarian uncertainties in ethics. It re-establishes the principle of a morality without dogma, of a social order without arbitrary privilege, and of a culture without empty pretension.[20] This re-establishment is carried out for ethics proper by insisting on the exclusiveness and primacy of the duty of justice to be practiced toward man and animal and by an amplification of the realm of duties by the realm of ideals. The classical ideals of truth, goodness, and beauty are unified into what may be called "the ideal of rational self-determination" (*vernünftige Selbstbestimmung*), and education and politics are shown to receive their ethical goals from that ideal. Consequently, the philosophy of education formulates ethical principles of an education for freedom from fear and freedom from intellectual bondage, and the philosophy of politics formulates ethical principles of a social order in which, under qualified leadership, peace, social justice, and cultural freedom are institutionally guaranteed.

The critical mirror Nelson places before mankind reflects the abyss that separates ideal and reality. To shrink from this abyss or

20. As those pretensions typically confuse empirical, ethical, and religious ideas, a sharp distinction among them is all the more important for the health of cultural life. Nelson's "The Scientific and Esthetic Conception of Nature" and his "The World-View of Ethics and Religion" (see this volume, pp. 44, 62) provide important and impressively formulated clarifications of such a distinction.

Nelson's approach to religion, which he never developed systematically, is guided by the Kantian attitude of distinguishing between the phenomenal and the noumenal aspects of the universe, which implies an awareness of human apartness from the eternal. This attitude is incompatible with mystical certainties about the "numinous objects" into which one of Nelson's early collaborators, Rudolf Otto, transformed Fries's antimystical philosophy of religion in his well-known and stimulating books, e.g., *The Idea of the Holy*. Through Otto's theory of religion, elements of Fries's philosophy swelled the broad stream of religious mysticism which had found its philosophical formulation in James's "religious experience" and later in Scheler's "religious intuitions." In addition to Otto, the psychiatrist Kronfeld and the distinguished physiologist Meyerhof belonged to Nelson's philosophical circle.

to seek consolation in forces beyond the human realm is a clear sign of ethical self-deception. Ethical integrity demands that we look into the mirror, evaluate what it reflects, and then arrive at a clarified ethical judgment. It may be confidently asserted that if we face Nelson's *Ethics* squarely, we shall come away with a new approach to the theoretically central and practically vital problem as to whether rational ethics—and that means also the rational foundation of educational and political theory—can be realized or is no more than a dream. If only part of Nelson's constructions should prove to be valid, they would substantially confirm the conviction of the greatest philosophers since Plato that rational ethics is within the reach of man.

Nelson's epistemology and his system of ethics have remained up to now a part of what may be termed the unofficial European philosophy of the beginning of the century. It awaits a rediscovery like Nelson's rediscovery of Fries's work. Official European philosophy, at first relativistic, then more and more mystical, had no use for Nelson's antirelativistic and antimystical ethics of practical reason. It therefore either ignored Nelson's work or ridiculed it as a "belated rebirth of eighteenth century rationalism"—disclosing thereby that it preferred high-sounding historistical superficialities to the effort of systematic penetration. Having dismissed Nelson condescendingly, official European philosophy indulged all the more in prophecies of destiny, abandoning the clarification of human tasks as an outdated prejudice. Instead, it brooded over the essence of human existence, which Heidegger painted in the grey of despair and to which Jaspers gave a no less illogical, if somewhat less monotonous, interpretation.[21] The price for this dismissal of rational ethics is the creation of an anthropological scholasticism that plays with Kierkegaardian paradoxes and Hegelian dialectics, a result to be seriously pondered by any philosophy that does not want to run afoul of logic.

Thanks to the efforts of Russell and Whitehead, Hilbert and many others, logic experienced a revival in the twentieth century. So far, however, it has had scant constructive results for philosophy as a whole. In fact, "the new logic" has been misused to bring about a

21. See the present writer's *Von Husserl zu Heidegger. Kritik der phänomenologischen Philosophie (From Husserl to Heidegger. Critique of Phenomenological Philosophy)* (1932), and "The Philosophy of Existence. Its Structure and Significance," *Philosophy and Phenomenological Research*, Vol. I. No. 3 (1941).

renewal of logicistic and even nominalistic claims, which debase philosophy to a system of tautologies, if not of meaningless symbols; a further impressive demonstration of the fact that new scientific devices, such as the invention of logical calculi, cease to be a blessing if they are subjected to arbitrary philosophical interpretations, in this case the interpretation that modern logic is incompatible with metaphysics, that is, speaking epistemologically, with systems based on synthetic propositions a priori.

Precisely the same incompatibility is being asserted concerning other fundamental sciences. Mathematics is claimed as a branch of logic; physics is considered a combination of observational and conventional elements. Behavioristic psychology has, of course, only contempt for "metaphysical fictions" like the concept of a mental reality. Finally, the social sciences and the humanities are objects of a fierce competitive struggle between those who want to compress them into more or less consistently developed physicalistic schemes and those who consider them fertile ground for the seeds of their particular political and religious preferences, thus transforming them from fields of knowledge into means of indoctrination.[22] Art and religion, too, share a similar fate in being treated alternatively by preconceived psychological and sociological schemes or by serving as pretexts for unchaining the unholy, age-old hatred of reason.

But all this—the denunciation of rational metaphysics in the name of science, art, and religion—is only a claim, and not a claim of modern science, art, and religion themselves but of the interpretation given to them by an antirational philosophy. Viewed in this light, this denunciation is nothing but a usurpation that ought to be overthrown by a rational reinterpretation of the widened intellectual horizon of the nineteenth and twentieth centuries. Such an intellectual endeavor will bring about fruitful interaction between old ideas and new achievements. The old ideas will be progressively freed from the dross of their historical shortcomings, and the new achievements will be understood as those of a human, that is, of a rational, mind with insurmountable limitations. Thereby it will become apparent that the radical wings of twentieth-century philosophy, empiricism as well as existentialism, have aims that find much more satis-

22. A typical expression of these fundamental uncertainties concerning the methodological interpretation of the social sciences and the humanities is the theory of *Geisteswissenschaft* established by Dilthey and radicalized by existentialist methodology of history. A systematic analysis and appraisal of the doctrine of *Geisteswissenschaft* will be found in the present writer's *Die Unmöglichkeit der Geisteswissenschaft* (*The Impossibility of "Geisteswissenschaft"*) (1934).

factory realization in a rational philosophy. These aims are, on the one hand, the rejection of obscurantism and, on the other, the search for a meaning of human existence. Rational philosophy pursues them by a nonempiricist philosophy of science and by its ethics and its philosophy of religion.

Nelson has set a great example by vastly enriching these disciplines in the spirit of Kant and Fries and by demonstrating thereby once again that it is not the eulogizing of and blind submission to great men but the meeting of unfettered minds that brings about deepening of philosophical judgment. It is almost superfluous to add that the attainment of this end is also a practical requirement of the hour. A famous historian of our day describes our predicament as "civilization on trial." In that trial history holds out no hope of a favorable judgment for a generation that indulges in intellectual self-mutilation. The rediscovery of reason—in science, in ethics, and in religion—thus becomes a prerequisite for recapturing the meaning of life. In this rediscovery and in this recapture Nelson's philosophical work can be a powerful ally.

JULIUS KRAFT

Washington and Jefferson College
  Washington, Pennsylvania
    November 1, 1948

SOCRATIC METHOD
AND
CRITICAL PHILOSOPHY

I

THE SOCRATIC METHOD *

AS A faithful disciple of Socrates and of his great successor Plato, I find it rather difficult to justify my acceptance of your invitation to talk to you about the Socratic method. You know the Socratic method as a method of teaching philosophy. But philosophy is different from other subjects of instruction; in Plato's own words: "It does not at all admit of verbal expression like other studies, but as a result of continued application to the subject itself and communion therewith, it is brought to birth in the soul on a sudden, as light that is kindled by a leaping spark, and thereafter it nourishes itself." [1]

I therefore find myself in a quandary, not unlike that of a violinist who, when asked how he goes about playing the violin, can of course demonstrate his art but cannot explain his technique in abstract terms.

The Socratic method, then, is the art of teaching not philosophy but philosophizing, the art not of teaching about philosophers but of making philosophers of the students. So, in order to give a true idea of the Socratic method, I should halt my discourse right here and, instead of lecturing to you, take up with you a philosophical problem and deal with it according to the Socratic method. But what did Plato say? Only "continued application to the subject itself and communion therewith" kindle the light of philosophical cognition.

Despite the short time at my disposal I shall nevertheless venture a description of the Socratic method and attempt through words to bring home to you its meaning and significance. I justify this compromise by limiting my task, the sole object of my exposition being to direct your attention to this method of teaching and thereby to promote an appreciation of it.

* A lecture, "Die sokratische Methode," delivered on December 11, 1922, before the Pedagogic Society of Göttingen. Published in *Abhandlungen der Fries'schen Schule*, V (Göttingen, 1929), No. 1.

1. Plato, *Epistles*, R. G. Bury, tr., in Loeb Classical Library (London, New York, 1929), VII, 531.

A person who knows no more about the Grand Inquisitor's speech in Dostoevsky's novel, *The Brothers Karamazov*, than that it is a most magnificent discussion of a fundamental ethical problem, knows little enough about it; yet that little will make him more disposed to read the speech attentively. Similarly, whoever looks at the memorial tablet here in the former Physics Institute [Göttingen] that tells of the first electric telegraph invented by Gauss and Wilhelm Weber and how it served to connect that institute with the astronomical observatory will at least feel inclined to follow up the history of this invention with greater reverence. And so I hope that in presenting my subject I, too, may arouse your interest in the significant and, for all its simplicity, profound method that bears the name of the Athenian sage to whom we owe its invention.

A stepchild of philosophy, slighted and rejected, the Socratic method has survived only in name beside its more popular older sister, the more insinuating and more easily manipulated dogmatic method.

You may perhaps suspect me of a personal inclination for the younger of the two sisters. And, indeed, I freely confess that the longer I enjoy her company, the more I am captivated by her charms; so that it has become a matter of chivalry with me to lead her back to life who has been forgotten and pronounced dead, and to win her here that place of honor hitherto reserved for the wanton sister who, though dead at heart, has time and again appeared all decked out.

Let me add, however—and this much I hope to demonstrate to you today—that it is not blind partiality that actuates me; it is the inner worth of her whose appearance is so plain that attracts me to her. But, you say, her sad fate—being disdained by the overwhelming majority of philosophers—could not have been undeserved and it is therefore idle to try to breathe new life into her by artificial means.

In reply I shall not resort to the general proposition that history shows no pre-established harmony between merit and success, for, indeed, the success or failure of a *method* as a means to an end is a very real test of its value.

However, a fair judgment requires consideration of a preliminary question, namely, whether a particular science is so far advanced that the solution of its problems is sought in a prescribed way; in other words, whether generally valid methods are recognized in it.

In mathematics and in the natural sciences based on it this question of method was long ago decided affirmatively. There is not a mathematician who is not familiar with and who does not employ the progressive method. All serious research in the natural sciences makes use of the inductive method. In fact, method enjoys in these sciences a recognition so unchallenged and matter of course that the students following its guidance are often hardly conscious of the assured course of their researches. All dispute about methods here turns exclusively on their reliability and fruitfulness. If, in this field, a method is dropped or retains merely a historic interest, the presumption is justified that it can offer nothing more to research.

It is quite otherwise, however, in a science where everyone still claims the right to make his own laws and rules, where methodological directives are evaluated *ab initio* as temporally or individually conditioned, subject only to historical appraisal. With luck one method may find favor and for a time determine the direction of future work. But in such a science errors, concomitants of every scientific achievement, do not inspire efforts in the already established direction to correct the defects; errors here are looked upon as faults of construction and must give way to entirely new structures, which in their turn all too soon meet the same fate.

What passes for philosophical science is still in this youthful stage of development. In this judgment I have the support of Windelband, the renowned historian of philosophy. He tells us that "even among the philosophers who claim a special method for their science"—and by no means all philosophers make such a claim—"there is not the least agreement concerning this 'philosophical method.' "[2]

This conclusion appears the more depressing in view of his previous admission that it is impossible to establish a constant criterion even for the very subject matter of philosophy.

2. Wilhelm Windelband, *Präludien* (Freiburg and Tübingen, 1884), p. 9.

In view of this, one wonders what such philosophers really think of their science. At any rate, in this anarchy the question is left open whether the disesteem into which a philosophical theory falls in itself proves that the theory is scientifically worthless. For how can we expect to judge the scientific value or lack of value of a philosophical achievement when generally valid criteria for passing judgment do not exist?

Now, it is not that the diversity of the *results* made it difficult for philosophers to set up a systematic guide to their science. On the contrary, the great philosophical truths have been from the beginning the common property of all the great thinkers. Here, then, a common starting point was provided. But the verification of these results according to unequivocal rules that preclude arbitrariness and even the mere formulation of the pertinent methodological task with definiteness and precision, both these tasks in the general interest of philosophy have thus far been given so little attention that we must not be surprised that the devoted efforts of a few men to satisfy this interest have proved in vain. True, the lifelong work of Socrates and of Kant in the service of this methodological task has earned immeasurable historical glory. But, as far as its revolutionary significance for the establishment of philosophy as a science is concerned, it has remained sterile and ineffectual.

Twice in its history there was some prospect of getting philosophy out of its groping stage and onto the certain path of science. The ancient world punished the first courageous attempt with death: Socrates was condemned as a corrupter of youth. The modern world disdains to execute the heretic. It has passed sentence by "going beyond" Kant—to let Windelband speak once more.[3]

But there is no need for labored interpretation to appreciate the significance of these two men. They themselves stressed the meaning of their endeavors, explicitly and unceasingly. As everyone knows, Socrates constructed no system. Time and again he admitted his not-knowing. He met every assertion with an invitation to seek the ground of its truth. As the *Apology* shows,

3. Windelband, *Präludien*, p. vi.

he "questioned and examined and cross-examined" [4] his fellow citizens, not to convey a new truth to them in the manner of an instructor but only to point out the path along which it might be found.

His ethical doctrine, in so far as this designation is appropriate to his inquiries, is based on the proposition that virtue can be taught, or, to put it in more precise terms, that ethics is a science. He did not develop this science because the initial question, *How do I gain knowledge about virtue?* continued to absorb him. He held fast to this initial question. He accepted the absence of fruitful results with composure, without a trace of skepticism as to the soundness of his method, unshakable in the conviction that with his question he was, in spite of everything, on the only right road.

All subsequent philosophy, with the sole exception of Plato, stands helpless before that memorable fact. Plato took over and adhered to the method of Socrates, even after his own researches had carried him far beyond the results reached by his master. He adopted it with all its imperfections. He failed to eliminate its weaknesses and inflexibilities, surely not because of reverence for the memory of his teacher but because he could not overcome these defects. Like Socrates, he was guided by a feeling for truth. Having dealt so boldly with the content of the Socratic philosophy that philosophical philologists are still quarreling about what is Socratic in Plato's doctrine and what Platonic, he turned this boldness into homage by putting all his own discoveries into the mouth of his great teacher. But he paid Socrates even greater homage by clothing these discoveries in the uneven, often dragging, often digressive form of the Socratic dialogue, burdening his own teachings with his teacher's faults. In this manner, of course, he safeguarded the yet unmined treasure and thus gave posterity the opportunity of taking possession of it anew and of developing its riches.

But in vain. Today, after two thousand years, opinion on Socrates is more uncertain and more divided than ever. Over against the judgment of an expert like Joel, that Socrates was "the first

4. Plato, *Apology*, H. N. Fowler, tr., in Loeb Classical Library (London, New York, 1913), I, 109.

and perhaps the last quite genuine, *quite pure* philosopher," [5] there is Heinrich Maier's statement "that Socrates has been labeled as what he quite certainly was *not*, a philosopher." [6]

This difference of opinion has its roots in the inadequacy of the criticism, which still exercises its ingenuity on the conclusions of Socrates' philosophy. But as these conclusions were handed down only indirectly and perhaps were never even given definite form by Socrates, they remain exposed to the most contradictory interpretations. Where criticism touches on the method, it either praises trivialities or assigns the value of the Socratic method exclusively to the personality of Socrates, as shown in the opinion voiced by Wilamowitz in his *Plato:* "The Socratic method without Socrates is no more than a pedagogy that, aping how some inspired spiritual leader clears his throat and spits, bottles his alleged method and then imagines it is dispensing the water of life." [7]

If Socrates' philosophy, lively as it was and rooted in concrete problems, found no emulators, it is little wonder then that the truth content of Kant's far more abstract methodological investigations failed to be understood and adopted—except by those few who comprehended his doctrine and developed it further, but who in their turn were pushed completely into the background by the irresistible *Zeitgeist* and passed over by history. The preconditions were lacking for the realization that Kant's critical method was the resumption of Socratic-Platonic philosophizing, and for the acceptance of the *Critique of Pure Reason* as a "treatise on the method," which its author, according to his own words, intended it to be. [8]

In addition to this treatise on method, Kant produced a system. He enriched the broad domain of philosophy with an abundance of fruitful results. It was these results that became the subject of controversy; but the hope of a satisfactory settlement was bound to remain illusory as long as no attempt was made to retrace the creative path by which Kant had reached his conclusions. Dog-

5. Karl Joel, *Geschichte der antiken Philosophie* (Tübingen, 1921), p. 770.
6. Heinrich Maier, *Sokrates* (Tübingen, 1913), p. 157.
7. Ulrich von Wilamowitz-Moellendorff, *Platon* (Berlin, 1919), I, 108.
8. Immanuel Kant, *Critique of Pure Reason,* Norman Kemp Smith, tr. (London, New York, 1933), p. 25.

matism remained dominant, more triumphant than ever in the erection of arbitrary systems that vied with one another in bizarreness and estranged public interest altogether from the sober and critical philosophizing of the Kantian period. Such fragments of Kant's results as were transplanted to this alien soil could not thrive there and maintained only an artificial existence, thanks to a fancy for the history of philosophy that displaced philosophy itself.

Why is it, asked Kant, that nothing is being done to prevent the "scandal" which, "sooner or later, is sure to become obvious even to the masses, as the result of the disputes in which metaphysicians . . . without critique inevitably become involved." [9]

It is manifestly the aim of every science to verify its judgments by reducing them to more general propositions, which themselves must be made certain. We can then proceed from these principles to the erection of the scientific system through logical inference. However difficult this may be in its details, in its essence it is accomplished in all sciences by the same method, that of progressive reasoning. The methodological problems are encountered in every science where the regress from the particular to the general has to be accomplished, where the task is to secure the most fundamental propositions, the most general principles.

The brilliant development of the science of mathematics and its universally acknowledged advance are explained by the fact that its principles—ignoring for the moment the problems of axiomatics—are easily grasped by the consciousness. They are intuitively clear and thus completely evident, so evident that, as Hilbert recently remarked on this same platform, mathematical comprehension can be forced on everyone. The mathematician does not even have to perform the laborious regress to these principles. He is free to start from arbitrarily formed concepts and go on confidently to propositions; in short, he can immediately proceed systematically, and in this sense dogmatically. He can do so because the fact that his concepts lend themselves to construction is a criterion of their reality, a sure indication that his theory does not deal with mere fictions.

9. Kant, *Critique of Pure Reason*, pp. 31–32. [Translation revised by T.K.B.]

The natural sciences, on their part, do not enjoy this advantage. The laws underlying natural phenomena can be uncovered only by induction. But since induction proceeds from the observation of facts, from which accidental elements are eliminated by experimentation; since, moreover, all events in space and in time are susceptible of mathematical calculation; and, finally, since the theoretical generalizations obtained are, as empirical propositions, subject to check by confirmatory or contradictory experience, the natural sciences have, in close relation to mathematics, likewise achieved the ascent to the scientific level. Where this claim is still contested, as in biology, the metaphysical premises within the inductive science are involved. There, to be sure, we find at once the confusion that is encountered whenever we pass into the realm of philosophy.

Philosophy does not rest on principles that are self-evident truths. On the contrary, its principles are the focus of obscurity, uncertainty, and controversy. There is unanimity only with respect to the concrete application of these principles. But the moment we try to disregard the particular instance of application and to isolate the principles from experience, that is, if we try to formulate them in pure abstraction, then our search gets lost in metaphysical darkness unless we illuminate our way by the artificial light of a method.

Under these circumstances one would expect to find interest in the problem of method nowhere so great as among philosophers. It should be noted, however, that the consideration just put forward itself depends on a methodological point of view. It raises, in advance of any philosophical speculation proper, the question of the nature of philosophical cognition; and it is only through this preliminary question that light is shed on the real content of the problems besetting philosophy.

Let us pause here a moment and take a closer look at the concept of the method with which we are concerned. What, precisely, is meant by a method that subjects the thinking of philosophers to its rules? Obviously, it is something other than just the rules of logical thinking. Obedience to the laws of logic is an indispensable precondition of any science. The essential factor distinguishing a method of philosophy can therefore not be found in the fact that it avails itself of logic. That would too narrowly circumscribe the function devolving on it. On the other hand, the demands made on method must not go too far, nor should the impossible be expected of it, namely, the creative increase of philosophical knowledge.

The function to be performed by the philosophical method is nothing other than making secure the contemplated regress to principles, for without the guidance of method, such a regress would be merely a leap in the dark and would leave us where we were before—prey to the arbitrary.

But how to find the clarity requisite for discovering such a guide, since nothing is clear save only judgments relative to individual instances? For these judgments the concrete use of our intelligence, as applied in every empirical judgment in science and in daily life, suffices. Once we go beyond these judgments, how can we orient ourselves at all? The difficulty that seems to be present here is resolved upon critical examination of these empirical judgments. Each of them comprises, in addition to the particular data supplied by observation, a cognition hidden in the very form of the judgment. This cognition, however, is not separately perceived, but by virtue of it we already actually assume and apply the principle we seek.

To give a commonplace illustration: If we were here to discuss the meaning of the philosophical concept of substance, we should most probably become involved in a hopeless dispute, in which the skeptics would very likely soon get the best of it. But if, on the conclusion of our debate, one of the skeptics failed to find his overcoat beside the door where he had hung it, he would hardly reconcile himself to the unfortunate loss of his coat on the ground that it simply confirmed his philosophical doubt of the permanence of substance. Like anyone else hunting for a lost object, the skeptic assumes in the judgment that motivates his search the universal truth that no thing can become nothing, and thus, without being conscious of the inconsistency with his doctrine, he employs the metaphysical principle of the permanence of substance.

Or, suppose we discussed the universal validity of the idea of justice. Our discussion would have the same outcome and once more seem to favor the skeptic who denies the universal validity of ethical truths. When, however, this skeptic reads in his evening paper that farmers are still holding back grain deliveries to exploit a favorable market and that bread will therefore have to be rationed again, he will not readily be disposed to suppress his indignation on the ground that there is no common principle of right applicable to producer and consumer. Like everyone else he condemns profiteering and thereby demonstrates that in fact he acknowledges the metaphysical assumption of equal rights to the satisfaction of interests, regardless of the favorableness or unfavorableness of any individual's personal situation.

It is the same with all experiential judgments. If we inquire into the conditions of their possibility, we come upon more general propositions that constitute the basis of the particular judgments passed. By analyzing conceded judgments we go back to their presuppositions. We operate regressively from the consequences to the reason. In this regression we eliminate the accidental facts to which the particular judgment relates and by this separation bring into relief the originally obscure assumption that lies at the bottom of the judgment on the concrete instance. The regressive method of abstraction, which serves to disclose philosophical principles, produces no new knowledge either of facts or of laws. It merely utilizes reflection to transform into clear concepts what reposed in our reason as an original possession and made itself obscurely heard in every individual judgment.

It seems as though this discussion has carried us far from our real theme, the method of teaching philosophy. Let us then find the connection. We have discovered philosophy to be the sum total of those universal rational truths that become clear only through reflection. To philosophize, then, is simply to isolate these rational truths with our intellect and to express them in general judgments.

What implications does this hold for the teaching of philosophy? When expressed in words, these universal truths will be heard, but it does not necessarily follow that they will be comprehended. We can understand them only when, beginning with their application in our judgments, we then personally undertake the regress to the premises of these empirical judgments and recognize in them our own presuppositions.

It is accordingly impossible to communicate philosophy, the sum total of these philosophical principles, by instruction as we communicate historical facts or even geometrical theorems. The facts of history as such are not objects of insight; they can only be noted.

True, the principles of mathematics are comprehensible, but we gain insight into them without treading the circuitous path of our own creative thinking. They become immediately evident as soon as attention is directed to their content. The mathematics teacher who anticipates his pupil's independent investigation by presenting these principles in lectures does not thereby impair their clarity. In this case the pupil is able to follow even though he does not himself travel the exploratory path to them. To what extent such instruction makes sure that the pupil follows with real comprehension is of course another question.

But to present philosophy in this manner is to treat it as a science of facts that are to be accepted as such. The result is at best a mere history of philosophy. For what the instructor communicates is not philosophical truth itself but merely the fact that he or somebody else considers this or that to be a philosophical truth. In claiming that he is teaching philosophy, he deceives both himself and his students.

The teacher who seriously wishes to impart philosophical insight can aim only at teaching the art of philosophizing. He can do no more than show his students how to undertake, each for himself, the laborious regress that alone affords insight into basic principles. If there is such a thing at all as instruction in philosophy, it can only be instruction in doing one's own thinking; more precisely, in the independent practice of the art of abstraction. The meaning of my initial remark, that the Socratic method, as a method of instruction in philosophy, is the art not of teaching philosophy but of teaching philosophizing, will now become clear. But we have gone further than that. We also know now that, in order to succeed, this art must be guided by the rules of the regressive method.

We have still to examine the subsidiary question, whether this, the only appropriate method of teaching philosophy, is rightfully called the Socratic method. For my earlier references to the significance of Socrates bore only on the fact that his procedure pertained to method.

To begin with, it goes without saying that his way of teaching is full of faults. Every intelligent college freshman reading Plato's dialogues raises the objection that Socrates, at the most decisive points, engages in monologues and that his pupils are scarcely more than yes men—at times, as Fries remarks, one does not even quite see how they arrived at the "yes." [10] In addition to these didactic defects, there are grave philosophical errors, so that we often find ourselves concurring in the dissenting opinions of some of the participants.

In order to reach a conclusion concerning truth and error, the valuable and the valueless, let us take another glance at Plato's account. No one has appraised Socrates' manner of teaching and its effect on his pupils with greater objectivity or deeper knowledge of human nature. Whenever the reader is moved to protest against long-windedness or hair splitting in the conversations, against the monotony of the deductions, against the futility of the battle of words, a like protest arises at once from some participant in the dialogue. How openly Plato allows the pupils to voice their displeasure, their doubt, their boredom—just think of the railing of Callicles in the *Gorgias*.[11] He even has conversations breaking off because the patience of the participants is exhausted; and the reader's judgment is by no means always in favor of Socrates. But does this criticism reveal anything except the sovereign assurance with which Plato stands by the method of his teacher for all its shortcomings? Is there any better proof of confidence in the inherent value of a cause than to depict it with all its imperfections, certain that it will nevertheless prevail? Plato's attitude toward his teacher's work is like that displayed toward Socrates, the man, in the well-known oration by Alcibiades in the *Symposium*. There, by contrasting the uncouth

10. J. F. Fries, *Die Geschichte der Philosophie* (Halle, 1837), I, 253.
11. Plato, *Gorgias*, W. R. M. Lamb, tr., in Loeb Classical Library (London, New York, 1926), V, 381–395.

physical appearance of Socrates with his inner nature, he makes his noble personality shine forth with greater radiance and compares him to a silenus who bears within him the mark of the gods.

What, then, is the positive element in the work of Socrates? Where do we find the beginnings of the art of teaching philosophy? Surely not in the mere transition from the rhetoric of the sophists to the dialogue with pupils, even though we ignore the fact that, as I have already indicated, the questions put by Socrates are for the most part leading questions eliciting no more than "Undoubtedly, Socrates!" "Truly, so it is, by Zeus! How could it be otherwise?"

But suppose Socrates' philosophical ardor and his awkwardness had allowed the pupils more self-expression. We should still have to inquire first into the deeper significance of the dialogue in philosophical instruction and into the lessons to be derived from Plato's use of it.

We find dialogue employed as an art form in fiction and drama and as a pedagogic form in instruction. Theoretically these forms are separable but actually we require of every conversation liveliness, clarity, and beauty of expression, as well as espousal of truth, decisiveness, and strength of conviction. Even though the emphasis varies, we like to recognize the teacher in the artist and the artist in the teacher.

We must furthermore distinguish between a conversation reduced to writing—even though it is a reproduction of actual speech—and a real conversation carried on between persons. Conversations that are written down lose their original liveliness, "like the flower in the botanist's case." If, in spite of this, we are to find them satisfactory, the atmosphere must be spiritualized and purified, standards must be raised; and then there may come forth some rare and admirable production as the conversation of the Grand Inquisitor, which is carried on with a silent opponent who by his silence defeats him.

Conversation as a pedagogic form, however, must sound like actual talk; otherwise it does not fulfill its task of being model and guide. To catch, in the mirror of a written reproduction, the fleeting form of such talk with its irregularities, to strike the mean between fidelity to the sense and fidelity to the word—this is a problem that can perhaps be solved didactically; but the solution, serving as it does a definite purpose, will rarely meet the demands of free art and therefore as a whole will nearly always produce a mixed impression. I know of only a few didactic conversations in literature from which this discord has been even partially eliminated. I have in mind, for instance, some passages in the three well-known dialogues by Solovyeff; then there is the Socratic dialogue with which the American socialist writer Bellamy opens his didactic novel, *Looking Backward;* and finally —by no means the least successful—the conversations in August Niemann's novel, *Bakchen und Thyrsosträger*, which is imbued with the true Socratic spirit.

To the difficulty just described one must add another, more basic objection, that to reduce the evolving didactic conversation to writing borders on the absurd. For by offering the solution along with the problem, the transcription violates, with respect to the reader, the rule of individual effort and honesty and thus, as Socrates puts it in the *Phaedrus,* imparts to the novice "the appearance of wisdom, not true wisdom." [12] Such writing has meaning only for those to whom it recalls their own intellectual efforts. On all others it acts as an obstacle to insight—it seduces them into the naive notion that, as Socrates says further on, "anything in writing will be clear and certain." [13] Thus Plato speaks of his own "perplexity and uncertainty" [14] in setting down his thoughts in writing.

It does not at all admit of verbal expression. . . . But were I to undertake this task it would not, as I think, prove a good thing for men, save for some few who are able to discover the truth themselves with but little instruction; for as to the rest, some it would most unseasonably fill with mistaken contempt, and others with an overweening empty aspiration, as though they had learnt some sublime mysteries. [15]

12. Plato, *Phaedrus*, H. N. Fowler, tr., in Loeb Classical Library (London, New York, 1913), I, 563.
13. *Ibid.*, p. 565.
14. Plato, *Epistles*, p. 537.
15. *Ibid.*, pp. 531–533.

. . . Whenever one sees a man's written compositions—whether they be the laws of a legislator or anything else in any other form—these are not his most serious works, if so be that the writer himself is serious: rather those works abide in the fairest region he possesses. If, however, these really are his serious efforts, and put into writing, it is not "the gods" but mortal men who "then of a truth themselves have utterly ruined his senses." [16]

We must bear this discord in mind as we scrutinize the Platonic dialogue to discover how Socrates accomplished his pedagogic task.

One achievement is universally conceded to him: that by his questioning he leads his pupils to confess their ignorance and thus cuts through the roots of their dogmatism. This result, which indeed cannot be *forced* in any other way, discloses the significance of the dialogue as an instrument of instruction. The lecture, too, can stimulate spontaneous thinking, particularly in more mature students; but no matter what allure such stimulus may possess, it is not *irresistible*. Only persistent pressure to speak one's mind, to meet every counterquestion, and to state the reasons for every assertion transforms the power of that allure into an irresistible compulsion. This art of *forcing* minds *to freedom* constitutes the first secret of the Socratic method.

But only the first. For it does not take the pupil beyond the abandonment of his prejudices, the realization of his not-knowing, this negative determinant of all genuine and certain knowledge.

Socrates, after this higher level of ignorance is reached, far from directing the discussion toward the metaphysical problems, blocks every attempt of his pupils to push straight on to them with the injunction that they had better first learn about the life of the weavers, the blacksmiths, the carters. In this pattern of the discussion we recognize the philosophical instinct for the only correct method: first to derive the general premises from the observed facts of everyday life, and thus to proceed from judgments of which we are sure to those that are less sure.

It is astonishing how little understood this simple guiding idea

16. Plato, *Epistles*, p. 541.

of method is even in our own day. Take, for example, the assertion that his use of the affairs of the workaday world as a point of departure exhibits merely the practical interest Socrates took in the moral jolting of his fellow citizens. No, had Socrates been concerned with natural philosophy rather than with ethics, he would still have introduced his ideas in the same way.

We arrive at no better understanding of the Socratic method when we consider the way it works back from particulars to universals as a method of regressive inference, thereby identifying it with the inductive method. Though Aristotle praised him for it, Socrates was not the inventor of the inductive method. Rather, he pursued the path of abstraction, which employs reflection to lift the knowledge we already possess into consciousness. Had Aristotle been correct in his interpretation, we should not be surprised at the failure of Socrates' endeavors. For ethical principles cannot be derived from observed facts.

The truth is that in the execution of his design Socrates does fail. His sense of truth guides him surely through the introduction of the abstraction; but further on so many erroneous methodological ideas intrude that the success of the conversation is almost always frustrated.

In this process of separation from the particulars of experience and in his search for the more universal truths, Socrates concentrates his attention wholly on the general characteristics of concepts as we grasp them and devotes himself to the task of making these concepts explicit by definition. Without concepts, of course, there is no definite comprehension of general rational truths; but the elucidation of concepts and the discussion of their interrelations do not suffice to gain the content of the synthetic truths that are the true object of his quest.

What holds Socrates on his futile course is a mistake that comes to light only in Plato and gives his doctrine of ideas its ambivalent, half-mystic, half-logicizing character. This doctrine assumes that concepts are images of the ideas that constitute ultimate reality. This is why the Socratic-Platonic dialogues see the summit of scientific knowledge in the elucidation of concepts.

It is not difficult for us to discern in retrospect the error that caused philosophy here to stray from the right path, and consequently hindered the elaboration of methods of abstraction requisite for scientific metaphysics. However, it would be beside the point to dwell on the shortcomings of a philosophy that made for the first time an attempt at critical self-analysis. Our present concern is not with its errors or with the incompleteness of its system but with its bold and sure beginnings that opened the road to philosophical truth.

Socrates was the first to combine with confidence in the ability of the human mind to recognize philosophical truth the conviction that this truth is not arrived at through occasional bright ideas or mechanical teaching but that only planned, unremitting, and consistent thinking leads us from darkness into its light. Therein lies Socrates' greatness as a philosopher. His greatness as a pedagogue is based on another innovation: he made his pupils do their own thinking and introduced the interchange of ideas as a safeguard against self-deception.

In the light of this evaluation, the Socratic method, for all its deficiencies, remains the only method for teaching philosophy. Conversely, all philosophical instruction is fruitless if it conflicts with Socrates' basic methodic requirements.

Of course, the development of philosophical knowledge had to free from its entanglement with Platonic mysticism the doctrine of reminiscence, the truth of which constitutes the real and most profound reason for the possibility of and necessity for the Socratic method. This liberation was achieved after two thousand years by the critical philosophies of Kant and Fries. They carried the regressive method of abstraction to completion. Beyond this, they firmly secured the results of abstraction—which as basic principles do not admit of proof but as propositions must nevertheless be verified—by the method of *deduction.**

In the idea of this deduction—with which only Fries really succeeded—the doctrine of reminiscence experienced its resurrection. It is not too much to say that the Socratic-Platonic concept was thus transmuted from the prophetic-symbolic form, in which it had been confined by the two Greek sages, into the solidly welded and unshakably established form of a science.

Deduction, this master achievement of philosophy, is not easy

* Regarding the use of the word "deduction," see p. 119, n.

to explain. If I were to attempt to convey some idea of it, I could not indicate its nature more succinctly than by saying that it is quite literally the instrumentality for carrying out the Socratic design to instruct the ignorant by compelling them to realize that they actually know what they did not know they knew.

Kant and Fries did not pursue the problem of instruction in philosophy beyond some incidental pedagogic observations of a general character. But, thanks to critical philosophy, philosophical science has made such progress in surmounting its inherent methodological difficulties that now the most urgent task of critical philosophy is the revival and furtherance of the Socratic method, especially in its bearing on teaching. Must another two thousand years elapse before a kindred genius appears and rediscovers the ancient truth? Our science requires a continuous succession of trained philosophers, at once independent and well schooled, to avert the danger that critical philosophy may either fall a victim of incomprehension or, though continuing in name, it yet may become petrified into dogmatism.

In view of the importance of this task, we shall do well to pause once more and scrutinize the whole of the difficulty we must face. The exposition of our problem has disclosed the profound relation between critical philosophy and the Socratic method, on the basis of which we determine that the essence of the Socratic method consists in freeing instruction from dogmatism; in other words, in excluding all didactic judgments from instruction. Now we are confronted with the full gravity of the pedagogic problem we are to solve. Consider the question: How is any instruction and therefore any teaching at all possible when every instructive judgment is forbidden? Let us not attempt evasion by assuming that the requirement cannot possibly be meant to go to the extreme of prohibiting an occasional discreet helpful hint from teacher to student. No, there must be an honest choice: either dogmatism or following Socrates. The question then becomes all the more insistent: How is Socratic instruction possible?

Here we actually come up against the basic problem of education, which in its general form points to the question: How is education at all possible? If the end of education is rational self-determination, i.e., a condition in which the individual does not allow his behavior to be determined by outside influences but judges and acts according to his own insight, the question arises: How can we affect a person by outside influences so that he will not permit himself to be affected by outside influences? We must resolve this paradox or abandon the task of education.

The first thing to note is that in nature the human mind is always under external influences and, indeed, that the mind cannot develop without external stimulus. We then are confronted with the still broader question: Is self-determination compatible with the fact that in nature the mind is subject to external influence?

It will help us to clarify our thinking if we distinguish between the two senses in which the term "external influence" is used. It may mean external influence in general or an external determinant. Similarly, in teaching it may mean external stimulation of the mind or molding the mind to the acceptance of outside judgments.

Now, it is clearly no contradiction to hold both that the human mind finds within itself the cognitive source of philosophical truth and that insight into this truth is awakened in the mind by external stimuli. Indeed, the mind requires such external stimulation if the initial obscurity of philosophical truth is to grow into clear knowledge. Within the limits set by these conditions, instruction in philosophy is possible and even necessary if the development of the pupil is to be independent of mere chance.

Philosophical instruction fulfills its task when it systematically weakens the influences that obstruct the growth of philosophical comprehension and reinforces those that promote it. Without going into the question of other relevant influences, let us keep firmly in mind the one that must be excluded unconditionally: the influence that may emanate from the instructor's assertions. If this influence is not eliminated, all labor is vain. The instructor will have done everything possible to forestall the pupil's own judgment by offering him a ready-made judgment.

We are now arrived at a point from which we have a clear view both of the task of the Socratic method and of the possibility of fulfilling it. The rest must be left to the experiment and the degree of conviction it may carry.

But it would be underrating the difficulty presented not to consider what the experiment must call for if from its outcome we are to decide whether or not our goal is attainable. Although I have been taxing your patience for some time, I should render a poor service to our cause, and thus to you too, if I did not engage your attention a while longer to consider the *procedure* of such an experiment.

There is a danger inherent in the nature of an exacting enterprise, whose success has met with little recognition, and it is this: that the participants in it, once they become involved in its mounting difficulties and unexpected distractions, will repent of their good intentions or at least will begin to think of ways of modifying the method to make it easier. This tendency, springing from purely subjective discomfort, is likely to distort or completely frustrate the object of the undertaking. It is therefore advisable, lest expectations be disappointed, to envisage in advance as clearly as possible the manifold difficulties that will surely arise and, with due appreciation of these difficulties, to set down what will be required of teachers and students.

We must bear in mind that instruction in philosophy is not concerned with heaping solution on solution, nor indeed with establishing results, but solely with learning the method of reaching solutions. If we do this, we shall observe at once that the teacher's proper role cannot be that of a guide keeping his party from wrong paths and accidents. Nor yet is he a guide going in the lead while his party simply follow in the expectation that this will prepare them to find the same path later on by themselves. On the contrary, the essential thing is the skill with which the teacher puts the pupils on their own responsibility at the very beginning by teaching them to go by themselves—although they would not on that account go alone—and by so developing this independence that one day they may be able to venture forth alone, self-guidance having replaced the teacher's supervision.

As to the observations I am about to make, I must beg to be

allowed to cull incidental examples from my own long experience as a teacher of philosophy, for unfortunately the experiences of others are not at my disposal.

Let me take up first the requirements imposed on the teacher and then go on to those placed on the pupil. Once a student of mine, endeavoring to reproduce a Socratically conducted exercise, presented a version in which he put the replies now into the teacher's mouth, now into the pupil's. Only my astonished question, "Have you ever heard me say 'yes' or 'no'?" stopped him short. Thrasymachus saw the point more clearly; in Plato's *Republic* he calls out to Socrates: "Ye gods! . . . I knew it . . . that you would refuse and do anything rather than answer." [17] The teacher who follows the Socratic model does not answer. Neither does he question. More precisely, he puts no philosophical questions, and when such questions are addressed to him, he under no circumstances gives the answer sought. Does he then remain silent? We shall see. During such a session we may often hear the despairing appeal to the teacher: "I don't know what it is you want!" Whereupon the teacher replies: "I? I want nothing at all." This certainly does not convey the desired information. What is it, then, that the teacher actually does? He sets the interplay of question and answer going between the students, perhaps by the introductory remark: "Has anyone a question?"

Now, everyone will realize that, as Kant said, "to know what questions may reasonably be asked is already a great and necessary proof of sagacity and insight." [18] What about foolish questions, or what if there are no questions at all? Suppose nobody answers?

You see, at the very beginning the difficulty presents itself of getting the students to the point of spontaneous activity, and with it arises the temptation for the teacher to pay out a clue like Ariadne's thread. But the teacher must be firm from the beginning, and especially at the beginning. If a student approaches philosophy without having a single question to put to it, what can

---

17. Plato, *The Republic*, Paul Shorey, tr., in Loeb Classical Library (London, New York), p. 41.
18. Kant, *Critique of Pure Reason*, p. 97.

we expect in the way of his capacity to persevere in exploring its complex and profound problems?

What should the teacher do if there are no questions? He should wait—until questions come. At most, he should request that in the future, in order to save time, questions be thought over in advance. But he should not, just to save time, save the students the effort of formulating their own questions. If he does, he may for the moment temper their impatience, but only at the cost of nipping in the bud the philosophical impatience we seek to awaken.

Once questions start coming—one by one, hesitantly, good ones and foolish ones—how does the teacher receive them, how does he handle them? He now seems to have easy going since the rule of the Socratic method forbids his answering them. He submits the questions to discussion.

All of them? The appropriate and the inappropriate?

By no means. He ignores all questions uttered in too low a voice. Likewise those that are phrased incoherently. How can difficult ideas be grasped when they are expressed in mutilated language?

Thanks to the extraordinary instruction in the mother tongue given in our schools, over half the questions are thus eliminated.* As for the rest, many are confused or vague. Sometimes clarification comes with the counterquestion: "Just what do you mean by that?" But very often this will not work because the speaker does not know what he means himself. The work of the discussion group thus tends automatically either to take up the clear, simple questions or to clear up unclear, vague ones first.

We are not so fortunate in the problems of philosophy as we are in the problems of mathematics, which, as Hilbert says, fairly call to us: "Here I am, find the solution!" The philosophical problem is wrapped in obscurity. To be able to come to grips with it by framing clear-cut, searching questions demands many trials and much effort. It will therefore scarcely surprise you to learn that a semester's work in a seminar in ethics yielded nothing

---

* Nelson refers, of course, to German schools. The reader may judge to what degree this criticism also applies to schools in the United States and England.

except agreement on the fact that the initial question was incongruous. The question was, "Is it not stupid to act morally?"

Of course, the instructor will not submit every incongruous question to such protracted examination. He will seek to advance the discussion through his own appraisal of the questions. But he will do no more than allow a certain question to come to the fore because it is instructive in itself or because threshing it out will bring to light typical errors. And he will do this by some such expedient as following the question up with the query: "Who understood what was said just now?" This contains no indication of the relevance or irrelevance of the question; it is merely an invitation to consider it, to extract its meaning by intensive cross-examination.

What is his policy as regards the answers? How are they handled? They are treated like the questions. Unintelligible answers are ignored in order to teach the students to meet the requirements of scientific speech. Answers, too, are probed through such questions as:

"What has this answer to do with our question?"

"Which word do you wish to emphasize?"

"Who has been following?"

"Do you still know what you said a few moments ago?"

"What question are we talking about?"

The simpler these questions, the more flustered the students become. Then, if some fellow student takes pity on his colleague's distress and comes to his aid with the explanation, "He surely wanted to say . . . ," this helpful gesture is unfeelingly cut short with the request to let the art of mind reading alone and cultivate instead the more modest art of saying what one actually wants to say.

By this time you will have gathered that the investigations run a far from even course. Questions and answers tumble over one another. Some of the students understand the development, some do not. The latter cut in with groping questions, trying to re-establish contact, but the others will not be stopped from going ahead. They disregard the interruptions. New questions crop up, wider of the mark. Here and there a debater falls silent; then whole groups. Meanwhile, the agitation continues, and questions become constantly more pointless. Even those who were originally sure of their ground become confused. They, too, lose the thread and do not know how to find it again. Finally, nobody knows where the discussion is headed.

The bewilderment famed in the Socratic circle closes in. Everyone is at his wit's end. What had been certain at the outset has become uncertain. The students, instead of clarifying their own conceptions, now feel as though they had been robbed of their capacity to make anything clear by thinking.

And does the teacher tolerate this too?

"I consider," says Meno to his teacher Socrates, in the dialogue bearing his name, "that both in appearance and in other respects you are extremely like the flat torpedo fish; for it benumbs anyone who approaches and touches it. . . . For in truth I feel my soul and my tongue quite benumbed and I am at a loss what answer to give you." [19]

When Socrates replies, "It is from being in more doubt than anyone else that I cause doubts in others," Meno counters with the celebrated question: "Why, on what lines will you look, Socrates, for a thing of whose nature you know nothing at all?" And this draws from Socrates the more celebrated answer: "Because the soul should be able to recollect all that she knew before." [20] We all know that these words are an echo of the Platonic doctrine of ideas, which the historic Socrates did not teach. Yet there is in them the Socratic spirit, the stout spirit of reason's self-confidence, its reverence for its own self-sufficient strength. This strength gives Socrates the composure that permits him to let the seekers after truth go astray and stumble. More than that, it gives him the courage to send them astray in order to test their convictions, to separate knowledge simply taken over from the truth that slowly attains clarity in us through our own reflection. He is unafraid of the confession of not-knowing; indeed, he even induces it. In this he is guided by an attitude of thinking so far from skeptical that he regards this admission as the first step

19. Plato, *Meno*, W. R. M. Lamb, tr., in Loeb Classical Library (London, New York, 1924), IV, 297.
20. *Ibid.*, pp. 299 ff.

toward deeper knowledge. "He does not think he knows . . . and is he not better off in respect of the matter which he did not know?" he says of the slave to whom he gives instruction in mathematics. "For now he will push on in the search gladly, as lacking knowledge." [21]

To Socrates the test of whether a man loves wisdom is whether he welcomes his ignorance in order to attain to better knowledge. The slave in the *Meno* does this and goes on with the task. Many, however, slacken and tire of the effort when they find their knowledge belittled, when they find that their first few unaided steps do not get them far. The teacher of philosophy who lacks the courage to put his pupils to the test of perplexity and discouragement not only deprives them of the opportunity to develop the endurance needed for research but also deludes them concerning their capabilities and makes them dishonest with themselves.

Now we can discern one of the sources of error that provoke the familiar unjust criticisms of the Socratic method. This method is charged with a defect which it merely reveals and which it must reveal to prepare the ground on which alone the continuation of serious work is possible. It simply uncovers the harm that has been done to men's minds by dogmatic teaching.

Is it a fault of the Socratic method that it must take time for such elementary matters as ascertaining what question is being discussed or determining what the speaker intended to say about it? It is easy for dogmatic instruction to soar into higher regions. Indifferent to self-understanding, it purchases its illusory success at the cost of more and more deeply rooted dishonesty. It is not surprising, then, that the Socratic method is compelled to fight a desperate battle for integrity of thought and speech before it can turn to larger tasks. It must also suffer the additional reproach of being unphilosophical enough to orient itself by means of examples and facts.

The only way one can learn to recognize and avoid the pitfalls of reflection is to become acquainted with them in *application*, even at the risk of gaining wisdom only by sad experience. It is useless to preface philosophizing proper with an introductory

21. Plato, *Meno*, p. 313.

course in logic in the hope of thus saving the novice from the risk of taking the wrong path. Knowledge of the principles of logic and the rules of the syllogism, even the ability to illustrate every fallacy by examples, remains after all an art *in abstracto*. An individual is far from learning to think logically even though he has learned to conclude by all the syllogistic rules that Caius is mortal. The test of one's own conclusions and their subjection to the rules of logic is the province of one's faculty of judgment, not at all the province of logic. The faculty of judgment, said Kant, being the power of rightly employing given rules, "must belong to the learner himself; and in the absence of such a natural gift no rule that may be prescribed to him for this purpose can ensure against misuse." [22] If, therefore, this natural gift is weak, it must be strengthened. But it can be strengthened only by exercise.

Thus, after our instructor breaks the spell of numbness by calling for a return to the original question, and the students trace their way back to the point from which they started, each must, by critical examination of every one of his steps, study the sources of error and work out for himself his own school of logic. Rules of logic derived from personal experience retain a living relation with the judgments they are to govern. Furthermore, the fact that dialectics, though indispensable, is introduced as an auxiliary only prevents attaching an exaggerated value to it in the manner of scholasticism, to which the most trivial metaphysical problem served for the exercise of logical ingenuity. Segregation of the philosophical disciplines with a view to reducing the difficulties of instruction by separate treatment would be worse than a waste of time. Other ways will have to be found to satisfy the pedagogic maxim that our requirements of the pupil should become progressively more stringent.

This question, if examined carefully, presents no further difficulties for us. If there is such a thing as a research method for philosophy, its essential element must consist of practical directives for the step-by-step solution of problems. It is therefore simply a question of letting the student himself follow the path of the regressive method. The first step, obviously, is to have him

22. Kant, *Critique of Pure Reason*, p. 178.

secure a firm footing in experience—which is harder to do than an outsider might think. For your adept in philosophy scorns nothing so much as using his intelligence concretely in forming judgments on real facts, an operation that obliges him to remember those lowly instruments of cognition, his five senses. Ask anyone at a philosophy seminar, "What do you see on the blackboard?" and depend on it, he will look at the floor. Upon your repeating, "What do you see *on the blackboard?*" he will finally wrench out a sentence that begins with "If" and demonstrates that for him the world of facts does not exist.

He shows the same disdain for reality when asked to give an example. Forthwith he goes off into a world of fantasy or, if forced to stay on this planet, he at least makes off to the sea or into the desert, so that one wonders whether being attacked by lions and saved from drowning are typical experiences among the acquaintances of a philosopher. The "if" sentences, the farfetched examples, and the premature desire for definitions characterize not the ingenuous beginner but rather the philosophically indoctrinated dilettante. And it is always he, with his pseudowisdom, who disturbs the quiet and simple progress of an investigation.

I recall a seminar in logic, in which the desire to start from general definitions—under the impression that otherwise the concepts being discussed could not be employed—caused much fruitless trouble. Despite my warning, the group stuck to the opening question: "What is a concept?"

It was not long before a casual reference to the concept "lamp" as an example was followed by the appearance of the "lamp in general" provided with all the essential characteristics of all particular lamps. The students waxed warm in vehement dispute regarding the proof of the existence of this lamp furnished with all the essential features of all particular lamps. My diffident question, whether the lamp-in-general was fed with gas, electricity, or kerosene, went unanswered as unworthy of philosophical debate until, hours later, the resumption of this very question of the source of energy forced the negation of the existence of the lamp-in-general. That is to say, the disputants discovered that different illuminants for one and the same lamp, be it ever so general, were mutually exclusive. Thus, starting with practical application, they had unexpectedly found the law of contradiction by the regressive method. But to define the concept of a concept had proved a vain endeavor; just as in the Socratic circle the definitions nearly always miscarried.

Are we justified, however, in assuming that the cause of such failures always lies in conditions unconnected with the Socratic method itself? Does not this method perhaps suffer from an inherent limitation that makes the solution of deeper problems impossible?

Before coming to a final decision on this point, we must consider one more factor that creates difficulty in the employment of the Socratic method. Though intimately associated with the latter, it lies outside it, yet demands consideration before we can set the limits of the method itself.

The significance of the Socratic dialogue has been sought in the assumption that deliberating with others makes us more easily cognizant of truth than silent reflection. Obviously, there is much soundness in this view. Yet many a person may be moved to doubt this praise after he has listened to the hodgepodge of questions and answers at a philosophical debate and noted the absence, despite the outward discipline, of the tranquillity that belongs to reflection. It is inevitable that what is said by one participant may prove disturbing to another, whether he feels himself placed in a dependent position by intelligent remarks or is distracted by poor ones. It is inevitable that collaboration should progressively become a trial of nerves, made more difficult by increasing demands on personal tact and tolerance.

To a great extent these disturbances can be obviated by an instructor who, for instance, will ignore the innumerable senseless answers, cast doubt on the right ones with Socratic irony, or ease nervous unrest with some understanding word. But his power to restore harmony to the play of ideas is limited unless the others are willing to pursue the common task with determination.

It should be admitted that many disturbances are unavoidable because of the students' imperfect understanding; but the obstacles I have in mind do not lie in the intellectual sphere and for that reason even the most skillful teacher finds them an insurmountable barrier. He can enforce intellectual discipline only if the students are possessed of a disciplined will. This may sound strange but it is a fact that one becomes a philosopher, not by virtue of intellectual gifts but by the exercise of will.

True, philosophizing demands considerable power of intellect. But who will exercise it? Surely not the man who relies merely on his intellectual power. As he delves more deeply into his studies and his difficulties multiply, he will without fail weaken. Because of his intelligence he will recognize these difficulties, even see them very clearly. But the elasticity required to face a problem again and again, to stay with it until it is solved, and not to succumb to disintegrating doubt—this elasticity is achieved only through the power of an iron will, a power of which the entertaining ingenuity of the mere sophist knows nothing. In the end, his intellectual fireworks are as sterile for science as the intellectual dullness that shrinks back at the first obstacle. It is no accident that the investigators whom the history of philosophy records as having made the most decisive advances in dialectics were at the same time philosophers in the original meaning of the word. Only because they loved wisdom were they able to take upon themselves the "many preliminary subjects it entails and [so] much labor," as Plato says in a letter that continues:

For on hearing this, if the pupil be truly philosophical, in sympathy with the subject and worthy of it, because divinely gifted, he believes that he has been shown a marvelous pathway and that he must brace himself at once to follow it, and that life will not be worth living if he does otherwise. . . .

Those, on the other hand, who are in reality not philosophical, but superficially tinged with opinions—like men whose bodies are sunburnt on the surface—when they see how many studies are required and how great labor, and how the disciplined mode of daily life is that which benefits the subject, they deem it difficult or impossible for themselves.[23]

That is the clear and most definite characteristic of "those who are luxurious and incapable of enduring labor, since [the test] prevents any of them from ever casting the blame on his instruc-

23. Plato, *Epistles*, pp. 527 ff.

tor instead of on himself and his own inability to pursue all the studies which are necessary to his subject." [23]

"In one word, neither receptivity nor memory will ever produce knowledge in him who has no affinity with the object, since it does not germinate to start with in alien states of mind." [24]

We, in common with Plato, require of the philosopher that he strengthen his will power, but it is impossible to achieve this as a by-product in the course of philosophical instruction. The student's will power must be the fruit of his prior education. It is the instructor's duty to make no concession in maintaining the rigorous and indispensable demands on the will; indeed, he must do so out of respect for the students themselves. If, for the want of requisite firmness, he allows himself to be persuaded to relax his stand, or if he does so of his own accord to hold his following, he will have betrayed his philosophical goal. He has no alternative: he must insist on his demands or give up the task. Everything else is abject compromise.

Of course, the student should know the details of the demands to be made on his will. They constitute the minimum required for examining ideas in a group. This means, first, the communication of thoughts, not of acquired fragments of knowledge, not even the knowledge of other people's thoughts. It means, further, the use of clear, unambiguous language. Only the compulsion to communicate provides a means of testing the definiteness and clarity of one's own conceptions. Here, protesting that one has the right feeling but cannot express it will not avail. Feeling is indeed the first and best guide on the path to truth, but it is just as often the protector of prejudice. In a scientific matter, therefore, feeling must be interpreted so that it may be evaluated in accordance with concepts and ordered logic. Moreover, our investigation demands the communication of ideas in distinctly audible and generally comprehensible speech, free from ambiguities. A technical terminology is not only unnecessary for philosophizing but is actually detrimental to its steady progress. It imparts to metaphysical matters, abstract and difficult in any case, the appearance of an esoteric science, which only superior

24. Plato, *Epistles*, p. 539.

minds are qualified to penetrate. It prevents us from considering the conclusions of unprejudiced judgment, which we have seen to be the starting point of meaningful philosophizing. Unprejudiced judgment, in its operation, relies on concepts that we have, not on artificial reflections, and it makes its conclusions understood by strict adherence to current linguistic usage.

In order to grasp those concepts clearly it is necessary, of course, to isolate them. By the process of abstraction it is possible to separate them from other ideas, to reduce them gradually to their elements, and through such analyses to advance to basic concepts. By holding fast to existing concepts, the philosopher guards himself against peopling his future system with the products of mere speculation and with fantastic brain children. For, if he does not consult unprejudiced judgment, he will allow himself to be lured into forming philosophical concepts by the arbitrary combination of specific characteristics, without any assurance that objects corresponding to his constructions actually exist. Only the use of the same vocabulary still connects him with the critical philosopher. He denotes his artificial concept by the same word the critical philosopher uses to denote his real concept, although, to be sure, he uses this word in a different sense. He says "I" and means "cosmic reason." He says "God" and means "peace of mind." He says "state" and means "power subject to no law." He says "marriage" and means "indissoluble communion of love." He says "space" and means "the labyrinth of the ear." His language is full of artificial meanings. Although it is not apparent, his is actually a technical language; and because this is so, the situation is far more dangerous than it would be if the philosopher indicated the special sense of his language by coining specific new terms. For the sameness of the words tricks the unwary into associating their own familiar concepts with them, and a misunderstanding results. What is more pernicious, this artificial language tempts its own creator to the covert use of the same words in different meanings, and by such a shift of concepts he produces sham proofs. In this abuse of purely verbal definitions we encounter one of the most prevalent and profound of dialectical errors, an error that is rendered more difficult to track down by the fact that the shift of concepts cannot be discovered simply by calling on intuition. However, it betrays itself through its consequences, through the curious phenomenon that with the help of the same verbal definition the pseudoproof presented can be confronted with a contrary proof that has the same air of validity.

The most celebrated and memorable instance of such antitheses is found in the antinomies that Kant discovered and solved. Kant said of these classic examples of contradiction that they were the most beneficent aberration in the history of reason because they furnished the incentive to investigate the cause of the illusion and to reconcile reason to itself. This remark is applicable to every instance of such dialectical conflict.

It will seem, perhaps, that in these last considerations we have strayed somewhat from our subject: the requirement that the student use distinctly audible and generally comprehensible language. But, as a matter of fact, we have secured a deeper understanding of the significance of that requirement.

After all that we have said, what is it that we gain with this demand on the pupil? Only those who, by using comprehensible language, adhere to the concepts we have and become practiced in discussing them will sharpen their critical sense for every arbitrary definition and for every sham proof adroitly derived from such verbal definition. If the requirement of simple and clear language is observed, it is possible, in Socratic teaching, merely by writing the theses of two mutually contradictory doctrines on the blackboard, to focus attention on the verbal definition underlying them, disclose its abuse, and thereby overthrow both doctrinal opinions. The success of such a dialectical performance is achieved—and this is its significant feature—not by flashes of inspiration but methodically, i.e., through a step-by-step search for the hidden premise at the bottom of the contradictory judgments. This method will succeed if the student, struck with suspicion at such a sophism, attends closely to the meaning of the words, for these words, when used in an inartificial sense, put him on the track of the error.

Do not misunderstand me. I do not advocate the point of view that so-called common sense and its language can satisfy the demands of scientific philosophizing. Nor is it my purpose, in dwelling on simple elementary conditions seemingly easy to fulfill, to veil the fact that the pursuit of philosophizing requires rigorous training in the art of abstraction, one difficult to master. My point is this: We cannot with impunity skip the first steps in the development of this art. Abstraction must have something to abstract from. The immediate and tangible material of philosophy is language which presents concepts through words. In its wealth, supplied from many sources, reason dwells concealed. Reflection discloses this rational knowledge by separating it from intuitive notions.

Just as Socrates took pains to question locksmiths and blacksmiths and made their activities the first subject of discussion with his pupils, so every philosopher ought to start out with the vernacular and develop the language of his abstract science from its pure elements.

I am now done with the requirements that apply to the students. Their difficulty lies not in the fulfillment of details but in the observance of the whole. I said earlier that the working agreement with the students requires of them nothing but the communication of their ideas. You will understand if I now express the same demand in another form: It requires of the students submission to the method of philosophizing, for it is the sole aim of Socratic instruction to enable the students to judge for themselves their observance of the agreement.

Our examination of the Socratic method is nearing its conclusion. Now that we have discussed the difficulties of its application, there remains only one query: May not the reason for the unfavorable reception of the method lie, in part at least, within itself? Is there not perhaps some limitation inherent in it that restricts its usefulness?

One singular fact, more than any other, is calculated to make us consider this doubt seriously. Fries, the one man who actually completed critical philosophy and restored the Socratic-Platonic doctrine of reminiscence and the self-certainty of intelligence, Fries, the most genuine of all Socrateans, gave the Socratic method only qualified recognition because he considered it inadequate for achieving complete self-examination of the intellect. He acknowledged its capacity to guide the novice in the early stages; he even demanded emphatically that all instruction in philosophy follow the spirit of the Socratic method, the essence of which, he held, lay not in its use of dialogue but in its "starting from the common things of everyday life and only then going on from these to scientific views." [25] "But as soon as higher truths, further removed from intuition and everyday experience, are involved," [26] Fries did not approve of letting the students find these truths by themselves. "Here the instructor must employ a language molded upon subtle abstractions, of which the student does not yet have complete command, and to which he must be educated by instruction." [27]

In Fries's own words, this lecture method of instruction "step by step invites cooperative thinking." [28] An illustration of it is given in his didactic novel, *Julius und Evagoras*. And indeed it is not a form of Socratic instruction.

I should not think of choosing a really successful dialogue of Plato's—were there such—as subject matter for a philosophy seminar as it would forestall the creative thinking of the students, but there is nothing in *Julius und Evagoras* to preclude its use for such a purpose. For the development of abstract ideas which it presents to the reader does indeed "invite" critical verification by the students, as Fries desires. However, though otherwise exemplary, it offers no assurance that the students will accept the invitation or, if made to stand on their own feet, that they will master such difficulties as they may encounter on their way. Have your students study the fine and instructive chapter on "The Sources of Certainty," and I stand ready to demonstrate in a Socratic discussion that those students will still lack everything that would enable them to defend what they have learned. The key to this riddle is to be found in Goethe's words: "One sees only what one already knows."

It is futile to lay a sound, clear, and well-grounded theory before the students; futile though they respond to the invitation to follow in their thinking. It is even useless to point out to them

25. J. F. Fries, *System der Logik* (3d ed., reissued, Leipzig, 1914), p. 449.
26. Fries, *Die Geschichte der Philosophie*, I, 253.
27. Fries, *System der Logik*, p. 436.
28. *Ibid.*

the difficulties they would have to overcome in order to work out such results independently. If they are to become independent masters of philosophical theory, it is imperative that they go beyond the mere learning of problems and their difficulties; they must wrestle with them in constant practical application so that, through day-by-day dealing with them, they may learn to overcome them with all their snares and pitfalls and diversities of form. However, the instructor's lecture that Fries would have delivered "in language molded upon subtle abstractions," just because of its definiteness and clearness, will obscure the difficulties that hamper the development of this very lucidity of thought and verbal precision. The outcome will be that in the end only those already expert in Socratic thinking will assimilate the philosophical substance and appreciate the solidness and originality of the exposition.

Fries underrated the Socratic method because, for one thing, he did not and could not find the Socratic method in the method of Socrates, and he considered this fact as confirming his opinion of the inadequacy of the Socratic method. Another reason—and the more profound, I think—lay in the particular character of Fries's genius. He combined with a sense of truth unparalleled in the history of philosophy a linguistic gift that produced with the assurance of a somnambulist the words that were most appropriate to a philosophical idea. A man with a mind so superior, rich, and free will always find it difficult to maintain close contact with the minds of less independent thinkers. He is prone to overlook the danger of dogmatism that threatens the more dependent mind even when the instructor's lecture has reached the highest degree of lucidity and exactitude of expression. A man of such superiority can become a leader of generations of men. But this is contingent on the appearance of teachers who will find the key to his language by resorting to the "maieutic" services * of the Socratic method, instituting the laborious and protracted exercises that must not frighten away those who plan to dedicate themselves to philosophy.

* Maieutic: "The word means performing midwife's service (to thought or ideas); Socrates figured himself as a midwife (*maia*) bringing others' thoughts to birth with his questionings; . . ." (H. D. Fowler, *A Dictionary of Modern English Usage* [New York, 1944], p. 339.) See the quotation from Plato's *Theætetus* at the end of this essay.

I maintain that this art has no limitations. I have seen a Socratic seminar not only deal successfully with such an abstract subject as the philosophy of law but even proceed to the construction of its system.

This is claiming a good deal, you will say. Well, I have enough Socratic irony to acknowledge the awkwardness of my position, which, incidentally, I admitted in the opening sentence of my address. For when all is said and done, no one will be won over to the cause I am pleading here except by the evidence of the experiment, that is, through his own experience.

But let us look about us: Can we not find some sufficiently simple and well-known control experiment that permits a valid conclusion on the question at issue? What sort of experiment might that be? If non-Socratically conducted instruction could accomplish the designated end in philosophy, such a procedure should succeed all the more readily in a science that does not have to struggle with the particular difficulties of philosophical knowledge—a science in which, on the contrary, everything from first to last becomes absolutely and completely clear even when set forth in a dogmatic lecture.

If we inquire whether there is such a science and, if so, whether it has a place among the subjects of instruction in our schools and universities, we find that such a science actually does exist. Mathematics satisfies both conditions. "We are in possession," said a classic French mathematician. The relevant experiment is thus available, and we need only consider its outcome with an unprejudiced mind.

What does it teach? Just among ourselves and without glossing over anything or blaming anyone, we teachers might as well confess to what is a public secret: on the whole the result is negative. We all know from personal experience that diligent and even gifted students in our secondary schools and colleges, if seriously put to the test, are not sure of even the rudiments of mathematics and discover their own ignorance.

Our experiment therefore points to the conclusion I spoke of; as a matter of fact, there is no escaping it. Suppose someone were to say there is no such thing as understanding, regardless of the kind of instruction. That is arguable, but not for us as pedagogues. We start from the assumption that meaningful instruction is possible. And then we must come to the conclusion that, if there is any assurance that a subject can be understood, Socratic instruction offers such assurance. And with that we have found more than we sought, for this conclusion applies not only to philosophy but to every subject that involves comprehension.

An experiment conducted by history itself on a grand scale confirms the fact that the pedagogic inadequacy in the field of mathematics is not due merely to incompetent teachers but must have a more fundamental cause; or, to put it differently, that even the best mathematics instruction, if it follows the dogmatic method, cannot, despite all its clearness, bring about thorough understanding. This experiment deserves the attention of everyone interested in the teaching of mathematics.

The basic principles of calculus (nowadays included in the curricula of some of our high schools) became the secure and acknowledged possession of science only about the middle of the nineteenth century, when they were first established with clarity and exactitude. Although the most important results had been a matter of general knowledge ever since Newton and Leibniz, their foundations remained in dispute. Endlessly repeated attempts at elucidation only resulted in new obscurities and paradoxes. Considering the state of this branch of mathematics at that time, Berkeley was not unjustified when he undertook to prove that in the unintelligibility of its theories it was not one whit behind the dogmas and mysteries of theology.[29] We know today that those riddles were solvable, that, thanks to the work of Cauchy and Weierstrass, they have been solved, and that this branch of mathematics is susceptible of the same clarity and lucidity of structure as elementary geometry. Here, too, everything becomes evident as soon as attention is focused on the decisive point. But it is precisely this that is hard to achieve, an art each student must acquire by his own efforts.

29. George Berkeley, *The Analyst; or a Discourse Addressed to an Infidel Mathematician, Wherein It Is Examined Whether the Object, Principles, and Inferences of the Modern Analysis Are More Distinctly Conceived, or More Evidently Deduced, Than Religious Mysteries and Points of Faith.* Selected Pamphlets, Vol. XVI (London, 1734).

To demonstrate how true this is, I shall mention two especially noteworthy facts. The first is this: Newton's treatise, widely known and celebrated since its appearance, not only expounds the decisive point of view established by Cauchy and Weierstrass but formulates it with a clarity, precision, and succinctness that would satisfy the most exacting requirements contemporary science could lay down. Moreover, it contains an explicit warning against that very misunderstanding which, as we now know, kept succeeding generations of mathematicians so completely in bondage that their minds remained closed to the emphatic "Cave!" of the classic passage in Newton's work,[30] familiar to all of them.

The second, the complement, as it were, of the first, is that, even after Weierstrass and after the argument had at long last been settled, it was possible to revive it not only among dilettanti, whom we shall always have with us, but even under the leadership of a man of research as distinguished for his work on the theory of functions as Paul du Bois-Reymond. In his own words, his "solution is that it remains and will remain a riddle." [31]

There is an impressive warning in this instance of the disparity between the objective lucidity and systematic completeness of a scientific theory, on the one hand, and any pedagogic assurance that it will be understood, on the other. It is precisely the man with a philosophical turn of mind who is unwilling, in mathematics as elsewhere, simply to accept a result; he philosophizes about it, i.e., he strives to understand its fundamentals and bring it into harmony with the rest of his knowledge. But it is just he who is sure to fail unless he is one of the few who find their way to clarity by their own efforts. We thus discover that even mathematics, instead of remaining the unassailable standard and model that might help philosophy, is drawn along by it into the whirlpool of confusion.

Herewith, I believe, I have also answered the weightiest comment I know on the value of the Socratic method in teaching mathematics. It comes from no less a man than Weierstrass. He

30. Isaac Newton, *Philosophiae naturalis principia mathematica* (1687), Liber primus, scholium.
31. Paul du Bois-Reymond, *Die allgemeine Funktionentheorie* (Tübingen, 1882), Pt. I, p. 2.

devoted a special essay to the Socratic method,[32] an indication of the esteem and comprehension this profound mathematician and pedagogue had for our subject. His detailed argument is proof of this. He demonstrated the basic practicability of the Socratic method in philosophy and pure mathematics, in contradistinction to the empirical sciences. That he nevertheless rated it as of little value for use in the school was due, for one thing, to the fact that he considered insurmountable the external difficulties which undeniably exist, and which I have dwelt on extensively. For another, he was obviously partial to the coherent lecture with its large perspectives and architectonic beauty of structure, a partiality easily understandable in a scientist of his genius. Still, he admitted that such a lecture "presupposes students of rather more mature intelligence, if it is to be effective." Since, however, it was also his opinion that "the Socratic method, carried out in its true spirit, . . . is less suitable for boys than for more mature youths," one is impelled to ask (but in vain) how the maturity of mind can develop that will assure success to a non-Socratic mode of instruction.

What maturity of mind our students must have if they are to surpass Paul du Bois-Reymond, the pupil of Weierstrass, and Euler, the pupil of Newton, in depth of understanding!

Our findings might lead us to pessimism. But, if we view the matter rightly, we are not yet finished. What we have found actually indicates the way we can remove the cause of this lamentable state of affairs, which itself can hardly be regarded pessimistically enough.

The way lies in mathematics. It is within the power of the mathematicians to end the scandal that not only has completely undermined the authority of philosophy but also threatens mathematics itself with the loss of the prestige that, thanks to its powerful position in education, it has until now maintained in the intellectual life of mankind. In view of the deplorable situation in which the cause of the Socratic method finds itself, help can come only through a science that combines the several advantages

32. Karl Weierstrass, *Mathematische Werke* (Berlin, 1903), III, Appendix, 315–329.

I have discussed, advantages that only mathematics has and that assure it a head start which philosophy can never overcome by its own efforts.

The character and repute of mathematics as a science still stand quite firm. In the long run, the evidence of its results cannot be obscured by any teaching, however wretched, and it will always offer a means of orientation though all else be plunged into darkness and confusion. I therefore appeal to the mathematicians. May they become aware of the spiritual power they hold and of their consequent mission of leadership in the fields of science and education. Philosophy cannot now assume the role, originally hers, of guardian of the intellectual values whose fate is bound up with that of the Socratic method. Having disowned her stepchild and thus deprived herself of its vitalizing and rejuvenating influence, philosophy has become so infirm that she must now beg of her sister science asylum and aid for her cast-off daughter.

Though I said at the beginning that a sense of chivalry has made me champion of the disdained one, I am nevertheless far from blind to my powerlessness. I can fulfill this command of chivalry only by commending my protégée to the care of mathematics—confident that the outcast will be nurtured by it and grow vigorously until, her strength renewed, she returns to her own home and there establishes law and order, thus requiting with good the evil done her.

APPENDIX *

A MIDWIFERY FOR MEN

Theætetus. I can assure you, Socrates, that I have tried very often to answer your questions; but I can neither persuade myself that I have any answer to give, nor hear of anyone who answers as you would have him. I cannot shake off a feeling of anxiety.

Socrates. These are the pangs of labor, my dear Theætetus; you have something within you which you are bringing to birth.

Theæt. I do not know, Socrates; I only say what I feel.

Soc. And did you never hear, simpleton, that I am the son of a mid-wife, brave and burly, whose name was Phænarete?

Theæt. Yes, I have.

Soc. And that I myself practise midwifery?

Theæt. No, never.

Soc. Let me tell you that I do, my friend; but you must not reveal the secret, as the world in general has not found me out; and there-fore they only say of me, that I am the strangest of mortals, and drive men to their wits' end. Did you ever hear that too?

Theæt. Yes.

Soc. Shall I tell you the reason?

Theæt. By all means.

Soc. Bear in mind the whole business of the midwives, and then you will see my meaning better. By the use of potions and incanta-tions they are able to arouse the pangs and to soothe them at will; they can make those bear who have a difficulty in bearing, and if they think fit, they can smother the embryo in the womb.

Theæt. They can.

Soc. Did you ever remark that they are also most cunning match-makers, and have a thorough knowledge of what unions are likely to produce a brave brood?

Theæt. No, never.

Soc. Then let me tell you that this is their greatest pride, more than cutting the umbilical cord. And if you reflect, you will see that the same art which cultivates and gathers in the fruits of the earth, will be most likely to know in what soils the several plants or seeds should be deposited.

* See p. 35, n.

Theæt. Yes, the same art.

Soc. And do you suppose that with women the case is otherwise?

Theæt. I should think not.

Soc. Certainly not; but midwives are respectable women and have a character to lose, and they avoid this department of their profession, because they are afraid of being called procuresses, which is a name given to those who join together man and woman in an unlawful and unscientific way; and yet the true midwife is also the true and only matchmaker.

Theæt. Clearly.

Soc. Such are the midwives, whose task is a very important one, but not so important as mine; for women do not bring into the world at one time real children, and at another time counterfeits which are with difficulty distinguished from them; if they did, then the discernment of the true and false birth would be the crowning achievement of the art of midwifery—you would think so?

Theæt. Indeed I should.

Soc. Well, my art of midwifery is in most respects like theirs; but differs in that I attend men and not women, and I look after their souls when they are in labor, and not after their bodies; and the triumph of my art is in thoroughly examining whether the thought which the mind of the young man is bringing to birth, is a false idol or a noble and true spirit.

And like the midwives, I am barren, and the reproach which is often made against me, that I ask questions of others and have not the wit to answer them myself, is very just; the reason is, that the god compels me to be a midwife, but forbids me to bring forth.

And therefore I am not myself at all wise, nor have I anything to show which is the invention or birth of my own soul, but those who converse with me profit. Some of them appear dull enough at first, but afterwards, as our acquaintance ripens, if the god is gracious to them, they all make astonishing progress; and this in the opinion of others as well as their own.

It is quite clear that they had never learned anything from me; the many fine discoveries to which they cling are of their own making. But to me and the god they owe their delivery. And the proof of my words is, that many of them in their ignorance, either in their self-conceit despising me, or falling under the influence of others, have gone away too soon; and have not only lost the children of whom I had previously delivered them by an ill bringing up, but have stifled whatever else they had in them by evil communications, being fonder of lies and shams than of the truth; and they have at last ended by seeing themselves, as others see them, to be great fools. Dire are the pangs which my art is able to arouse and to allay in those who consort with me, just like the pangs of women in childbirth; night and day they are full of perplexity and travail which is even worse than that of the women.

So much for them. And there are others, Theætetus, who come to me apparently having nothing in them; and as I know that they have no need of my art, I coax them into marrying some one, and by the grace of God I can generally tell who is likely to do them good. Many of them I have given away to Prodicus, and many to other inspired sages.

I tell you this long story, friend Theætetus, because I suspect, as indeed you seem to think yourself, that you are in labor—great with some conception. Come then to me, who am a midwife's son and myself a midwife, and try to answer the questions which I will ask you. And if I abstract and expose your first-born, because I discover upon inspection that the conception which you have formed is a vain shadow, do not quarrel with me on that account, as the manner of women is when their first children are taken from them. For I have actually known some who were ready to bite me when I deprived them of a darling folly; they did not perceive that I acted from good will, not knowing that no god is the enemy of man—that was not within the range of their ideas; neither am I their enemy in all this, but it would be wrong in me to admit falsehood, or to stifle the truth.

Once more, then, Theætetus, I repeat my old question, "What is knowledge?" and do not say that you cannot tell; but quit yourself like a man, and by the help of God you will be able to tell.

—Plato, *Theætetus*

II

THE SCIENTIFIC AND THE ESTHETIC
CONCEPTION OF NATURE *

IF we compare the picture of nature that our scientists have
drawn up in the last centuries with the way in which the
Greeks viewed it, a striking difference is at once apparent.
An inner harmony that satisfies the need for beauty is as characteristic of the Greek conception of nature as it is uncharacter-
istic of ours. There is in the former a certain poetic freedom, in
the latter a strict and prosaic constraint. In the former an esthetic
point of view dictates the world-picture; in the latter there is
exclusively the idea of an inviolable conformity with law in all
that happens. The Greeks saw the objects of nature as anthro-
pomorphic, animate beings; they were not familiar with the laws
of the conservation of mass and energy and of the inertia of
matter, which are so much a matter of course with us.† We are
so accustomed to thinking in terms of these laws and observing

* An address, "Über wissenschaftliche und ästhetische Naturbetrachtung," 1908.
Published in *Die Reformation der Philosophie* (Leipzig, 1918).

† This address was delivered almost forty years ago—that is to say, *before* the
determinative discoveries of the general theory of relativity and quantum mechanics.
The scientific conception of nature, basic to Nelson, is that of classical physics or,
more precisely, classical mechanics; and to the extent that this is relevant, his statements on physics require revision. Such presuppositions as, for example, that it is
theoretically possible to calculate every event in advance provided sufficient knowledge of natural laws and certain observable physical data is available, or that all
natural events take place in a unified, infinite, Euclidean space, can no longer be
maintained today.
But the modern corrections in no way affect our interpretation of the scientific
cognition of nature through which Nelson differentiates between the scientific and
the esthetic world views. It is true of modern physics likewise that it explains
natural phenomena by subordinating them to laws; but its explanations, too, can
never advance to a complete knowledge of reality. Indeed, Nelson's thesis, that
science cannot achieve a complete and adequate knowledge of reality, finds renewed corroboration in modern physics; and the conclusions he draws from this
thesis are still valid today. (See Introduction, n. 13.)
In view of numerous modern attempts to exploit recent physical discoveries for
purposes of romantic and religious speculation, his warning against confusing scientific and esthetic viewpoints takes on a new and especially urgent significance.

the things around us in their light that we are prone to forget that this manner of thinking is by no means self-evident but has been achieved in the course of a very ingenious scientific development.

When we subject this antithesis between the classic and the modern conceptions of nature to historical scrutiny, we see that its appearance was by no means abrupt. If we disregard the dark centuries of the Middle Ages, in which no intellectual progress was made at all, we find a continuous development from Pythagoras' doctrine of the harmony of the spheres to Laplace's celestial mechanics. The further we follow this development, the more the poetic coloring of the world-picture yields to constructions of the calculating intelligence, and the more the vagrant dream-figures of fantasy are superseded by a despiritualized system of masses under necessary natural laws. Kepler hearkened still to the music of the spheres; but Newton, on the basis of the laws of planetary motion that he himself discovered, made those gigantic discoveries that bound the motion of heavenly bodies to the laws of mechanics and once for all shattered the crystal spheres. The supernatural powers who formerly had guided the stars through the heavens were resolved to a rigid mechanism the motive power of which is self-contained. Without doubt, the esthetic point of view has been entirely eliminated from the science of our day. There is no room for ideas of the beautiful and the sublime in a domain in which one is concerned solely with material masses and their definitely calculable movements.

Perhaps no one has more movingly portrayed the contrast between these two conceptions than Schiller in his poem *Die Götter Griechenlands*. This poem laments in pensive verses the way the Greeks' esthetic conception of nature has little by little been supplanted by the physicists' modern scientific conception. But is the poet justified in portraying esthetic imagery as a permanently lost possession and in bemoaning its downfall as an irreplaceable loss? Indeed, the law of gravity has dethroned the gods of nature, and the time will never return

> Da der Dichtung zauberische Hülle
> Sich noch lieblich um die Wahrheit wand.*

* ". . . when the magical cloak of poetry still tenderly enfolded the truth."

But has science robbed the esthetic conception of nature of its independent importance? Has beauty vanished from nature, to exist henceforth only in the illusory fairyland of song?

Is our knowledge, we must ask ourselves, able to comprehend everything, without exception, from natural laws, or is there perhaps an insurmountable limit to the explanations of science? Is there a realm inaccessible to the calculations of the reflection; is there a region beyond the theoretically explicable, no matter how far science may extend its sway? If there is *no* such region, then, to be sure, we shall have to grant unconditional sovereignty to the scientific conception of the universe and renounce all pretensions of the esthetic as illusory.

Before we decide to recommend this renunciation, it may be worth while for us to examine the data that might guide us to an unprejudiced solution of this problem. If we wish to pass impartial judgment on the struggle for ascendency between the two Weltanschauungen, we should do well to try to understand the real foundations of their so disparate methods of approach. Accordingly, I shall attempt a brief delineation of these foundations and their relation to one another.

All scientific knowledge of nature begins with sensory intuition, with the observation of the phenomena that take place before our senses. But it is not content merely to record the multifarious facts that it observes; it seeks to explore the deeper connection between the phenomena; for the basic motive that governs all the various manifestations of our cognition is the demand for unity in multiplicity. But this unity of events does not appear immediately before our eyes. It is not itself perceptible; we can find a clue to it only via a derived and often very laborious comparison of the contents of our perceptions. We find it in *laws*, in which alone the necessary connection between the diverse individual phenomena resides. The exploration of this necessary lawfulness in natural events is the entire and only task of science. The subordination of the objects of sensory intuition under universal and necessary laws is effectuated by logical syllogisms; and the essence of *theory* consists in the systematic erection of such syllogisms. What we call *nature* is not the disorderly confusion of the phenomena as they stream past before our senses; it is, rather, an interconnection ordered according to universal laws, which we ourselves can no longer intuit but only think. For the law itself is not an object of intuition, although it is a necessary precondition on which the existence of the objects of intuition depends.

What we call the *explanation* of a phenomenon is nothing but the process of referring it back to a law; and the explanation is the more complete the more universal the laws are to which it has been successfully referred back. The most universal laws are the basic principles of mechanics, i.e., the theory of the forces that determine the motion of bodies. For the complete explanation of a phenomenon, of whatever sort it may be, we must insist therefore on referring it back to mechanical principles. Thus we explain acoustic phenomena by disclosing the vibrations that produce the sounds and by deriving the laws according to which these vibrations occur from the basic laws of mechanics.

Now, the possibility of all explanation rests—a fact on which I cannot dwell here at greater length—on the application of the concepts of measurement and number. We must measure and count the phenomena, that is, we must explore the size-relationships that are to be found in them, if we wish to relate them to a scientific law and thus make them theoretically comprehensible. The application of *mathematics* to the phenomena is the necessary precondition of all scientific explanation. And also conversely: everything to which the concepts of mathematics are applicable is accessible to scientific explanation. Whatever can be measured in terms of spatial or temporal magnitude is subject to the authority of scientific theory; it must be explicable in terms of law. That many phenomena have not yet been explained is not to be attributed to an inadequacy in scientific method but solely to the fact either that sufficient evidence has not yet been collected or that the mathematical relations in question are too complicated.

Thus the natural scientist conceives his world as a system of inert masses every condition of which is determined, in accordance with necessary laws, by the condition preceding it, so that a person who is able to survey the condition of the system at any arbitrarily selected time can discover simply through calculation, in accordance with these laws, all the rest of the history of the system. He can discover through calculation how one movement follows another, how life is born from life, how thoughts develop from thoughts; and he can trace this sequence to any moment in time, no matter how remote in past or future. An intellect that has reached this highest level of the knowledge of nature would be superior only in degree to our astronomers, whose art enables them to calculate to the second, from *one* formula of Newton's law of gravity, the past and future history of planetary motion. In Du Bois-Reymond's brilliant statement:

Just as the astronomer has only to give time the proper negative value in his equations concerning lunar motion in order to ascertain whether the sun over Piraeus was in eclipse when Pericles embarked for Epidaurus, that superior intellect could tell us, through the pertinent consultation of his world-formula, who the Iron Mask was or how the *President* foundered. Just as the astronomer can predict the day on which a comet, hidden for years in the profundities of the universe, will again appear in the firmament, that superior intellect could read in his equations the day on which the Greek Cross will blaze from the Hagia Sophia or England will burn its last lump of coal.

Now let us consider what is characteristic of the *esthetic* evaluation of nature. The antithesis between it and the scientific evaluation manifests itself first of all in the fact that in the former we remain entirely within the realm of *intuition*. The individual entity is of interest to the scientist only in so far as it lends itself as an exemplification of a universal law. The esthetic attitude, on the other hand, endows the individual entity with a discrete meaning that could never be attributed to it from the scientific point of view. Physiology informs us that what we call a plant possesses as such absolutely no reality but is simply the law-determined form of continually changing substances. But when we admire the beauty of a plant we do not inquire into the chemical laws of metabolism nor into the morphology of cell formation. We immerse ourselves in the *gestalt* as it presents itself immediately to our vision; we separate it, in effect, from the law-determined order of things, in which it appears as a transitional event, unimportant in itself, in an infinite series of necessarily related occurrences. Or let us assume, to take another example, that on a cloudless night we find ourselves under the open sky and are contemplating the constellations of the firmament. The exaltation that is here awakened in us depends, in this case also, only on the content of immediate intuition and not on our more or less extensive astronomical information. The astronomer will tell us that the stars whose luster gladdens us are so far away from us that their light travels for decades before it reaches our eyes and that consequently we may be watching a star long after it may have ceased to shine. This information may be of interest to us otherwise, but it has no influence on our esthetic judgment. One acquainted with astronomy is also well aware that the stars are in no physical interrelation corresponding to the intuitive order in which we combine them in the constellations but simply, according to the laws of optics and perspective, *appear* to us to be so interrelated. But this, too, is of no importance to the delight we experience in the image that we perceive.

There is, however, a vast difference between attributing esthetic significance to an object and simply feeling it to be *pleasant*. We call a thing pleasant when it affects our senses agreeably: its pleasantness consists always only in the effect it has on us, the sentient subject. The beauty of a thing, on the other hand, is altogether independent of its relation to the observing subject. The salad that one man sweetens with sugar is thereby made unpalatable to another. One man abominates touching a caterpillar and even the mere sight of one disgusts him; the other does so with pleasure. In all such cases it is a question only of the effect of the things on ourselves, and we are quite satisfied to say, "This is pleasant to *me*," without thereby predicating any value to the *object* and without thereby entering into controversy with those whose opinions differ from ours.

In esthetics it is quite another matter. When we call a Bach prelude beautiful we claim that every educated person should be of the same opinion; and we do so not because of any accidental homogeneity in man's sense of hearing but because we attribute beauty to the object as such, independently of its effect on the organ of the perceiving subject.*

This claim to universal validity that distinguishes the esthetic judgment is a highly remarkable fact. This apodictic character of the esthetic judgment is remarkable because the object that we are judging esthetically is always perceived through intuition and can therefore be only an individual entity. But outside of esthetics we are able to form apodictic judgments on individual entities only if we know a universal law from which we can deduce the particular case. Thus we can assert apodictically that a stone we throw will describe a parabola, since we know the universal law of which such trajectories are only a particular illustration. But in the esthetic field such a law is nowhere to be found. We assert the beauty of a sonata with the most positive awareness that our judgment is valid, but we can cite no law from which its beauty can be deduced and made comprehensible through a logical syllogism in the way that we can derive and explain the parabola of the stone's trajectory through a logical syllogism from the laws of falling bodies. If someone should dispute our esthetic judgment we could find no logical grounds on which to instruct him; we could only direct his attention to the beautiful object itself and urge him to develop his taste by observing it.

The beautiful is likewise differentiated from the *useful* by this same property. If inquiry is made into the usefulness of a tool or a machine, we need only ascertain whether or not the thing is suited to the fulfillment of its purpose, and we shall be able to

---

* To this statement of Nelson's the objection has been raised that not everyone likes Bach's music, and that people's esthetic judgments often differ radically. But this is not to say that the question where the truth lies in such disputes is meaningless. With other differences of opinion, we take for granted that it makes sense to ask what is true and what is false. We believe it is possible to confront the convictions of one person with those of another and to decide the issue by scrutinizing the evidence on both sides. To be sure, conceptually analyzable grounds are lacking in the esthetic field, and consequently the argument cannot be settled with logical reasons. But there can be a kind of discussion where one party to the dispute points out to the other beauties which previously had escaped him; there is such a thing as developing and educating appreciation. The differentiation we make between good and bad taste, between more and less educated taste, shows that we actually do associate the claim to objective validity with esthetic judgments.

determine its value or lack of value from its suitability or un-
suitability for the fulfillment of its purpose. But this is not so in
the evaluation of the beautiful—for what might be the purpose
of a beautiful flower, a beautiful constellation, a beautiful sonata?
The very inquiry into the purpose of the beautiful must appear
grotesque to us. The beautiful does not serve as the means to an
end, from which it derives its value; it is as little useful as it is
pleasant: it is simply satisfying in itself, with no need of comparison. Its purpose and value are immanent in it.

The unique significance of the beautiful can therefore be made
comprehensible neither by a natural law nor by a law of teleology. The magnificence of a play of color, the harmony of musical tones, the grace of forms—all these are invested with a
mysterious import, which we can feel but which we are unable
to define in concepts.

I said above that we should understand under "nature" the
existence of things in so far as it is determined by universal and
necessary laws. On the basis of this formulation we can now
make the assertion that beauty is never an attribute of a thing
qua object of nature. It is true that the beautiful is inconceivable
without a certain inner order, but this order, this regularity and
harmony that please us in the beautiful are not to be determined
through universal laws of the intellect. They must manifest
themselves to our intuition and simply cannot be reduced to
concepts.

Herewith we return to the question posed in the beginning.
If we are unwilling to repudiate the reality of the beautiful as a
snare and a delusion, it would appear that we come into conflict
with the claims of science. Or can perhaps a domain be found,
no matter how remote, in which elucidating theory has no juris-
diction, a domain permanently exempt from scientific treatment?
And if we are obliged to confess that we know of no such domain
and that we can never hope to find it, what escape remains for
an esthetic conception of the world?

The infinite extension and divisibility of space and time make
it impossible for science to terminate its exploration of causes at
any one point; rather, the infinite diversity of phenomena pre-

sents it continually with new tasks. But precisely this boundlessness of its domain impels us on closer scrutiny to recognize an insurmountable limit to human knowledge; since we can never complete our knowledge, we are obliged to recognize that complete knowledge of the world is impossible for us. Our knowledge can never become a finished whole; it must always remain fragmentary, and fragmentary in such a way that we cannot even in our thoughts perfect it to a complete whole. If, for instance, we should at any time in our progressive discovery of the galaxies come to a boundary of the universe, that could never justify our holding this boundary for anything more than the limit of our experience up till then. For in order to know that there could be no other stars outside it we should have to have searched through all the rest of space; but since space is infinite this is impossible. The perfecting of our limited scientific knowledge to a completed whole is therefore inconceivable. Consequently, our knowledge is limited not only in degree but also in its essential nature.

We cannot conceive of achieving a complete or omniscient knowledge of the world through a gradual consummation of our present knowledge; rather, we must think of the former as different in its essence from the latter. But we can form no positive notion of such an omniscient knowledge; the concept of it remains entirely without content for us. We can only define it *negatively*, as a knowledge that is *not* subject to any limit but can command a view of the world as a complete whole; that is, we must think of the world as a complete whole even though our limited *knowledge* of it is necessarily not susceptible of completion. Therefore, we can form a concept of the world as it exists independent of our limited knowledge of it only by thinking of the bounds that circumscribe our knowledge as abrogated.

Something that exists independent of the way in which we have knowledge of it is called a *thing-in-itself* (*Ding an sich*). A thing-in-itself can therefore never become the object of scientific knowledge. We can express this by saying that we have only *ideas* of the things-in-themselves. An idea is a notion the object of which cannot be found in any specific cognition. Two qualities are necessary to make a cognition specific: intuition and concept. Intuition informs us of the diversity of the individual phenomena; by means of the concept we think out the law under which the individual phenomena are subordinated. Only by connecting intuition and concept does science find unity in diversity. There does not exist for our knowledge any phenomenon that does not adhere to the lawfulness of our reflection; and no more does there exist a law under which not real phenomena are subordinated. We observed at the outset how the unity of our knowledge of nature is brought about by the reciprocal determination of intuition and concept, phenomenon and law. Now we see clearly in what respect this knowledge of nature is limited, in what respect it must necessarily remain unsatisfactory: the longing of our reason for unity cannot be *entirely* satisfied by science. We can conceive of the complete unity of the universe only in ideas; science can never attain it.

But how does all this bear on the esthetic conception of nature? Very closely, as we shall see at once. I said above that an *idea* is a notion the object of which cannot be given in any specific cognition. Accordingly, we can discriminate between two sorts of ideas: on the one hand there can be *concepts*, which allow of no *intuitive* determination, concepts of whose objects we can achieve no intuition; on the other hand there can be *intuitive* notions, which allow of no *conceptual* determination, intuitions that cannot be reduced to concepts. Of the first sort are the above-mentioned concepts of the things-in-themselves, which we form by negating the limits of our knowledge. To differentiate them from the other sort of ideas we can designate these limit-negating ideas of the things-in-themselves as *logical* ideas. The ideas of the other sort are forms of intuition that cannot be reduced to concepts; and it is just such forms that we previously recognized as those characteristic of the esthetic way of conceiving things. We might therefore call them *esthetic* ideas.

It is now no longer difficult to make clear the possibility of the esthetic conception of nature and its relation to the scientific. We can now specify how it is that there is room for an esthetic conception alongside the scientific and that each can exist without infringing on the claims of the other. We have found that the esthetic attitude does not judge its object as an object of nature but, as it were, isolates it, detaches it from its interconnection with the infinite mechanism of the phenomena. Now, when science explains for us the mechanism of events, what more does it accomplish than point out to us with every given phenomenon another from which according to law the necessary succession of the first can be understood? And this other phenomenon can in its turn only be explained by our pointing out a third, in which the necessity of its occurrence is grounded. Thus every explanation refers back to something unexplained: we solve one problem by setting another in its place. Since we come to no final point in the series of phenomena, we reach no final point in our explanations. The necessity which characterizes events in nature proves therefore to be limited; the original fortuitousness of phenomena cannot be set aside, it can only be pushed back.

I pointed out above that whoever knew the condition of all the parts of a material system at any one moment would then be in a position to deduce the entire history of the system. *Which* moment of time one chooses is immaterial; but it is significant for the question with which we are now concerned to affirm that such a condition, not deducible from law and therefore fortuitous, *must* necessarily be assumed. Even the most complete scientific theory cannot suspend this fortuitousness. The astronomer who is able with infallible mathematical certainty to calculate the position of the stars for any past or future time still needs the *empirical* knowledge of their constellation at some particular time. Although he can choose this time at his discretion, nevertheless the geometric arrangement of the stars that he observes and uses as the chosen point of departure for his calculations is plainly accidental.

This fortuitousness of the original arrangement leaves room for the esthetic conception of nature. Whereas science observes the given substance of sensory intuition only with reference to its dependence on universal laws, the esthetic evaluation rests precisely on the recognition of the original fortuitousness of the

intuitive arrangement of this substance. For it is just this fortuitousness that allows us to accord the objects of intuition an
importance of their own, one independent of the mechanism of
which they are a part.

Herewith the nature of the esthetic judgment, which seemed
so inscrutable, becomes comprehensible to us. We understand
first of all why it is only objects of intuition that we can evaluate
esthetically. But while intuitiveness is a necessary condition of
the beautiful, it is not the essence of beauty. The content of the
intuition must harmonize to a unified whole in order to be invested with esthetic significance. The beautiful must have the
unified form of an individual whole, through which it is isolated
from the infinite flux of the phenomena. Not every sequence of
musical notes is beautiful, but only a sequence so ordered as to
take the form of a melody. This individual form, this inner unity
and harmony of the beautiful, is truly the indescribable and in-
effable core, which cannot be articulated in words or reduced to
concepts. The true enchantment of the beautiful resides in this
form. This enchantment reposes in the fact that things satisfy the
need of our reason for unity where we could not have expected
it, that they respond to this need without our being able to grasp
the necessity of such a response. We can now easily understand
the inscrutability of this enchantment and the impossibility of
explaining it, when we recall that we explain something by deriving it from a natural law; but the form of the beautiful must
be regarded as that which is absolutely accidental and therefore
not to be derived from natural laws.

But although beauty cannot be traced back theoretically to a
law, the esthetic judgment's claim to apodictic validity, which
we have already considered, betrays the fact that it must be
grounded on some universal principle. There must be some
ground, concealed though it may be, on which the universal
validity and necessity of the esthetic judgments rest. Since this
principle is not to be found in our knowledge of nature, we can
look for it only in ideas. Now, there exist outside the esthetic
ideas no others but the logical ideas of the things-in-themselves.
Therefore, these latter must underlie the esthetic conception in a

way analogous to that in which the laws of the intellect underlie the theoretical conception. But whereas the theoretical subordination of the phenomena under a law is established by a *syllogism*, it is in the esthetic conception merely a *feeling* that relates the phenomena to the ideas.

This explains the deeper meaning that we attach to the beautiful, as well as the unique effect that it has on the spiritual temper of the beholder. The beautiful, because of its immediate relation to ideas, towers, as it were, above the world of phenomena up into the world of things in themselves. Every truly beautiful object evokes the idea of consummated unity. A loftier, mysterious truth is annunciated in the beautiful forms of nature, in a language that, to be sure, no intellect can decipher but every refined sensibility will apprehend.

Consequently the anxiety lest the development of science choke off the feeling for beauty in man is unfounded. This feeling, both in its origins and its essence, is superior to all scientific explanations and can never be stolen from us by any sort of scientific insight. The scientific and the esthetic attitudes toward nature do not exclude one another but are complementary. But we must keep well in mind that an amicable coexistence of the two points of view is possible only if they are kept separate, and that each must be careful not to trespass on the preserve of the other, if they are not both to suffer injury.

It is implicit in this matter that the necessity of a discrete development of the theoretical and esthetic conceptions made itself felt only rather late in the course of history. The discovery of the true order of the universe and the natural laws necessitated the final divorce of physics and esthetics. The Greeks were still able in large measure to adapt their ideas of art and mythology to their undeveloped science; they could still imagine nature as a *cosmos*, i.e., as an architectonically ordered whole, on the analogy of a work of art. This is clearly demonstrated in the Pythagorean picture of the world, in which the heavenly spheres are ordered at various levels around the divine fire at the center: at the lowest level the terrestrial region of clouds and winds, and of the orbit of the earth; thereafter, the spheres, wheeling in their eternal rotation, of the moon, the sun, and the planets; and so out to the farthest sphere, on which the stars are embossed and which is engirded by Olympus, the dwelling of the gods. This cosmos manifests in its architectonic arrangement a plurality of heavenly regions, which nevertheless together form a whole; and the unity of this whole reposes in intuition. Hence the world-structure presents itself in the form of an esthetic idea.

The esthetic allurement of this astronomical image had to disappear as soon as the discovery of the infinity of space rent its unity asunder. It has often been remarked that Ptolemy's world-concept had this advantage over Copernicus', that it provided the poetic imagination with a more congenial field of activity. The truth of this observation is made clear by a comparison of Dante's *Divine Comedy* with Klopstock's *Messias*. The former sets before our eyes, in our wanderings through Hell, Purgatory, and Heaven, the various stories of the world-edifice; the latter extends its picture into the immeasurable, and while the scene of action proper is limited to the narrow confines of Palestine, we are expected to follow the flight of the spirits through stellar space: the attempt to satisfy both imagination and intellect has resulted in a strident discordance in the execution.

But in the last analysis what has deprived the new world-picture of esthetic significance is not really the circumstance that the earth has been moved from its firm position nor that it has become a subordinate member of a subordinate system. As a matter of fact, the view taken in the Copernican system does not absolutely exclude a poetic treatment. When Klopstock sings, in the spirit of this view:

> Um Erden wandeln Monde,
> Erden um Sonnen,
> Aller Sonnen Heere wandeln
> Um eine grosse Sonne—*

the picture of the world-structure painted in these verses still manifests, in its well-ordered arrangement and grouping of the heavenly bodies around a central sun, the architectonic unity of

* "Moons revolve around earths, earths around suns; the hosts of all the suns revolve around one great sun."

an esthetic idea. But this picture no longer corresponds to the theories of modern astronomy. First of all, the center of gravity of the system of stars need not be located within a star but can lie somewhere in empty space; moreover (and this is the essential factor), we must necessarily think of the universe in space as incompletable, and this thought deprives of all meaning the notion of a spatial center and hence of a universal sun. Therewith the architectonic unity of the earlier world-picture is definitively destroyed, since that which is illimitably extended has no form or shape. We can no longer imagine the totality of the universe intuitively; we can conceive of it only in logical ideas.

Immersion in this infinity of astronomical space leaves one with no other impression than the stupefying sensation of an unrelenting desolation, a benumbing frigidity—an impression that, to be sure, can achieve indirectly, through the infinite humility with which it strikes us and which seems to destroy our own physical existence, a lofty ethical significance, but still an impression that remains esthetically meaningless. He who hopes that a deeper penetration into this picture will satisfy the needs of his spirit will soon find himself bitterly disappointed. We can confront his expectations with the words that stand at the threshold of Dante's Hell:

All hope abandon, ye who enter here.

Nevertheless, a few have tried to animate this modern astronomical picture poetically by portraying, on the analogy of the ancient doctrine of the migration of souls, a journey of departed spirits through space, in which the soul, after it has achieved the degree of perfection possible on one heavenly body, travels to another and thus progresses through ever higher stages of perfection toward its consummation. But this notion simply leads us along an endless path of progress, without ever affording us the prospect of a resting place: it can only make us the more conscious, through the hopelessness of this restless and never satisfied nomadism, how despairing and devoid of taste such a conception is.

Thus we had better not appraise the various astronomical systems in terms of their esthetic value. If it is once for all impossible to satisfy the demands of both esthetics and science in one picture, why should we not content our esthetic needs with the sublime spectacle that the star-strewn vault of the night offers directly to our senses? Is not this spectacle in its inexhaustible magic superior to the constructions of the calculating intellect?

This esthetic view has its proper significance and will never lose it, if we but adhere to the principle of not letting it lay any claim to being scientific. The attempt to elaborate the one view with the means of the other betrays both gross scientific ignorance and crudity of taste. Nevertheless, there has grown up in quite recent times a considerable school, which has sought the true ideal of a harmonic spiritual development in just such an alliance and interpenetration of the esthetic and the theoretical conception—a school which just recently has achieved new fame and seems to be winning more and more adherents among us. I refer to the *romanticists*. "If thou wouldst penetrate to the inmost essence of physics, allow thyself to be initiated in the mysteries of poetry," says Friedrich Schlegel, enunciating in one sentence the gospel of romanticism. This school has made demands on science that its very nature does not permit it to fulfill. Discontented with the prosaic sobriety of theoretical natural science, this school turned with contempt from the mathematical clarity of science's methods and results, back to the ill-contrived anthropomorphisms of Greek natural philosophy: the old dream of the world soul was to come true as a physical poem or a poetic physics, in an absurd hodgepodge of theoretical thought-processes and mythological fantasies—an undertaking that must, if persisted in, be pernicious to all healthy thinking and feeling.

Schiller never participated in any such fantastic business. He always held the earnestness of exact science in high regard, and in his later years he even succeeded, through a philosophical investigation of the beautiful, in rising above the mood of resignation to which he had given expression in his poem *Die Götter Griechenlands*. What he sought was, in his own words, nothing less than the objective principle of esthetic judgments. His lucid establishment of his formulation, "Beauty is freedom in the phenomenon" (*Schönheit ist Freiheit in der Erscheinung*), shows that he came amazingly close to the true solution of the problem.

On the other hand, we cannot declare Goethe innocent of an offense through which he involved not so much himself as the great multitude of his less independent contemporaries in a participation in the confusions of romanticism. Goethe was, of all the moderns, the most eloquent herald of the objective reality of the beautiful, but he did not always note and respect the line of demarcation between the provinces of esthetics and theory. It is undeniable that natural science is indebted to him for various fruitful discoveries, but these all belong to the field of merely *descriptive* science and natural *history*. He regarded the soulless mechanism that characterizes nature in the mathematical physics of Newton and his successors as a caricature of nature which aroused his liveliest repugnance. His evolutionary studies, too, have their source more in an esthetic idea than in a striving for scientific explanation. He did not want, as has been correctly pointed out, to reduce man to a mechanism, as modern biology has done, but rather to elevate all of nature to the heights that man represents.

The first meeting between Goethe and Schiller took place at a gathering of natural scientists at which both happened to be present. As they were leaving a lecture on botany they became involved in a conversation on science. Goethe began to elaborate the basic thought of his metamorphosis of plants; but Schiller interrupted him soon with the words, "That is not experience, that is an idea." This statement of Schiller's formulates in the clearest way possible the inner antithesis between the direction of his own thought and Goethe's; but it has also a more universal significance in the history of ideas. Goethe, in commingling experience with ideas, paved the way for romanticism.

That delusive mirage of romanticism, the mirage of a science compounded of ideas, should no longer deceive us today. Because of the autonomy of natural law and the fact that the sensory world cannot be completely apprehended, we shall never succeed in discovering for the visible universe a form of intuition that bears the stamp of completion and that might again marry theory to esthetics through the magic of an esthetic idea. To be sure, there is and there always will be an esthetic *truth*, but this truth is not the truth of science. The consummated unity of the world becomes manifest to us, not in a universal natural law, but only in the diversity of esthetic ideas. Let us therefore disclaim all efforts to intermix the pure feeling for beauty with the scientifically exact concepts of the intellect.

Even today nature speaks its divine language to us through her esthetic ideas; but science is unable to interpret its meaning.

III

THE WORLD-VIEW OF ETHICS
AND RELIGION *

ROMAIN ROLLAND says a beautiful and simple thing about
Jean Christophe: "After all, he was far too religious to
think much about God." We cannot say that of our time.
Our time thinks much about God, but it is not religious.

Behind us lies the sudden change from security and prosperity
to insecurity and want. Men no longer see their way. No longer
can they cover their expenses. Violent fluctuations in prices have
completely obscured the value of material goods, and spiritual
values have become altogether vague. What some reject assumes
for others an all the more exaggerated worth.

Most people stand perplexed at these fluctuations in moral
currency. They follow the impulse of the moment, but, for all
that, they long for some security of mind, some firm foundation
for life. They feel the need of learning how to judge and understand events and of forming their judgments in relation to a
harmonious and ordered world about them.

Certainly there have been times in the past when the calamities
that have befallen men have been as great as—nay, even greater
than—today; times in which decades of wars and invasions or
the hostile powers of nature have defeated men. But men had
then that which our generation lacks to help them see their way
and begin anew. Their thought and faith rested in a "closed"
concept of the world. This view might have been naive, superstitious, shortsighted, and earth-bound, or visionary and mystical,
now nearer to, now farther from, the truth; yet it formed the
firm foundation of their existence, the ground upon which they

* An address, "Sittliche und religiöse Weltansicht," given at the twenty-sixth
Student Conference at Aarau, March 13 to 15, 1922. Published in *XXVI Aarauer
Studenten-Konferenz* (Leipzig, 1922) and *Abhandlungen der Fries'schen Schule*, VI
(Berlin, 1933), No. 1. Published in English as "The Moral and Religious View of the
World" in *Politics and Education* by Leonard Nelson (London, Allen & Unwin,
1928), tr. by W. Lansdell and revised for this volume by Thomas K. Brown III.
Used by permission of the publishers.

could build again after the flood of events had passed over them.

Since the time of the Reformation this circumscribed world has fallen into ruin. The cleavage of faith, initiated by Luther, soon developed into a mere cleavage of the churches, in which dogma opposed dogma. This gulf could be bridged by edicts of toleration. But the gulf formed by the reformation of astronomy went deeper and was unbridgeable. When Kepler subjected the orbits of the planets to the geometry of conic sections and Newton explained the movements of the heavenly bodies by the law of gravity, then knowledge detached itself from faith and conceived a world whose riddles could all be solved by the calculating and measuring intellect. In this view of the world the colorful and varied drama of development was reduced to movements that the laws of mechanics were capable of explaining. The thought of a creation and the idea that nature was bound by laws of value have become, in this conception, a hypothesis that is simply superfluous.

The next step toward the destruction of the idea of the systematic unity of our knowledge was taken when ethics was finally emancipated from physics, on the one hand, and (even more important) from faith, on the other. This advance, however, has hardly penetrated the general consciousness. When Kant discovered the distinction between categorical and hypothetical imperatives, he divorced the obligation of the moral law from any kind of compulsion, from the necessity of nature, as well as from any sanction through the power of a lawgiver superior to man.

This doctrine of Kant's, by which the dignity of man was for the first time really set forth, definitely marked the overthrow of the medieval view of the world. For of what use is insight into the laws governing the mechanism of nature if we do not also have free insight into the moral law, which sets the standard for our personal conduct? Without such knowledge man, no matter how profound his penetration into the secrets of nature, would still remain, in his highest practical decisions, dependent everywhere upon the tutelage of higher powers.

Obviously, it was only slowly and amid great struggles that these bold scientific conquests could transform man's views on his life and the universe.

A deep and sustained effort of the human spirit was naturally required to lay the foundations of the new sciences and to construct on these foundations the system of exact sciences and of ethics. No wonder, therefore, that the gradual advance of science has been hampered by errors and mistakes, which made understanding more difficult, and that, further, the presentation of the completed research and findings demanded a language so carefully considered, restrained, and abstract that the general public had neither the capacity to understand nor the willingness to keep pace with it.

But there was a deeper reason still, a purely emotional one, which made the introduction and the recognition of these scientific achievements difficult. Natural science posited a world unbounded in time and space, in opposition to faith, which held to the conviction of a "closed" world, defined and complete in itself. Furthermore, ethics set the law of human conduct free from any dependence on the aims of a divine world government. Thus the idea—deeply rooted in the reason of man—of the unity of the world seemed to be assailed.

The efforts of monistic thought to enforce a unified view of the world were just as little able to satisfy the feeling for truth as were the efforts of pluralism, which postulated the existence of several worlds. And since, in the conflicting doctrines, the idea of the unity of the world no longer found a secure foothold, each one stood by his own view without considering that of others, and so interest in the solution of this problem dwindled. The religious view of the world remained in unadjusted disagreement with the achievements of human progress, maintaining a shadowy existence in churches and sects. The natural sciences allowed only experience to pass as assured truth. And on both sides efforts were made to keep ethics in bondage—efforts whose combined effect was to starve the moral life more and more.

With this confused inheritance the European nations entered into the chaos of the World War, and even before it was ended they were obliged to admit the bankruptcy of their view of the world, which long had been unsound.

Can we hope for a reconstruction?

When Frederick the Great had ended the Seven Years' War,

he immediately began the reconstruction of his state. He made good his promise to build up in seven years what seven years had demolished. The reconstruction of Europe will take longer, if it is accomplished at all; and it will succeed only when to the political treaties of peace is added a treaty far more comprehensive and radical—a treaty of peace between the reformations and revolutions, which since the beginning of modern times have been struggling among themselves for their rights.

This peace, too, can come about only through the efforts of men. And only those are qualified to negotiate who know no fear, least of all fear of the truth. For in this peace negotiation it will avail men nothing to indulge their weaknesses. Nothing short of absolute honesty will help them.

Today I would attempt to lay before you such a treaty of peace, or at least that part of it which I take to be the chief article. I am prompted chiefly by a practical interest; but I believe that I can best serve this practical interest if I abide by my calling, which is that of philosophical investigator. To philosophize demands sobriety, and the test of this sobriety lies in clearness and definiteness of language; the unequivocal relation between word and thought. What, in this way, the language of the philosopher loses in force of imagery and immediate emotional appeal, it must make good by its power to lead the student to think for himself and thereby to achieve a calm certainty of judgment. Without such independence of thought, the result is at best only a lifeless repetition of formulae. You will therefore understand that I must make some demands on your attention if I am to treat my subject in a manner in keeping with my respect for this gathering.

Permit me, however, in order to avoid making unnecessary difficulties for you and to facilitate your understanding, to approach our subject by way of a simple consideration.

Lloyd George has declared that all the governments more or less stumbled into the war. To many it seems that this phrase puts the question of guilt at last in the right light; since no one is at fault, it is meaningless to seek for the culprit.

I attach another meaning to the pronouncement of the English statesman. Granted that his assertion is correct, it has not proved the question of guilt to be futile, but, on the contrary, it has contributed a good deal to its solution—indeed, his assertion contains directly the answer to the question as to the guilty party. Those men stumbled into the World War who built up the enormous war machines, which needed, as it were, only the pressure of a finger in order to perform irresistibly their work of destruction, and who have thus, without knowing what they did, set in motion the machinery of destruction, leaving things to take their course. The responsibility for the war, then, rests with the fatalism with which governments and governed have let things go as they have gone. With that judgment, it is believed, the question of guilt may be dismissed. But what would be the reaction if a judge chose to pronounce the following sentence on a group of drunken men who had smashed a shop window: "They were all drunk; they all stumbled into the window; therefore no one is guilty"?

Not to repudiate such fatalism is to surrender oneself to it. But if it is to be opposed successfully, the roots which nourish it must be discovered and dug up. I see two varieties of this aberration. There is, first of all, a fatalism arising from moral weakness, whether this rests upon weakness of will or upon light-mindedness. Fatalism of this sort carries its own condemnation. It seeks no justification. But there is a fatalism more deeply rooted, well known to history as characteristic of Eastern peoples, but which one would hardly expect to find in the advanced life of modern Europe. It springs basically from a misguided religious feeling and draws from this an apparent justification, of which the fatalism arising from moral weakness takes advantage, using it as a cloak to hide its own true nature. Its demoralizing effects are hypocrisy and cynicism.

Fatalism, then, must be attacked at the point at which, as an erroneous conviction, it influences the will of men. If indeed fatalism is derived from a misguided religious feeling, then it is at once clear that there is some want of harmony between the fatalist's ethical and religious views.

If we wish to investigate the relation of two views to each other, we must first of all try to be clear as to what these views are; and if we are guided by the practical interest of setting the conduct of men on the right road, we shall not discuss farfetched opinions on ethics and religion; instead we shall ask ourselves: What does ethics demand, and what is religion?

I begin with the first, the question of ethics, because where science makes the decisions, the truth is more readily grasped and is more easily accessible. Not that faith is any less certain than science. But the certitude of faith finds expression only in negative ideas—that is, in concepts of a reality that we can apprehend only by opposing it to what is found in experience. From this, then, we must set out—not, indeed, in order to have faith but in order to achieve real understanding of it.

Ethics sets us tasks—tasks for our conduct—but it does not offer us any inducement, such as the profit, comfort, or pleasure to be gained from an action. It gives us no counsel of prudence and entices us by no hopes; on the contrary, everything which otherwise might seem to man worthy of effort it conditions on morality—that is, on the fulfillment of duty.

Duty commands absolutely, without regard to any other end, without regard to our inclinations, not even to our love. When something happens that *ought not* to happen, then any advantage arising therefrom loses its merit. When anyone strives after an apparent ideal, which involves setting aside the requirements of duty, or indeed has the presumption to outbid duty, we have a more despicable behavior than when crude impulse openly rides roughshod over the consciousness of duty.

If duty pays no regard to inclination, then it is clear that moral action cannot take place under the influence of emotion or from mere habit. It demands deliberateness and thus insight into what we "ought." Without such insight it is only by chance that conduct can harmonize with what is morally enjoined. The moral command, however, claims mandatory validity. But that is realized only when man has the insight to perceive the duty laid upon him and thereby eliminates the element of chance from its fulfillment. Without such insight, indeed, the demands of duty would never be brought home to him. The obligation we call duty is not a fact but a law. We cannot gain knowledge of laws by observation as we do of facts; we apprehend laws only through thinking. If, therefore, there is any such thing as a moral law at all, then we can act morally only on the basis of our own insight. Morality stands or falls with the possibility of personal insight into duty. Any command imposed by an outside will is entirely beyond the range of our insight. We can take cognizance of the claim of this will as a fact; we can even submit ourselves to it; but never can such a will establish its validity. If the autonomy of ethics is done away with; if, in other words, the law of duty springs from a higher will, then it is the law of duty itself that is done away with. An "ought" because another wills it, is a contradiction in terms.

With this exposition of the concept of duty the autonomy of ethics and its independence of any authority is established. And for this it has been entirely unnecessary to define what is specifically commanded by duty. It is enough that we are able to apprehend the mere concept of duty in order for the autonomy of ethics to be established.

We stand now at the point where we can fix our eyes on the relation of the ethical to the religious view of the world. The fatalist who undertakes to explain his conduct as dependent on the divine will surrenders the possibility of moral action. Perhaps he does not even claim to *know* the divine will. It suffices him that history is directed by the will of God, and this makes null and void the task of realizing the good among men by personal effort.

If human life is guided by a higher providence, then it is under the dominion of eternal goodness. But where eternal goodness reigns, there it is only possible to *be* good, not to *become* good. Though the world may appear imperfect to the limited vision of man, it cannot—being ruled by divine goodness—be so in fact. Therefore, all man's attempts to improve the world must be just as meaningless as if he were to bid the wind to blow or command the sun to bestow warmth and light.

The fatalist who accepts the course of life as an inevitable fate and denies personal responsibility merely represents, in so doing, the only truly valid consequence of the religious interpretation of history. For if, in order to save morality, one tried the evasion,

"Perhaps just this development of man toward the good is God's will," then the fatalist—not merely with better logic but even with better faith—would answer by pointing to God's perfection. It is impossible to think of God as creator of the insufficient. His ends cannot be represented as subject to development in nature and as dependent upon the help of His creatures.

Whoever combines the religious view of the world with the ethical in *one* view is inevitably led not only to the subordination of human aims to God's aims but also to the abandonment of the ethical task altogether. Any attempt to maintain the unconditional necessity of the "ought," which is the essence of duty, leads him to insolvable contradictions with the idea of faith.

The sovereignty of the good in nature can only be conceived as a demand upon the human will, as an end to be realized only through human activity. Though the ethical view of the world by no means excludes the recognition of divine ends, it cannot conceive of them as being valid in nature. The principles of faith and the principles of ethics can never be united in one world-view; for our limited human knowledge they are apart. The ethical view of the world has no reference to the highest good in the world, not even to the destiny of man in respect to the world-purpose, but only to the aims which man, from his own insight into the law of duty, sets himself in nature and according to which he himself should shape his life and his history.

The religious view of the world rises above this view of the worth and aim of man in nature. We have faith in the reality of a world under the sway of the divine will but, owing to the limitations of our reason, the hope of developing this religious view of the world in positive concepts and of uniting it theoretically with the ethical view under one principle remains forever vain.

The fatalist who misunderstands the law of the separation of truth into the different views of the world carries over the principles of the divine order of the universe into human life in nature. His religious feeling is misguided. He is lured into a view of the world which denies the autonomy, and therewith the moral destiny, of man. He makes of man a mere creature, blindly guided by an invisible hand. Men stumbled into the World War.

To this statement, laden with cynicism, the fatalist must sub-scribe.

The bridge fatalism builds between the eternal and the finite world-order does not hold up. Fatalism does not satisfy the deeper convictions of men. We cannot renounce the truth of the moral demands that are perceptible to everyone in the voice of conscience. Where the fatalist comes up against a conflict be-tween the ethical and the religious view, he abandons the ethical truth without reflecting that such a conflict should make him suspect his own premises; for one truth cannot exclude another truth.

There would, indeed, be an insoluble contradiction, so that we should be compelled to sacrifice the one view in favor of the other, if it should prove true that we are capable of unlimited knowledge, for in that case, indeed, the systematic unity of our *subjectively* perceived world-view must really correspond to the *objective* unity of the world.

I cannot introduce here the proof of the necessary limitation of our knowledge as it is developed by critical philosophy in the doctrine of transcendental idealism. Yet we may here observe—and that is sufficient for our purpose—that, without the tacit presumption of capacity for unlimited knowledge, we cannot conclude that there is a contradiction between the ethical and the religious view from the fact that it is impossible to unite them in one system. Conversely, from the separation of these two views we can infer the falsity of that presumption—that is to say, we can directly prove transcendental idealism, according to which we cannot have positive knowledge of the world of things-in-themselves (*Dinge an sich*).

But with regard to the relation between the ethical and the religious conception there arises an even more profound question, which goes beyond that of the compatibility of these two world-views. We have the definite, though vague, notion that an inti-mate bond exists between religion and morality. For all positive religions, which have based ethics on the revelation of the divine will, there is no problem here. But as the notion of duty, origi-nally obscure, has now been made clear, and the autonomy of ethics has therewith been recognized, the relation between the ethical and the religious view of the world has become indefinite and uncertain and requires further clarification.

Regarding the problem of man and his duty, we have up to now considered only whether he can *recognize* the moral law, and we have found his autonomy in the fact that he can perceive it only through his personal insight. But it may still seem necessary to inquire whether man has in himself sufficient strength to *fulfill* the law.

If the autonomy of human reason does not include this capacity, then man remains, at the crucial point, still dependent on aid from above. The emancipation of ethics from religion must then be held to have failed. The separation of the ethical from the religious view cannot be sustained. Interest in this problem is by no means merely theoretical; on the contrary, it is a matter of immediate practical interest to man, indeed, his highest practical interest: whether man as a moral being, left to his own resources, is capable of the fulfillment of duty.

At this particular turn in our argument a phalanx of opposition is concentrated against what seems to be an overweening presumption of reason in order to force it at last to a humble capitulation, and so to save humanity from taking on a responsibility under the burden of which it must inevitably break down.

Thus Kant's declaration of the emancipation of moral reason has challenged all those who would keep humanity in tutelage.

The conflict is waged more openly by those who, under the protection of assured traditions and because of their superior insight into human nature, do not fear defeat. By all others the issue is confused, on the one hand by fruitless insistence on what is generally agreed upon, such as the existence of duties, and on the other hand by the appeal to personalities who have won the pure love of men and with whom piety and reverence shrink from contending.

Putting aside the doctrines and sayings of these personalities and confining ourselves to the law of duty in all its rigor, let us ask ourselves: Can the simple consciousness of duty become the motive of conduct for man?

The challenge of duty comes to man only when he is faced with a choice, and indeed with a choice that compels him to an "either-or." Either he resolves upon the one course of action and in that way fulfills his duty, or he resolves upon the other and violates his duty. There is no third possibility. There is no tragic conflict of duties, only the conflict of having to renounce the satisfaction of an interest for the sake of duty—for duty alone. For duty does not commend itself to us through a value obtainable by its fulfillment. It brings no reward with it. It is no merit. Duty, moreover, does not command an action because it is good and worthy of our effort. What does "good" mean here? An action is good only in so far as it fulfills duty, and it is not good and is no longer worthy of effort if it infringes duty. Thus, in the conflict of contending inclinations no positive value sways the will to side with duty. And just as little does a threat or fear of harm and punishment compel the will. The law can exert no force on man, and man can soften and silence the voice of conscience.

But does not duty, through that which it commands, necessarily awaken motives that mitigate its own severity? Do not sympathy and love and inner satisfaction bolster up the consciousness of duty? The words "Thou shalt" give the answer. There is no necessary connection between duty and love, between duty and inner satisfaction. There is the command, "Thou shalt," and the exhortation, "Love thy neighbor," but there is no command, "Thou shalt love thy neighbor." Such a command contradicts itself. Love is a free gift. Duty, on the other hand, is a law, and he who is resolved to fulfill this law must be prepared to act against his love.

But as to inner satisfaction, it is the *result* of a disposition loyal to duty, and it vanishes if speculation as to satisfaction takes the place of loyalty to duty. Moreover, the happiness afforded by this inner satisfaction does not necessarily outweigh the suffering that the very man who is loyal to duty must at times undergo. He would be a foolish dreamer who, for the sake of the enjoyment of that satisfaction alone, would take upon himself the burden of all the painful conflicts into which duty leads man.

So, then, we ask once more: What gives man the strength to carry out his duty? What is it that affords him—man who is sensuous and rejoices in beauty, who is lighthearted and passionate—the steadfastness to defy all temptations and to follow the voice of conscience? What has enabled him throughout the ages to risk happiness and life where no renown was in prospect, no tangible advantage beckoned, no encouragement sustained him —where he has resolved upon that *alone* which he recognized to be right?

There is a doctrine that says in reply to this: Man does not act in this way. He does not do his duty merely because it is his duty. He knows that there is a sanction in another world. "If there were no sanction in the life beyond," asks a Jesuit moral philosopher of our time,

what could have restrained the Christian martyrs from yielding to the demands of their persecutors, and so save their lives? Was it the baseness of the deed? The fear of the categorical imperative? . . . I believe that every unprejudiced man feels the paltriness of such motives in such solemnly earnest moments, when the highest good is at stake and the question is one of "to be or not to be."

But had the clever Jesuit put the counterquestion: What kept the *heretics* from yielding to the demands of *their* persecutors, and so save their lives? he could then scarcely have missed the answer. Does not the explanation he sought lie in the fact that in those solemnly earnest moments, when the question of the highest good was at stake, these men were conscious that life is *not* the highest good, but that of all evils the greatest is guilt?

What gave strength to martyrs and to heretics, what enables every earnest man to do what he has recognized as his duty, is the calm reflection on his dignity as a man, the surrender of which would make him despicable in his own eyes. Self-respect, directly bound up with man's awareness of duty, without any additional motive, is the sufficient driving force of the moral man.

Perhaps duty has never yet been fulfilled simply for its own sake, without the alloy of some other impulse. No one, indeed, can guarantee the unconditional morality of his conduct. But what has such speculation to do with the consciousness of the binding character of the obligation, with the certainty that one could always make the moral impulse prevail, and that will power would have sufficed for that?

No will has power over duty; rather, the consciousness of duty gives the will power to reject all motives that conflict with duty. It is not slavish subjection when man resolves upon what he ought, for his moral will does not yield to a higher power; on the contrary, sovereign freedom prevails, the *absolute* supremacy of the pure moral will over all impulses and necessities that otherwise hold man in bondage.

There is as yet no freedom if in the surge of desire a man forgets everything that is wont to move him. Carried along by the joy of action, he may feel himself strong because his conduct has been given a clear direction; but he remains determined by an alien influence and dependent on an impulse he himself has not chosen.

It is only in moral self-determination that man emancipates himself from all such dependence, since, free from any compulsion, he resolves upon the good simply from insight into the law. In recognizing the unconditional necessity of duty, however, we feel confident of more than our mere ability to overcome all hindrances to the fulfillment of duty *as each individual occasion arises*. We are conscious of an unqualified capacity, of a power superior to *any possible* counterimpulse that nature may present. Such a power presupposes nothing less than *infinite* strength of the rational will.

This certitude of the infinite strength of the rational will is not derived from experience. It essentially surpasses the limits of experience. In each particular moral action the strength of the moral impulse shows itself only as a definite finite force. Experience never allows us to know other than finite forces. For each force in nature there may be a greater force, by which the former is overcome. The certainty of the infinite strength of the good will, therefore, goes beyond all experience. In this assurance man rises above the limitations of his knowledge. He no longer judges himself according to concepts derived from nature; he presses forward to a judgment according to ideas. There is manifested to him the idea of freedom, and, subordinating his will to this idea, he *believes* in the freedom of his will.

Within the conception of nature man sees himself as a finite being, determined according to natural laws of which he has knowledge. He has knowledge at the same time of his moral task —indeed, his knowledge extends to the recognition that the fulfillment of this task presupposes freedom, and that this does not contradict the merely natural order.

But the reality of such freedom, and with it the reality of an order of things without the compulsion of "must," surpasses the limits of nature. Its certainty belongs to faith. It is of a religious nature. As a moral being man becomes conscious of the freedom of his will and so determines himself as belonging to an order of things pointing beyond nature. He determines himself as a member of a world under the law of freedom and of the good. The recognition of this world of faith is religion. Here, then, is the bond between religion and ethics. In moral self-determination, and in it alone, and with the fullest preservation of ethical autonomy, the faith that slumbers in the depths of reason comes into the light of consciousness and opens the way for man to religion.

But religion does not exhaust itself in the recognition of a world under the idea of freedom and of the good, by which nature is reduced to a mere phenomenon. Religion is more than what we can comprehend in the ideas of faith, in which we oppose the eternal to the finite. Religion has its true life in *feeling:* in the religious feelings that go hand in hand with the ideas of faith.

Here alone lies the positive element of a religion free from all superstition. That which is unattainable to all the concepts of knowledge, and which is expressed only negatively in the ideas of faith, we do actually possess in those feelings of *Ahndung* ["inkling," surmise, presage, divine],* to use the concept established by Fries, which embraces the deepest significance of the word. In these feelings that move us in the face of what is beautiful and sublime in nature and in the actions of men, there lives the certainty that in the objects of our knowledge appears the very reality which is the object of our faith. This wholly affirmative conviction recognizes the eternal significance of the finite appearance and brings about, in the realms of action and of

* See Rudolf Otto's discussion of *Ahndung* in *The Idea of the Holy,* John W. Harvey, tr. (New York, 1943), p. 150.

truth, the unity of the views of the world. But, precisely because it consists in a sensing that is inexpressible and cannot be analyzed into concepts, it can never suffice to disclose for us a definite knowledge of the eternal.

Those who are unacquainted with psychology are at this point always exposed to the danger of mistaking the convincing strength of this feeling for intuitive evidence, and so of claiming it as an immediately intuitive knowledge of the eternal. The pretensions of *mysticism* rest upon this psychological illusion.

After all that has been said, it is clear that the mystical doctrine of the immediate contact of the soul with God, which soars to the vision of God, must be at variance with ethics, just as it is not consistent with *Ahndung*, the essence of which is that the eternal is unfathomable.

Mysticism values morality at most as an exercise for the development of its higher powers. For, in addition to spontaneous conversion, it has always recognized the way of effort. Yet almost always, in the case of the mystics, a divorce from ethics has occurred, and that quite consistently. The really mystical experience of illumination falls to the lot of only a chosen few. It cannot be forced—at least not by merely moral conduct. Morality proves insufficient and therefore sinks in value for the devout. But it also proves itself superfluous as soon as the mystic begins to tread the path of vision. For how, if he succeeds in beholding his eternal destiny in all its clearness, can the doctrine of the end that man sets for himself hold its own? Mysticism destroys ethics. In its place it puts *asceticism*, meaning here a turning away from the world.

In like manner it destroys *Ahndung* and substitutes *ecstasy*— the intoxication of a union with God that breaks through the barriers of reason.

But let us ask ourselves: What is the relation of the unperverted religious feeling to the moral life?

The consciousness of the infinite strength of the moral will is accompanied by the elation of feeling we call *enthusiasm*. With the fulfillment of duty often comes satisfaction, which may indeed be intensified to delight when a man has at last trodden the path of action and finds his moral victory within sight. But enthusiasm leaves these feelings far behind. It grips man's inmost soul and lifts him above himself. When man has attained his moral victory through the efforts of his understanding and his will, he becomes conscious of the dignity of his free self. Then, in the clear conception of the moral law, the feeling seizes him of which Kant says "that it would rather be necessary to moderate the flight of an unlimited power of imagination, in order not to allow it to rise to enthusiasm, than, from fear of the powerlessness of these ideas, to seek help for them in pictures and childish apparatus."

Enthusiasm arises where inner emotion, nay, still more, where vigorous self-activity lives and the idea of our eternal destiny finds a response. From this enthusiasm luster and warmth radiate on that activity, adding beauty to its purity and constancy.

But morality in its purity and constancy is here the primary and decisive thing. Enthusiasm, once aroused, can for a time sustain the will and lend wings to action. But it has no life of its own and, when artificially nourished, it becomes shallow, boastful fantasticism, which inevitably destroys the real nature of enthusiasm.

It it different with morality. Morality has nothing to recommend it other than that it is the sober observance of the law. But for that very reason, in nature, where the idea of the good can only find expression in self-conquest, morality as an activity is superior to any mere feeling.

Far more even than that. This autonomous consciousness of duty, requiring no alien motive, this pure consciousness of duty alone leads man to the consciousness of his freedom and thus to faith. Those who hold that observance of duty needs the inspiration and stimulation of devout feelings, those who believe that it is necessary to curb the supposed pride of a self-sufficient rectitude by offering edifying religious teachings, they destroy the foundations of all morality; they choke the springs from which enthusiasm flows; they rob man of the possibility of becoming conscious of his faith.

What good are pious teachings and stories, mysteries and solemn rites, designed to arouse these devout feelings and to support virtue? They remain words and empty symbols, mere edifying spiritual entertainment, so long as personal living faith does not fill them with independent meaning, or they become substitutes and narcotics for those who, only from cowardice, bow themselves before God.

But, as regards pride of spirit, we should not forget that the conception of Pharisaism is derived from the conduct of theologians.

Moral autonomy is inseparably bound up with moral accountability. Moral accountability judges the conduct of man by the moral law as he perceives it by his own insight. This judgment, which evaluates the sincerity of man's character, prevents self-pride.

These considerations, however, which deal only with the individual isolated acts of man, lead to a still more profound problem. Man violates the moral law not only now and then. Every earnest man feels that the fulfillment of duty will always be for him a struggle; that an inclination to evil is inseparably bound up with his nature. He knows himself, as Kant puts it, to be essentially evil.

This idea of guilt has led, in the positive religions, to doctrines of redemption, and in philosophy to theodicies. But these attempts to justify the divine government of the world are frustrated by the contradictions inherent in the problem. The doctrines of redemption are theories of salvation that presuppose a positive and definite knowledge of the divine will. They rest, therefore, on superstition.

What then is the significance of the idea of essential evil to the philosophically enlightened, for whom the moral and religious views of the world are distinct?

Holding to the idea of the eternal good, we believe in a world contrasting with nature—a realm where being and being good are necessarily one. According to the idea of freedom, we judge ourselves as free authors of our deeds and attribute to ourselves our moral insufficiency. The idea of moral insufficiency thus has religious significance. Within our conception of nature the power of man is limited and can therefore be overcome. The fact that such defeat is possible, a possibility that always exists in nature and that is not excluded by the *possibility* of mastering the counterimpulses, necessarily separates man from the *holy* will. This holy will, in its very essence, without having to overcome possible counterimpulses, is directed toward the good. This insufficiency, man, bound within the limits of finite nature, can never cancel by his own power. There is in nature no conversion or sanctification of man. At this point the mystery of death gains religious significance, but any attempt to approach it through positive notions is excluded as a blasphemous absurdity.

In his belief in the infinite power of his good will, man is capable of enthusiasm. But there also remains in him the conviction of his own unholiness. We understand now that enthusiasm cannot be the pervading mood of the educated man.

Man sees the insufficiency of his knowledge. He sees the insufficiency of his will. A part of nature and subject to its laws, yet he remains a stranger in it, one who is not sufficient unto himself. Only the moral obligation that he recognizes as his task keeps him from despair. It heartens him and strengthens him in his loneliness in nature. But this mood lacks the reconciling element which the ethical view alone cannot give but which nevertheless does live in the feelings of the educated person. This reconciling element springs from the faith that man belongs to a world in which the imperfection that clings to him here is removed. Anything further is for faith an insoluble mystery, before which man bows in trustful humility. For the educated man moral courage and humility fuse together into the mood of resignation, in which his ethical view meets his religious view.

Let us pause here for a moment and look back on the way that lies behind us. We shall then see how steep was the ascent, how narrow the basis from which we set out.

We have presupposed nothing beyond the mere concept of duty. We have only asked: What is the meaning of "we ought"? And, advancing from this single premise, we have arrived at the point where the transition from ethics to religion is found. In doing so I was not actuated by the theoretical pleasure of applying the principle of economy of hypothesis to our investigations; rather, I felt the need of choosing our starting point so as to exclude as far as possible all controversy, and for that reason I wished to start only from what was self-evident. But because the content of our premise is so limited, we are compelled to amplify it if, beyond the results we have gained, we wish to gain at least some impression of their significance and implications for life.

The concept of duty, and all the considerations based on it, remain without any application so long as we have not answered the question, *What* ought we, what really is the object of duty? We need a principle determining the characteristic that distinguishes all the various dutiful acts as such.

But remarkable! Just here, where everything depends on receiving from philosophy a firm and unambiguous decision, we discover, when we freely reflect and exclude thereby the sophistic play of our interests, that a not lesser difficulty for common understanding arises from the original obscurity of philosophical knowledge itself. Indeed, the solution appears so unattainably remote that even the mere right to put the general question as to the content of duty is contested.

It would therefore be vain, especially as I must hasten to a conclusion, if I were to try to develop a really abstract solution to our question. Let us leave, therefore, all the controversies of the philosophers and rather consult simply the unprejudiced judgment passed, in their active daily life, by common men conscious of their responsibility. Let us also ask ourselves what it was for which, in the great progressing epochs of human life, men have freely made those sacrifices to which history again and again bears witness.

Put the question to yourselves in this way, and you will agree with me when, without further proof, I say: It is the idea of justice that guides the conscience of the man of action aware of his responsibility. It is the command to treat every other man as his equal and to ask the same from him. However difficult it may be to express this idea with scientific clarity, or to verify it by scientific method, you will nevertheless agree with me in this, too, that if any philosophy cannot consistently hold fast to this idea of justice as the fundamental law of all ethics, we may know at once that it can be only a product of confusion or sophistry.

But certainly, where a philosophy thus confused or sophistic prevails—at least in an epoch which, under the influence of a complex, and in many ways degenerate, civilization, has lost the simplicity of its healthy instincts—there even the usually sound judgment of the common man ultimately becomes confused and lapses into affected intellectualism or dull indifference. On the other hand, where the moral attitude is nurtured and where one seeks the wellsprings of progressive forces, but where men yet fail to give to this attitude a firm direction toward an aim, there the assumed purity of disposition yields to an empty fervor that comes easier than doing good.

This sickly weakness of the sense of justice is very evident today. It is, moreover, no accidental and passing phenomenon but manifests itself as a symptom of the rotten core of the intellectual life of Europe—a disease that poisons the healthy powers of the Western peoples and threatens them with complete ruin.

Its clearest manifestation is the ever deepening cleavage between an inwardness that is introspective and alienated from the business of everyday life and an outward activity that is undirected and devoid of ideals. This ruinous gulf divides the peoples of the West into the camp of the so-called good men, who hold themselves aloof from the rough business of the world and in a spirit of fatalism rely on the inherent power of the good itself, and the camp of those who are busy in Vanity Fair, who bargain for its power and profit knowing full well that the pious optimism of the others will never trouble their sphere.

People approve the separation of church and state, and see in its realization an advance toward freedom of the spirit—an aim certainly worthy if it is meant thereby that the state should break off its alliance with superstition. But that is not in people's thoughts today. What they really intend is, rather, to deprive the state of any foundation on a Weltanschauung. Even this one might still agree to, in so far as it is imperative to prevent the state from arbitrarily preferring one world-view and permitting it to terrorize those who differ. But the tendency of the idea of separation is not confined to this. Its real tendency is, on the one hand, to prepare a place for the cult of the ideal, withdrawn from active life and from its moral tasks, though it is only in eager devotion to these moral tasks that religious life can truly flourish; and, on the other hand, to abandon the soulless state, as a mere institution of power, to the rude sport of forces guided by no higher ideal.

Is not the very possibility that the idea of such a separation, and the discord in life that it implies, could find acceptance, the symptom of a pitiful and shameful spiritual confusion?

A glance at reality, however, shows that we are no longer dealing with a mere postulate—indeed, our age presents a spectacle of churches frozen into dead forms and of states degenerated, in their greed, into beasts of prey. Moral life, and with it all life, has fled from both. And how should it be otherwise, since moral life has its being only in the union of mind and action?

This decay of life, as is now apparent, is just another aspect of that confused mentality which knows not how to separate the ethical view of the world from the religious. For, as we have seen, this must be the bitter consequence of this mistake: that the autonomy of the ethical task is abandoned; yet not even the grip on the religious life can be maintained.

Only where the independence of the ethical task is recognized, and hunger and thirst after justice lays hold of men, can true life unfold itself afresh and prepare the soil for a strong and decent public life, a public life which forces the state, with all its powers, into the service of justice, a state *beside* which there is no need of a church because such a state is itself the dwelling place of the religious life in all its fullness.

So, then, all our reflections blend into harmony in the one thought, that we should unite our forces and devote them to a militant life in the pure *service of justice*, quietly certain that the more exclusively and fully we consecrate ourselves to this task, the more freely and strongly the inspiration and warmth of religious life will awaken among us.

THE ART OF PHILOSOPHIZING *

THE name of philosophy has, for many, an unpleasant ring to it. To some it signifies an unrealistic brooding, which was perhaps appropriate in ancient Greece or faraway legendary India but which, in an age that has carried civilization to its highest accomplishments, must appear as an intellectual exercise that, if it is not distracting, is at least useless. Others again will have nothing to do with the philosopher because they suspect his business of being unscientific, a flimsy speculation the results of which cannot stand up against thoughtful criticism. It must be said that disdain for philosophy has already passed its peak: philosophical questions are once more beginning to arouse wide interest. On every hand the need for a unified attitude toward life and nature is making itself felt. Nevertheless, though this need for philosophy (which is above all a need for inner stability and for a standard by which to guide our personal life) gives us an inkling, because of its universality, of the importance philosophy could assume in the whole of human existence, and though it may succeed in recovering at least a glimmer of its former dignity, men of science are distrustful of the ways of the philosopher and dispute his right to a place among them. For the multifarious and often bizarre forms in which the philosophical urge manifests itself and the planless groping for philosophical truth exhibit nothing resembling a method such as has long characterized the other sciences and such as must indeed be demanded of a science if it is to have a rightful claim to this label.

What, then, is the nature of that which we call philosophy and of which we are here inquiring whether it deserves to rank among the sciences? If we are not to dissipate our energies in a futile battle of words, we must first of all agree on the meaning to be attached to the word "philosophy"—for if one person under-

* "Von der Kunst, zu philosophieren," *Die Reformation der Philosophie* (Leipzig, 1918).

stands one thing by the word and another person something else, it is not surprising that no unity is achieved.

I

The content of philosophy, if philosophy indeed exists, must be truth. But, conversely, not every truth is philosophical; for the faithful reporting of an observation also contains truth, and so do the propositions of mathematics. Philosophical truth, therefore, must in some way be differentiated from other truths. But that which differentiates it can be found only in the fact that *it becomes clear to us solely through thinking.* Knowledge that is clear independently of thought is not called philosophical; all knowledge, on the other hand, that becomes clear only through thinking is of a philosophical nature.

But there are two ways of finding a truth by means of thought. In one of these, what we think of an object is simply that which is implicit in the concept of the object. In other words, the predicate by which we define the object in our mind cannot be omitted without thereby nullifying the concept of the object. For example, the knowledge that two is an even number or that one must not violate one's duty is of this kind. For the number two is defined as the double of one, and an even number is one that is double any whole number; therefore, it is a contradiction to think of two as not even. Nor can one, without annulling the concept of duty itself, think that it is permissible to violate one's duty. Judgments which contain no knowledge that extends beyond the concept of their object are called *analytic*, and that part of philosophy which embraces only analytic judgments is called *logic*.

All other judgments, namely, those through which we attribute to an object a predicate that is not already implicit in the concept of it, are called *synthetic*. For example, the judgment, "This rose is white," is a synthetic judgment, for it could be thought that this rose might not be white. Likewise the judgment, "The opposite sides of an equilateral quadrangle are parallel," is synthetic, since the parallelism of the opposite sides does not follow from the mere concept of the equilateral quadrangle.

Now it might appear (and indeed the illusion persisted until Kant) that all philosophical judgments have to be analytic; for all knowledge derived by thinking is knowledge through concepts, and consequently it would seem that knowledge can be philosophical only in so far as it springs from concepts.

However, though it is true that all analytic judgments (as we have defined the word) are philosophical, it does not follow that all philosophical judgments must be analytic. For it is one thing to say that a cognition becomes clear only through thinking, and something quite different that it is grounded in thinking alone. Hence it is not impossible that synthetic judgments be of a philosophical nature.

And in fact there are such; indeed, all of us are so familiar with them that we do not trouble to take note of them. Thus we presuppose, in the simplest sort of judgment based on experience, that no change occurs without cause. This proposition enunciates a philosophical truth since obviously it cannot be derived from intuition. Nevertheless, it is synthetic; for there is nothing in the mere concept of change that implies the necessity of a cause. Or, to give a quite different example: when we assert that crime should be punished, we are again expressing a philosophical, in fact, a synthetic, judgment. For neither can this assertion be grounded in intuition nor is anything regarding the legitimacy of punishment implicit in the concept of crime, that is, in the concept of an infringement of the law.

We call synthetic philosophical judgments briefly *metaphysical*.

Philosophy, therefore, in conformity with the difference between analytic and synthetic judgments, is divided into logic and metaphysics. Metaphysics constitutes the real content of philosophy because it is only through synthetic judgments that knowledge can be expanded beyond mere concepts. For this reason, then, we look above all to metaphysics when we weigh the possibility of a philosophical science.

II

The significance of this question varies, depending on what it is that first draws us to take an active interest in philosophy. It may be that the truth of a philosophical proposition interests us because of its importance for our conception of life and nature; or we may inquire into the relations among philosophical truths and into the sources from which we derive our comprehension of them.

Thus the proposition that every change has a cause interests us because from it we can judge whether or not a miracle is possible in the course of natural events. Similarly, it is of interest to us to know that every crime deserves punishment, because penal law stands or falls on the truth of this proposition. But it is not enough for us to be certain of this truth and to rely on it when applying the proposition. We seek also the sources of this certainty and the grounds to which we can have recourse in order to defend it against any possible doubt. The question arises here whether and in what way such a truth can be proved or, if it cannot be, in what other way we can reach a decision on it.

The interest that is directed only toward *results* arises immediately from our interest in the solution of the problems with which life itself confronts us. We demand of philosophy that it provide us with rules by which to evaluate the facts and events around us—rules which we need in order to act at all thoughtfully. Such thoughtfulness demands that we achieve an insight into the ultimate purposes and aims of human life; and it is precisely these purposes that philosophy should teach us to recognize. Its highest task, therefore, lies always in a practical sphere: in ethics as practical metaphysics. We could, with Socrates, designate philosophy's task as that of pointing out the unwritten laws, the laws that do not depend on authority and tradition for their validity but rather are prescribed by human reason itself.

Because of this relation to life, philosophy, like other phenomena of life, is part of the totality of human experience, and to this extent it, like them, can be examined historically as a phenomenon of human civilization.

The other interest, namely, the *verification* of philosophical truths, is the genuine scientific interest in philosophy. For philosophy does not become science simply because it contains truth; it is also necessary that philosophy verify the judgments whose truth it asserts. One may designate as *dialectics* the process of verifying a philosophical doctrine. This term, then, embraces all the means necessary for achieving with scientific certainty a general conception of life and nature.

Now, even though philosophy, understood as a conception of life and nature, is related to dialectics as purpose is related to mere means, the choice and employment of these means is of such decisive importance to philosophy *as a science* that we must first of all direct our attention exclusively to these means. For if we wish to achieve a well-grounded Weltanschauung, our first concern must be to develop the *art of philosophizing*, that is, to discover the methods by which we can trace philosophical judgments back to their ultimate sources. Therefore, we must guard against impatient eagerness to construct a system, an eagerness that, because it shies away from the tedium of work, always wants to have done and leads us off the path we *must* follow if philosophy is to become a science.

On occasion, to be sure, because of esteem for the method of philosophizing, the error has also been committed of neglecting the ultimate purpose of philosophy. Thus it has become usual in some schools to regard with contempt what is there called "Weltanschauung philosophy"—their notion being that a Weltanschauung does not fall within the scope of science and that philosophy as strict science must disavow any intention of achieving such a conception.

But this judgment, that a scientifically grounded conception of life is impossible, rests on an altogether arbitrary assumption, pre-empting thereby a function of philosophy as science without justification. For until proof itself has been furnished that it is impossible to achieve a clear and firm conception of life by way of strict science, the opinion of those who make this assertion is no more reliable than that of those who assert the contrary.

Nor does it avail to argue in support of this assumption by pointing out the alleged failure of all previous attempts to establish a Weltanschauung scientifically. Though this argument may carry some weight with the superficial observer, no one can seriously maintain that because something has not existed heretofore it therefore cannot become real in the future.

True, if we persist in the pessimistic prejudice inherent in this assumption, we shall carry our point: what has not been accomplished in the past will remain unaccomplished unto all eternity. But we shall have no one but ourselves to thank for this. For since success in this matter can be achieved only through the exertion of the human mind and since it is impossible to want to achieve that which seems impossible, it is precisely this disbelief that is at fault if the goal that is not pursued is not attained.

Physics itself, the pride of modern science, was possible only because men decided to break with a disbelief that had become impressed on their minds through the impact of the experience of past centuries. But this fundamental decision was not, even in the case of physics, enough to assure to science uninterrupted progress. There remained sufficient difficulties to put the self-reliance of human intellect again and again to the test. The problems were not solved overnight. The history of the theories of natural sciences is a continuous series of trials, which, only through a step-by-step approximation to truth and over the detour of manifold errors, met with gradually increasing success.

Although the perfecting of science succeeds only by way of a more or less faulty verification, this is not to say that the provisional stages through which science is obliged to pass must be false in their *results;* for a result insufficiently verified is not on that account necessarily false. Rather, it usually happens that the discovery of new truths anticipates the development of the methods necessary for their verification. The history of the empirical sciences and mathematics is rich in instances of how the genius of great scientists manifests itself precisely in their bringing to light discoveries the truth of which they themselves are unable to verify—discoveries for whose verification the methods of their age are simply not adequate. As a rule it is the disciples and followers of the masters who first succeed in working out this verification. The scientist's genius is guided by a feeling for truth which leads him further and more surely than the traditional application of methodic rules. Endowed with this feeling for truth, he anticipates results to which those who are not blessed with this gift must find their way through generations of united methodic labor.

If one insisted on condemning such ideas as fancies inconsequential for science because they are insufficiently verified, one would in so doing rob the strict methods of verification of their most fruitful field of application; for the discoveries anticipated by the feeling for truth not only precede in point of time the invention of the methods of verification but also indicate the direction of the refinement and the aim of these methods.

Gauss once said: "I have had my results for a long time; but I do not yet know how I am to arrive at them."

Kepler, as Poincaré cogently remarked, could never have discovered his famous laws if he had gone at his task equipped with the means of observation that are at our disposal today. Tycho Brahe's observations, which Kepler used, were sufficiently unprecise to allow Kepler to reach his conclusions. To be sure, these conclusions were not strictly correct; but for that very reason they paved the way for the greatest advances in astronomy. If, from the beginning, one had had to rely on exact observations, one would have been confronted with such complicated conditions that these advances would hardly have been possible.

The history of infinitesimal calculus provides us with another illustration. If those who were actually the creators of this science had had our present standards of precise proof when they approached their task, we can be sure that even today we should know nothing of infinitesimal calculus; for the difficulty of conforming to such strict norms in the very first attempt to erect this discipline would have proved insurmountable.

But one can go much further and assert that even those branches of present-day science, the methods of which have become most highly developed, could not withstand the criticism one would be obliged to subject them to if one carried this logical finicality to its ultimate conclusion and condemned as contraband every scientific proposition that was not verified with utmost strictness. What this would mean for the fate of science is at once evident from the fact that even the simplest principles of arithmetic, those on which the multiplication table is constructed, would then have to be abandoned. For it must be admitted that the theory of whole numbers has still to be definitively verified.

So it is that in philosophy too we must resign ourselves to provisional solutions of problems—solutions that are perfected only gradually. For if we set our sights too high, if we insist on dealing only with solved problems, we thereby bar to ourselves the only path to attain the truth.

And, as a matter of fact, the history of philosophy is replete with examples of how scientific progress is impeded when the followers of a great philosopher abandon his discoveries because they are not yet sufficiently verified. A classic example is the fate of Plato's doctrine of the ideas. Plato's pupil Aristotle discarded this doctrine because he saw that its verification was inadequate. Thus philosophy was robbed of so tremendous an advance that two millennia have not sufficed to guide thought back from its aberrations to the path that Plato marked out for it. The scientific verification of Plato's doctrine of the ideas was not successful until Kant's discovery of transcendental idealism. But, as it happens, the history of Kant's discovery provides us with a repetition of this very performance; the inclination to judge the truth of a discovery according to the strictness of its verification accounts for the fact that this doctrine of Kant's suffered the same misfortune. Kant's profound verification of transcendental idealism was in its turn encumbered with dialectical errors. It was the recognition of these errors which misled most of his successors into renouncing the discovery along with its faulty verification, and thus once more one of the greatest contributions to science was sacrificed.

The necessity of accepting incompletely verified results carries with it certain dangers. It may lead to a pupil's acquiescing in an opinion simply on his master's authority, and to his endorsing it as dogma; he parrots the words of his master, and tradition supersedes independent thought. The only safeguard against this is the development of truly critical thinking, which protects one against both unintelligent parroting and irresponsible rejection, and which the pupils of a pioneer thinker can least dispense with if they aspire to true faithfulness to their master; for this fidelity can only consist in their accepting his discovery in order to investigate its grounds and establish its truth dialectically.

Indeed, the history of philosophy teaches us that a new doctrine is seldom discovered and verified by one and the same person. Historically speaking, there exists between the world-view of a prominent philosopher and his dialectics this curious relationship: he achieves his world-view originally, not by way of dialectics, not through scientific research; rather, he is led to it by his experiences in life and only subsequently searches out its dialectical verification. This explains the inconsistencies that are often found in the systems of even the greatest discoverers. For no important philosopher doubts the results for which his feeling for truth vouches simply because they may contradict the principles of his system. Confronted with the choice either of denying his feeling for truth in order to preserve the logical consistency of his system or of adjusting his system through some inconsistency to those results, he will allow himself any inconsistency rather than sacrifice such a result. In general, it is the pupils of the great philosophers who, because they lack the creative gift and consequently depend only on the dead skeleton of the system, first go about providing the master's doctrine with such consistency that nothing remains in the system that cannot be traced back logically to the principles of the system. This often leads to the remarkable state of affairs that this system, logically elaborated by the pupils, lends support to a world-view altogether different from that of its creator.

Nevertheless, what in an important philosopher's doctrine is essential to the progress of science and really advances history lies not so much in the content of his conception of life as in what he contributes to the development of methods of verification. For it is not the world-view that distinguishes him from other important philosophers—it is not peculiar to any one thinker but indeed is common to all periods; it is immutable, like human reason itself. So far as its content is concerned, the sharpest thinker is not superior to the man wholly unschooled in dialectics; what distinguishes him from the latter is only the greater degree of clarity with which he is conscious of the *grounds* of the truths of that content. This also explains why one often finds the most modern ideas expounded by the philosophers of antiquity. Progress in the history of philosophy consists solely in the development of methods whereby the one philosophical truth that lies more or less confused in the minds of everyone may be more adequately verified. Hence, this progress is achieved in the field of dialectics, not in that of the world-view.

III

Philosophy, then, must meet two sharply distinct conditions: what it teaches must be truth, and the form in which it teaches must be science. Let us examine in detail the implications involved.

If philosophy is to instruct us in truth, it must be free of the authority of tradition, free of any sort of authority. This may seem self-evident, but it is not. Initially, thinking is not free. Every individual finds himself dependent on superior powers which, because of their inherited claims to hegemony, prescribe to him the rules for his thinking as for all his behavior. Thus thought must first liberate itself from all the shackles of authority; the struggle against every sort of intellectual despotism must be won before the work of philosophy can get under way.

But this liberation from the tyranny of authority does not in itself make thinking philosophical. The emancipation of the spirit from all outer restraints is, rather, only a precondition to the possibility of subjecting ourselves to those inner restraints that consist in subordinating thought to the services of truth. Here the interests of philosophy diverge from those of poetry and mythology.

They diverge also from all other interests, no matter how important and precious these other interests may appear; for only an interest in truth ought to affect the solution of philosophical problems.

In the case of philosophy this process of emancipation is attended by much more serious difficulties than in the case of any other science. Philosophical problems are intimately interwoven

with multifarious interests, and their solution has practical consequences that penetrate deeply into the life of the individual
and of society. The individual, depending on what he has to
hope or fear from a decision, will unintentionally incline to one
that favors his interests and will allow it an unperceived but
determining influence on the outcome of his investigations—a
danger that does not threaten other sciences to the same degree.
It is easy to keep a clear head in mathematics; but when one in-
quires into principles that will determine man's attitude toward
religious and ethical, legal and political matters, and when he
must be prepared, for the sake of truth, to renounce everything
dear to his heart, it is difficult for him to persevere in that dis-
passion without which there cannot be an unprejudiced examination and solution.

There seems to be the possibility of still another conflict. If
one's starting point is a nonautonomous ethics that binds one to
believe in certain things, a particular solution of certain problems
would thereby be prescribed and an unbiased investigation would
be impossible. Such an ethics, however, could not be accepted as
binding unless we were free to test its truth; it would have to
submit itself to free critical examination of the validity of its
claims.

For centuries philosophy was the handmaiden of theology.
We pride ourselves on having freed science from this bondage;
but whether thought is free today, or has perhaps simply changed
masters, is another question. Or is it settled that a science in servi-
tude to politics is freer than the erstwhile handmaiden of theology, and that it is more noble to yield to brute force and make
success the highest court of appeal than to do homage to a dogma
that, despite all its superstitious distortions, still reflects the splen-
dor of a higher idea?

Philosophical truth is rather of a special sort. It is not a matter
of knowledge but of insight. One masters it not by erudition but
by thinking it through for oneself. Therefore, what can be taught
is not so much philosophy as the art of philosophizing. To be
sure, one can acquire knowledge of the philosophical convictions
of another; but one does not thereby become a philosopher—one
merely learns what the other considers philosophy. When we

learn that Heraclitus asserted the flux of all things, this knowledge is no more philosophical than the knowledge that he lived in Ephesus or that Alexander the Great marched to Babylon. For this reason philosophy cannot be learned from the history of philosophy. The most accurate and comprehensive knowledge of the history of philosophy does not bring us a step nearer to even the simplest philosophical cognition; and nothing is more fatuous than the wish to make a philosopher of oneself through a study of the history of philosophy.

Philosophizing, however, the art of independent thinking through which one attains philosophy, can be learned and taken over from others who afford us an example of it. Indeed, it *must* be if we value the progress of philosophy and do not want to leave it entirely to chance whether or not we advance as far as our predecessors.

But philosophy demands something more than self-thinking, namely, *precision of thought*. Chaotic musing and brooding are not philosophizing, which requires sharply delimited concepts. In order not just to think but through thinking—and hence through concepts—to apprehend, one must differentiate between concepts. The ability to do this is acuity, and without it one cannot become a philosopher. Fancy may fly free and afford edification to the spirit when concepts intermingle, but philosophizing is a sober business which subjects the mind to the discipline of ordered thinking. And just as it cannot be the aim of philosophy to assuage the needs of the heart or compete with the creations of poetry through the wealth of its ideas or the grace of its forms, neither can philosophy tolerate any encroachment upon its proper field by mystical piety or ecstatic imaginings; for only unadorned thought belongs there.

Our aim, however, is not simply to reflect; if reflection is to have a purpose, it must be directed toward adequately significant problems. This does not imply that philosophical investigations are justified only if they serve a useful purpose. Philosophical inquiry, like any search for truth, is an end unto itself. But this higher interest in truth, which is independent of all usefulness, is nevertheless concerned with the relation of our thinking to reality, and only those intellectual efforts can appear valuable to it that further our knowledge of reality. In philosophy, too, the importance of the problems is determined by the extent to which their solution contributes to our knowledge of reality. It violates our requirement of *purposeful thought* to struggle with questions of no more than formal importance or with mere subtleties. And, indeed, a serious discussion of the problem whether Christ, if he had come to the world as a pumpkin, would have been able to redeem mankind, or whether a mouse that had nibbled at the Eucharistic host would thereby partake of heavenly bliss—questions that were of vital importance to the Scholastics—would appear ridiculous to us today.

And here it would be well to ask in what, precisely, philosophy's contribution to the knowledge of reality consists. It will be found that this contribution is of a very indirect kind, inasmuch as pure philosophy contains no knowledge of reality but simply provides us with a form, in itself empty, that receives its content only from experience. This does not deny the importance of the problems of pure philosophy; rather, it explains why this importance can be correctly appraised only in the light of the relation of pure to applied philosophy. No matter how slight the positive value of philosophy may appear in the light of this relation, the harm that the application of false philosophical doctrines can do is enormous. But since it is out of the question to renounce altogether the application of philosophical principles (because without them even the simplest empirical conclusion would be impossible), we are obliged, if we are to resist the blandishments of a false philosophy, to rely on the teachings of a correctly established one.

IV

It is easy to see that the particular nature of philosophical knowledge also sets certain conditions for its *presentation*—conditions that other branches of science have to meet, too, but that are uniquely important for philosophy.

The nature of philosophical knowledge requires that the words the philosopher uses to convey his thoughts designate sharply delimited and clearly defined concepts. Where this condition is not met, we can be sure in advance of finding no philosophical enlightenment. A word or an expression denotes either a definite thought or none at all. A word has *meaning* only through the unequivocality of its relation to the thought; and a word that intends more than one meaning has none. To be sure, there are some who feel it is a poor thing if a word stands for only a single thought: our fund of thought is obviously richer, the more thoughts that can be attached to one word. This notion would lead us to the ideal of a language that had infinite connotations, so that there would be no limit at all to the number of thoughts packed into one word. But whoever subscribes to this point of view merely betrays his ignorance of the purpose of language: the communication of thoughts through the use of symbols allocated to them—a purpose that would be frustrated by multiple implications. When the same word serves to connect many thoughts, this is not a sign of a wealth of thoughts but of the lack of thought on the part of him who uttered the words.

This indicates how we should regard the cliché with which confused philosophical books and speeches are sometimes excused or even praised, namely, that they admit of a variety of meanings. If an exposition does not oblige us to associate something definite, i.e., one single thought, with every expression, then it does not oblige us to think at all; we are dealing with sheer babble. We fool ourselves if we imagine that we are thinking, whereas we are only picking up words and parroting them. We should not be able to say of a scientific exposition that in its perusal we think of *something*, or even a variety of things, but that it *makes* us think something *definite*.

For this reason we must also reject a *metaphorical* philosophical language. For a metaphor as such is always indefinite and gives the mind too much free play. Every metaphor is a comparison; but every comparison is inexact. Therefore, a metaphorical expression can only serve as a clarifying example, never as the real means by which a specific thought is designated. One might counter this with the question what there would be left of a language if the principle of avoiding all metaphorical expressions were taken literally. But it must be remembered that most of the words originally used as metaphors have lost their former meaning, so that now immediate and definite concepts are associated with them. Thus, the word "ground" has today an abstract sense which we grasp immediately without considering that it originally meant the same as "earth." On the other hand, it is an unclear and actually metaphorical manner of speaking to talk of the "root" of the principle of sufficient reason. This expression is not definite in its meaning and like all such expressions is capable of misleading not only the listener or reader but also him who uses it.

One often hears attempts to excuse the inexactness of an expression by the profundity of the thought which prevents a comprehensible statement of it. But such a defense must be carefully scrutinized. Though it is true that the difficulty of expressing a thought increases with its profundity, one must beware of the tendency to look, as a matter of course, for special depth of thought in every incomprehensible statement. Philosophical impostors employ this illusion; they affect an unclear and pictorial speech, so that the obscurity of their talk may conceal from uncritical minds the turgidity and banality of their thoughts.

As a matter of fact, however, true profundity is by no means necessarily bound up with obscureness of presentation. We can reasonably assert only this: that *work* is necessary to the understanding of profound thoughts and that great acuity of thought is required for the comprehension of even the most exact presentation of difficult philosophical doctrines (indeed, the more exact the presentation, the greater is the need)—an acuity of thought of which the reader or listener is not always as capable as the expositor. We have no right to demand that the understanding of scientific doctrines be granted us without work; but we do have the right to demand—and indeed we ought to—that they become absolutely clear after sufficient work.

But along with these requirements, which pertain more or less to the presentation of every science, we must take into consideration another circumstance, one that is determined by the special quality of philosophical knowledge. It is characteristic of philosophical knowledge that it lacks the immediate perspicuity of intuition. This explains the peculiar difficulty in communicating philosophical thoughts, a difficulty that is foreign to other sciences. Whereas in other sciences we are able, by pointing out the object to intuition, to remove all doubt as to what thought we are trying to communicate, in philosophy we are limited exclusively to language. We are thus obliged to adhere strictly to *general* linguistic usage. If we should use our own arbitrarily invented linguistic formulae, an artificial terminology such as is permissible and often useful in other sciences, we should frustrate any understanding of our meaning. For how could we make our privately invented language comprehensible to others? If it can be translated into ordinary language, ordinary language will do; if not, we should have to have at our disposal some means of communicating thoughts other than language. Because of the nonintuitive nature of philosophical knowledge, such means are lacking; hence, understanding in philosophy depends entirely on a conscientious conformity with general linguistic usage. If this means of communication is abandoned, all possibility of intellectual exchange is lost.

Difficulties arise here, partly because general usage does not always have the precision necessary for scientific exposition, partly because it is not rich enough to keep up with the development of philosophical concepts. Nevertheless, there is nothing we can do except make the best of general usage; and we do so not by forcibly reinterpreting and thus corrupting the indispensable instrument of speech but by striving little by little to adjust the habits of speech to the needs of science. Where general usage fails us, we must have recourse to neologisms, i.e., symbols that have as yet no meaning and that heretofore have not appeared in the language at all; this is usually and best done through the introduction of words of foreign derivation. But two things must be kept in mind: first, such an artificial expression needs an explanation, the elements of which are defined in common linguistic terms; for an expression that is per se not comprehensible cannot be made so by reducing it to expressions that are just as incomprehensible; second, the introduction of such artificial expressions, even with this limitation, must always remain an emergency measure, since more is lost than gained through the misuse of this aid to understanding. It atrophies the roots from which the living language draws its strength, without which even the grafted shoots of an artificial terminology cannot hope to stay alive.

These requirements may seem self-evident to the ingenuous. And yet a single glance at contemporary philosophical literature suffices to demonstrate that even the most celebrated teachers are far from heeding these clear and simple demands.

V

We found that there are two conditions that philosophy must meet; one is concerned with its content, the other with its form. The first is met when philosophy contains knowledge, the second when it assumes the form of science. Now that we have seen what is necessary to the first of these, let us consider what is demanded for the second.

Philosophical knowledge, like every sort of knowledge, becomes science only when the diverse cognitions that go to make up the particular knowledge are given the form of systematic unity. The unity of a *system* consists in the fact that otherwise scattered knowledge is so ordered that every proposition expressing this knowledge occupies a definite position in the whole structure, either as a theorem, if it can be derived logically from other propositions in the same field of knowledge, or as a basic principle, if it cannot be derived through syllogisms from other propositions in this field but expresses a truth that is elsewhere established.

The most important step in assuring to philosophy the character of a science is the discovery and verification of its basic principles. We know that the consistency of a system does not depend on the correctness of its basic principles; an altogether consistent system may be erected on even the most absurd assumptions. But precisely for this reason it is not enough to rely on the inner consistency of a structure of theorems; for where the presuppositions are wrong, no amount of consistent thinking can bring us nearer the truth. Before the basic principles are established, therefore, it is a waste of energy to build a system on them. But once they are established the system may be constructed merely through syllogisms. Thus the chief methodological problem of all philosophizing is how to get hold of the basic philosophical principles, because they are not obvious as, for instance, the axioms of geometry are, for they are grounded on no intuition, so that we cannot start out from them as from something already established. Rather, they are the most controversial elements in the whole science, and their discovery and verification present us with the greatest difficulties.

The method of the discovery of the basic principles of a particular science must depend essentially on the nature of the knowledge that makes up the content of the science in question; thus philosophical method, too, is determined by the specific character of philosophical knowledge. When we say that those truths are philosophical which become clear to us only through reflection, we assert thereby that we are here concerned with a knowledge that we do not derive from experience, but that—if we are at all capable of acquiring it—has its basis in our own reason. We have also stated thereby that this knowledge does not stand clear and immediate in our consciousness but originally lies obscurely in our reason. The difficulty, therefore, is not in the actual acquisition of philosophical knowledge but in its illumination as it lies within us.

If the illumination of this knowledge is to be assured of success, we must not only reflect, we must do so according to a plan; and this means nothing else but that we must guide our reflection by a specific rule which, so far as possible, precludes our missing our goal.

But how are we to discover such a rule even before we know our goal?

No matter how obscurely philosophical knowledge lies in our reason, it still manifests itself in all everyday judgments; it is basic to every—even the simplest—empirical judgment. There is, therefore, no other way for us to find it but to start out with the concrete use of our intelligence, that is, with judgments whose truth we are certain of even though we cannot explain what this truth rests on. By analyzing such judgments we arrive at the basic principles we are seeking. This analysis consists in our examining what preassumptions we must make in order to form the judgment in question, thus ascending through constantly progressing abstraction from the accidental empirical content of the individual judgments to their most general presuppositions, the basic philosophical principles. And we are just as sure of the correctness of the preassumptions we have established as we are of our judgments.

The fact that there is a clash of philosophical opinions may seem to argue against the fitness of this method, for if philosophical principles can really be found by so simple a rule, how is it to be explained that not all philosophers agree on them? The answer is that it is as easy to state this rule as it is difficult to follow through with it and to refrain from all the detours and enticing side issues to which one is tempted by the mirage of a system patched together from elements arbitrarily assembled. The philosophers' hopeless quarrel over principles is simply the inevitable consequence of the fact that they do not find it worth the trouble to follow the guiding principle of steadily progressing abstraction—that, rather, driven by the lamentable craze for system, they immediately jump over to the most extreme abstractions, from which they can no longer orient themselves, because the thread has been broken that forms the connection with the one solid point of departure of abstraction.

Indeed, we observe that philosophers whose systems differ most radically are of one mind in using the same principles as soon as they turn from doctrine to its application—a circumstance demonstrating incontrovertibly that it is only digression from the straight path of abstraction that engenders disunity. If philosophers were to remain true in practice to their dogmatically erected system, how could the determinist, who denies the responsibility of man, ever make the mistake of passing an ethical judgment in daily life? If he is lied to and cheated, he should accept it as fate; at most, he might lament his misfortune, but he would have no grounds for moral indignation. Or has one ever found that the philosophical skeptic, who calls the assumption of a causal relation between phenomena an illusion, has stopped being interested in the causes of the events he observes, especially of those that touch him personally? Consistency would demand of him that he once and for all renounce the question "why?"

VI

Although the described procedure of abstraction is sufficient for the discovery of basic philosophical principles, it does not at the same time give us a verification of them. They are in this way only demonstrated to be the actual presuppositions of the analyzed judgments and hence their most general grounds; consequently, their legitimacy cannot, conversely, be grounded on these judgments. If, then, they are not to remain altogether unverified, we need a special procedure through which to ascertain the grounds of their validity.

Because of the peculiarity of philosophical knowledge we cannot here call intuition to our aid, as we can for the verification of the principles of other sciences. No more can we verify them in a purely logical manner; for that would presuppose that they, as secondary principles, could be traced back to—i.e., proved by —higher principles; but this would be a contradiction of the fact that they themselves already represent the highest principles of the system.

We found previously that the ground of cognition of philosophical judgments, if there is any at all, resides in ourselves, without any action on our part and independently of all experience. At the same time, also, we found that it does not reside in us with immediate clarity. It belongs, therefore, to the original components of our reason, as an immediate, although originally obscure, knowledge. Accordingly, it must be possible to disclose it by a sufficiently developed theory of reason.

And this disclosure, if it succeeds, is a sufficient verification of the basic philosophical principles. For it cannot again be asked if the immediate knowledge so revealed is in its turn valid. We may ask regarding a cognition whether we possess it or not; but when we confess that we really possess a cognition, it is a contradiction to ask whether what we apprehend through it as true is also really true. Thus doubt of the validity of the immediate cognition is an inner contradiction and annuls itself; and this circumstance makes further verification of the immediate cognition superfluous. Our certainty of it is for us the primary fact, anterior to all verifying and refuting thinking; it reposes in us, impregnable to all doubt arising from reflection by virtue of the *fact* of the self-confidence of reason.

Therefore, what is proved by the theory of reason is not the truth of the basic philosophical principles in question—they are, as basic principles, altogether unprovable—but simply the truth of the empirical proposition that we are actually in possession of an immediate rational knowledge that contains the ground of those philosophical propositions. Whoever demands more of the verification of philosophical principles, whoever thinks that philosophical knowledge can or should first be produced by way of dialectics, is simply deceived by the original obscurity of philosophical knowledge. Because this knowledge becomes clear only through thinking, he is of the opinion that its source, too, can lie only in thinking. And through this misconception of the real nature of philosophical knowledge he is driven to seek the secret of philosophy in the invention of a dialectics that artificially generates philosophical knowledge—an eternally fruitless exertion. Any attempt to bring about an extension of knowledge through reflection alone, without the preassumption of a knowledge derived from some other source, must come to nought on the intermediary nature and original emptiness of reflection, no matter how novel and ingenious this attempt may be. Reflection, *qua* the capacity to think, cannot enrich the content of our knowledge, though we need it in order to give this content scientific form and thus elevate it to the complete clarity of consciousness.

Once this confusion between reflection, which is in itself empty, and reason, which is the capacity for immediate cognition, has been removed, the foolish illusion automatically disappears that it lies within the power of thinking to distill a content from the forms of thinking by some sort of dialectical art.

As soon as it is recognized that this is the nature of philosophical knowledge, it will also become evident that there must be a system of pure philosophy that is immutably established and permits of no further elaboration. Since philosophical knowledge has its seat in pure reason, it cannot be dependent on extension through experience, and no expenditure of ingenuity can add anything to it or take anything away from it. If there is such a thing for us as philosophical knowledge, we possess it once and for all, and the development of philosophy consists only in our becoming more and more clearly and completely conscious of what philosophical knowledge we possess.

That this conclusion can be achieved is the source of an especial scientific allure, which pure philosophy has above all other sciences. Every other science draws on intuition and is susceptible of an extension into infinity because time and space are infinite. Philosophy, on the other hand, is capable of a final form, irrevocably prescribed to it by reason itself.

THE CRITICAL METHOD
AND THE RELATION OF
PSYCHOLOGY TO PHILOSOPHY *

AN ESSAY IN METHODOLOGY

"There are scholars whose philosophy consists simply in the history of philosophy (ancient as well as modern). Current prolegomena are not written for them."
— Immanuel Kant, *Prolegomena to Any Future Metaphysics.*

INTRODUCTION: TERMINOLOGY AND TASK

1. Since the concepts with which the following treatise will deal were first introduced into science as precise terms by Kant, I shall adhere strictly to Kantian terminology. Accordingly, I shall use the term "metaphysics" to denote the system of all philosophical judgments except logical judgments—in other words, all judgments not based on either empirical or mathematical intuition—that is to say, the system of synthetic a priori judgments evolved through mere concepts. And the term "critique of reason" will denote the demonstration of the validity of these judgments by disclosing the grounds of their possibility. I now ask myself the following question: To what extent does metaphysics need a critique of reason, and what method must the critique adopt to satisfy such a need?

I. THE REGRESSIVE METHOD: INDUCTION AND ABSTRACTION

Philosophy as Natural Disposition and as Science

2. There is a favorite old maxim: *Contra principia negantem non est disputandum* (I cannot argue with a person who disagrees

* "Die kritische Methode und das Verhältnis der Psychologie zur Philosophie," *Abhandlungen der Fries'schen Schule,* I (Göttingen, 1904), No. 1.

with me in principle). This saying is basically false in the field of philosophy. Every significant philosophical controversy is a controversy over principles. We are all in agreement on the application of these principles to experience and to life; it is only when we begin to philosophize about them *in abstracto* that differences appear. Thus, we assume in our calculations the continuity of motion without being disconcerted by Zeno's proof of the impossibility of continuous motion. Thus, every chemist expects a substance with which he experiments in a closed vessel to weigh, after his experiments, precisely what it weighed before; he does not concern himself with the metaphysical difficulties implicit in the principle of conservation of mass. Thus, everyone passes judgment on his own actions and on the actions of his fellow men without considering that he thereby presupposes a responsibility that contradicts his perhaps deterministic philosophical views. The materialist speaks of the spirit, the atheist of God, the fatalist of freedom, the atomist of continuum, the empiricist of natural law, the skeptic of truth. It is really only in the academies of philosophy that there is any dispute on these subjects; and after the discussion everyone abandons whatever decision has been reached and relapses into his previous convictions.

Let us therefore distinguish between the philosophical convictions that form, unconsciously, the basis for all our judgments and evaluations, and (on the other hand) the procedure by which we state these convictions as such and fit them into a system. If, in other words, we discriminate between philosophy as a natural disposition and philosophy as a scientific discipline, we can then say that no philosophical idea, in the sense of the first of these terms, is actually the subject of controversy, but that all difficulties in this matter arise when philosophical principles are stated without specific application *in abstracto*. This differentiation now gives us a means of arbitrating the quarrel over principles; for if we choose from the experiences of daily life those judgments and evaluations on which there is agreement, we can analyze them and thus, by a *regressive* procedure, search out the philosophical principles that have been applied in these judgments and evaluations and are presupposed in all of them. By a process of continuous analysis and abstraction from the specific applications we must eventually reach some essential and ultimate assumptions, which we can then separately denote.

Progressive and Regressive Methods

3. This process of abstracting reverses the usual method of objective establishment, which derives consequences from their reasons; it works its way from the consequences back to the reasons. We cannot say that in so doing we prove the principles but only that we reveal them as such. It is an *argumentum ad hominem.* We point out, for example, to the empiricist, who uses the catchword "experience," that synthetic a priori judgments constitute the precondition that makes his "experience" possible; we point out to the moralist, who speaks of "morality," that a belief in freedom of the will is the precondition that makes his "morality" possible. We prove nothing by doing this; we simply try to find the logical reasons for acknowledged consequences. These consequences are the accepted conclusions and evaluations; these we analyze, and they serve us as data for our *argumentum ad hominem.*

It is an altogether false logical prejudice that all truths must be provable. Indeed, no amount of proof can enable us to know or to discover anything that is not already implicit in our basic principles; we can only make it more obvious and clearer to our understanding. Proofs are necessary and possible only for secondary, derived propositions; they are both unnecessary and impossible for basic principles. As long as the premises of any proposition are not basic principles, we can doubt them and we can achieve no complete certainty. If we wish to achieve this certainty, we must ascend to the highest principles. But since these latter generally form the ground of our judgments and evaluations only in an obscure way, without our really stating them and without our becoming clearly aware of them, we must make use of an artificial regressive procedure to make them our own. In the case of those judgments of ours which are based on intuition, this is not difficult, because they force themselves clearly and evidently on our consciousness. But our knowledge is founded only in part on intuition; and it is precisely our non-intuitive knowledge, which we grasp only through concepts in judgments, for which evidence and clarity are lacking. It dwells in us obscurely, and we need a special method to bring it to the light of consciousness.

This, then, is the task of philosophy as science: to discover and to elevate from their original obscurity to the clarity of consciousness those basic principles that are not founded on intuition but arise solely from concepts. If we should succeed in making all of them our own, we should then have a means of definitely deciding all possible philosophical problems. Without the benefit of this regressive inquiry, on the other hand, we are exposed to all the caprice of dogmatic metaphysics, for unprovability is common both to basic principles and to all *false* doctrines—with this difference, that the latter can be refuted and exposed as false by comparison with the principles. The dogmatist, therefore, need only set up his doctrines as principles as soon as he is unable to prove them, and we can protect ourselves against his unjustified claims only if we are in possession of the system of all real principles and are thus able to make apparent to him the futility of his propositions by showing that they are derived.

Let us therefore define as *dogmatic* the procedure of a science that begins with the affirmation of its principles, and as *critical* the procedure of a science that submits even its principles to scrutiny. We shall then be able to state that a critical procedure is the very foundation of philosophy, and that critique in philosophy consists in an adherence to the regressive method.

Induction and Abstraction

4. Let us try to make this more definite.

All science has as its goal the progressive deduction of consequences from their reasons, the subordination of the particular under the general, of facts under laws—i.e., the formal system of theory. But preparatory work is often necessary before the general laws can be reached; it is not always possible, as it is in mathematics, to begin directly with a statement of the general laws. The natural sciences require first a regressive ascertainment of their laws through an examination of facts before they can undertake through theory to explain the facts by the laws. This regressive ascertainment of the natural laws from observed facts is the task of *induction*. Induction, however, never leads to basic principles but always only to theorems. We cannot even proceed inductively without first presupposing certain universal laws. Induction bases on the preassumption of the most universal, something less universal, something, therefore, that, in contrast to principles, is particular. Induction is not the way to necessary truths but only to the relation of necessary truths to contingent ones. For necessary truths consist in the ultimate universals which are already the a priori foundation of all induction from observations. The way to necessary truths, on the other hand, is *abstraction*.

For example: Newton's discovery of the law of gravitation led to the establishment of the theory of planetary motion.* The law of gravitation, however, is not a basic principle but a theorem; its validity could not be perceived a priori but had to be demonstrated inductively. For this induction, however, Newton had to *apply* certain general principles of mechanics. For instance, he had to borrow from the principles of mathematical natural philosophy the presupposition that all changes of motion are the result of constantly accelerating forces, which are subject to the law that every action has its equal and opposite reaction. But it had to be discovered from the empirically observable paths of the planets that acceleration is inversely proportional to the square of the distance of the acting masses.

Thus, Newton's law of gravity combines astronomical observations with the principles of mechanics. Without the latter it would lack universality and necessity; without the former it would lack empirical validity.

If we try, by analyzing Newton's train of thought, to discover the presuppositions of the law of gravity, we come finally to those most general principles of mechanics which are themselves the fundament of and the preconditions for the possibility of all induction, and which precisely for that reason are not inductively demonstrable.

There are, therefore, two different regressive methods: we must distinguish between the regressive method of *abstraction*

---

* This essay was written before the theory of relativity was discovered. See p. 44, n.

and that of *induction*. Accordingly, the analytic process of discovering philosophical principles is altogether different from all processes of proof, different not only from the progressive procedure of mathematics but also from the regressive procedure of induction.

Dogmatism and Criticism

5. Since all philosophizing is itself thinking and apprehending, we shall necessarily be obliged, when we philosophize, to presuppose and apply certain principles that we are really looking for. This is a circle on which every dogmatic method of proof must inevitably be frustrated and fall easy prey to skepticism. For the dogmatic method presupposes that which it sets out to prove, whether it be regressive like induction or progressive like mathematics. Only the critical method is free of this circle and therefore cannot be attacked by skepticism; for the critical method does not seek to prove the principles but only to recognize them as such. It does not prove but, on the contrary, searches out precisely what, in any proof, we have in fact presupposed and are necessarily obliged to presuppose.

Thus, whereas dogmatic philosophy starts naively with any arbitrarily collected pseudoprinciples, critical philosophy works its way up to the principles and seeks them out. The former starts from *hypotheses*. The latter starts only from *facts;* it accepts our judgments as they actually exist, examines and analyzes them, in order to state explicitly what was already implicit in them. Critical philosophy, therefore, does not have a particular part of things as the object of its investigation. It leaves the cognition of things entirely up to the induction of natural science, with which it has no quarrel regarding the knowledge either of physical or of psychical things, nor does it claim to be a science of the supernatural. Its theme is the principles of knowledge itself—the knowledge of all things, physical and psychical, material and immaterial. Critical philosophy does not try to explain anything; it seeks the ultimate grounds of all explanation. It is not limited to the apprehension of any one particular field but teaches how to avoid error in all fields. For this purpose it accepts knowledge as it finds it as *fact:* not to prove its truth or to explain its genesis but to abstract the purely conceptual knowledge and to trace it back to its ultimate principles. When it has discovered these, it then establishes them as the system of philosophy.

Historical Survey

6. Socrates and Plato long ago called for this method. But almost immediately Aristotle confused (under the name ἐπαγωγή) the Socratic method of abstraction with induction. This misunderstanding persisted in the history of philosophy until Kant.[1] Kant was the first to use the critical method precisely, in conscious opposition to both the progressive-mathematical procedure of his German predecessors and the inductive-psychological procedure of his English predecessors. This searching out of the principles through a logical analysis of the judgments and evaluations that lay claim to being apodictic he called *Grundlegung* or "metaphysical exposition," and he furthermore distinguished it from the "transcendental deduction" of principles, which is concerned with demonstrating their validity.

II. THE VERIFICATION OF JUDGMENTS: PROOF, DEMONSTRATION, AND DEDUCTION

Dependence of the Regressive Procedure on the Data of Analysis

7. What do we actually gain by the regressive procedure? New truths only in so far as we presuppose the truth of the data

---

1. Since Aristotle was led by this confusion to contrast induction as the regressive method with συλλογισμός, there remained to him as the original source of knowledge only logic and experience. He thus overlooked the emptiness of formal logic, on the one hand, and the lack of independence of mere experience, on the other. In this way he became the father of two opposing errors in the history of science: the founder of logical dogmatism in philosophy and of empiricism in the natural sciences, i.e., of the false doctrine of the independence of induction as well as of syllogism, which the majority of modern scientists have embraced and which has been most stubbornly defended by the English philosophers. The contrasting of induction and deduction—even today still popular in logic—rests on the same mistake. This second error in Aristotelian logic was not corrected until Ernst Friedrich Apelt published his *Theorie der Induktion*. [Regarding Apelt, see p. 156.]

Apelt supplements the Aristotelian theory of the progressive syllogism of the *dogmatic* method with the theory of regressive syllogism, thus providing a philosophical foundation for the *inductive* method of natural science. It now remains, as the third and last task of logic, to carry out the theory of the *critical* method as the doctrine of the scientific verification of philosophical basic judgments. It is this that we shall here attempt.

with which our analysis began. For, although the principles are logically independent of the consequences that we analyze to make the principles manifest, nevertheless our exposition of the principles remains dependent on their consequences. Since this procedure is not proof, nor any sort of objective verification, but simply a subjective appeal *ad hominem*, its results remain always dependent on these primary data accepted by us, which in their turn receive their objective verification only from the discovered principles. These principles must be valid as such, independent of any consequences derived from them, and cannot first be founded on these consequences.

An example will make this relation clear. The principle of the conservation of energy was not discovered by proof—indeed, because of its general nature, it could not be proved at all.[2] To be sure, with the help of this principle we are able to prove a great deal inductively, but the principle itself was discovered not by induction but by abstraction. Helmholtz discovered it by a process of purely logical analysis, by asking himself: What must the highest major premises of natural science be like if perpetual motion is to be impossible? If perpetual motion is impossible, then the principle of the conservation of energy is valid. But without this principle we can decide nothing a priori about the possibility or impossibility of perpetual motion. Therefore, the assumption of the law of the conservation of energy remains entirely dependent, after this regressive train of thought, on the expectation that someone might perhaps actually succeed in constructing a machine capable of perpetual motion. But this cannot be the last word on the matter, for no discerning physicist would think of making the validity of the law of the conservation of energy dependent on the degree of certainty of such an empirical proposition. Quite the contrary. He assumes it as the precondition for the validity of his observations; it serves him as norm and regulator for his inductions. We cannot, therefore, prove such

2. This is frequently overlooked through a confusion of the law of the conservation of energy with the first law of thermodynamics. But the latter proposition is only an application of the law of the conservation of energy and as such has been inductively proved. This proof does not say that energy is constant, but that heat is a form of energy, for which statement the law of the conservation of energy must already, in its most general form, be presupposed.

a principle by experience; on the other hand, we are unable to prove it a priori precisely in so far as it is really a basic principle. How, then, are we to accredit it as such? How are we to defend it if it becomes an object of doubt?

The regressive procedure of abstraction is thus in itself only a factual exposition: in so far as we in fact agree on certain propositions, we must also grant the logical conditions of their possibility. We thus simply point out the logical dependence and conditionality of one proposition on another; but we cannot in this way compel anyone to accept the disclosed proposition as true who is not convinced and who does not remain convinced of the truth of the consequence independently of our logical demonstration. Anyone who does not agree to those data will not be convinced, by analysis of them, of the principles that are their precondition. Indeed, the very opposite could happen: instead of acknowledging the reason with the consequence, he could deny the consequence with the reason; and thus we should achieve the very opposite of what we wanted. In the very process of putting a naively accepted proposition on a vague basis, we can easily make him suspicious of the proposition itself, since he can transfer his doubt of the reason to the consequence instead of transferring his certainty of the consequence to the reason. If, for instance, we show the naturalist that he himself, when he passes judgment on such matters as duty, right, and beauty, recognizes an objective teleology and sets it above natural law, we shall perhaps impel him to the point where, for the sake of his naturalistic philosophical system, he will be untrue to his ethical convictions and will deny them any justification—not in his active daily life but perhaps in his philosophical speculations.

Problem of the Independence and the Completeness of the System of Principles

8. What shall we do, then, if these data are doubted? They depend for their validity on principles and can be verified through principles. But it is the principles that are in dispute; it is precisely with their justification that we are concerned. The appeal to our awareness of the self-evidence of our own convic-

tion would afford only poor protection to the principles: how many errors have been trotted out as immediately evident truths? Insistence on the unshakable nature of our convictions is no more than the most outrageous sort of special pleading, by which we may sway our opponent but can never convince him. Now, we have already seen that there is no point in asking for proof of basic principles; *we must first determine whether a proposition is really a principle before we are justified in renouncing proof of it.*

The regressive procedure, however, is not in itself sufficient for this demonstration; analysis does not set for itself its own limits. On the one hand, it is always doubtful, without some further criterion, whether the analysis could not be pursued further or whether it has really arrived at principles. On the other hand, even if the latter were possible, there would still remain the question whether we had really exhausted the entire system of principles or whether it was not still incomplete. No matter how many data we analyze, it is always possible that we have overlooked some, the basic preconditions of which are still lacking in our system. Have we really reached the first and highest—the genuine—principles? Does not our system contain perhaps too many or too few of them? How can we elevate ourselves above the purely factual in our thought and feeling and secure the principles against doubt?

The Principle of Sufficient Reason

9. If we ask ourselves the general question: Why do our judgments need verification? we shall have to answer: Because our thinking is subject to the possibility of error. The determination of how to verify metaphysical principles depends, therefore, on the correct understanding of the difference between error and truth.

All thinking consists in the forming of concepts and in the combination of them into judgments, as well as in the combination of the judgments into conclusions. Thinking as such is not yet cognition. When we cognize, we do so only by thinking judgments, not mere concepts. But not all judgments are knowledge; there are judgments which simply analyze concepts, e.g.,

definitions. These are analytic judgments.[3] Among them belongs
also the syllogism. Every syllogism can be reduced to the form of
a (hypothetical) analytic judgment. Even a syllogism affords me
no new knowledge not already implicit in its premises; if it did,
it would be a fallacy. A syllogism does not assert that the premises
and the conclusion are true; it asserts the consequence of the conclusion from its premises, and this consequence is an analytic
judgment. Cognition is therefore contained in synthetic judgments but not in the derivation of one synthetic judgment from
others. This derivation, like all analytic judgments, is simply an
act of our consciousness by which it makes clearer in another
form the knowledge it already possesses from another source.

Every judgment is an act of thinking or of reflection and as
such (in contradistinction to the involuntary combination of
ideas through association) is arbitrarily formed. Herein lies the
possibility of error and the necessity of verifying all judgments.
For it is still questionable whether the voluntary combination
of ideas in a judgment took place in accordance with the canons
of truth; whether the claim to truth, which distinguishes reflection from association, is justified. Logic demands a reason for
every judgment. What does this mean? No knowledge is possi-

3. Concept and judgment must be sharply differentiated logically. (a) Only definitions, i.e., analytic judgments, are equivalent to concepts. But precisely for that
reason they have no value as knowledge: the existence of the defined concept must
first be proved. (b) Every complete conjunctive analytic judgment represents a
concept, but it is not conversely true that every concept can be represented by an
analytic judgment. Only for concepts resulting from combinations is this possible.
Originally metaphysical (in the sense of Kant's categories), mathematical, and empirical basic concepts cannot be defined. Anyone is at liberty not to *call* these basic
concepts "concepts"; that is simply logomachy. (c) Every judgment presupposes
concepts for its possibility.

To be sure, the merely problematic idea of a concept itself again presupposes for
its possibility assertoric ideas, i.e., knowledge. As Kant says, the analytic unity of
consciousness is not possible without the precondition of some sort of synthetic
unity. But this "original" synthesis is not one of judgments but of immediate knowledge without reflection. The obliteration of this distinction, which has often been
attempted lately, leads to the mystical notion of the reality of concepts and to the
transference to knowledge itself of the arbitrariness that pertains to the forming of
concepts; it leads to a confusion of thinking and knowing.

Furthermore, regarding the division of judgments into analytic and synthetic, it
can be said that this distinction is not grammatical but logical. Every judgment is
either analytic or synthetic depending on whether or not the predicate is contained
in the subject concept; but the same sentence can stand in one case for an analytic
and in another for a synthetic judgment. Concepts cannot change, but words can
change their meanings, that is, they can be associated with various concepts.

ble from mere concepts. If I am to form a judgment containing knowledge and truth, I need a ground for knowledge that is independent of the concept of the subject of my judgment. The truth of the judgment, therefore, lies not in itself but in something else from which the judgment derives the truth. What is this "something else," the cognitive ground of judgment? This ground can itself be another judgment; in this case verification is by proof. But all proofs must finally be derived from some unprovable judgments, the cognitive grounds of which cannot in their turn consist in judgments. These primary judgments, which are unprovable themselves and from which all proofs are derived, are called principles.

The Indirectness and Emptiness of Reflection

10. The statement of these principles is, to be sure, like every judgment, an act of reflection, but reflection cannot of itself create the truths that are stated in the principles. Reflection left to itself can only form analytic judgments; it can only derive, i.e., prove, consequences from given truths. But the truth of the principles is not dependent on proofs and they cannot, therefore, in so far as they are *synthetic* principles, be authenticated by reflection. The principles of geometry, for example, are, as synthetic principles, by no means logical necessities. Thus, the denial of the parallel postulate does not contradict any law of logic; consequently, logic is simply not in a position to determine its validity.

The ground of these ultimate principles, therefore, being independent of reflection, must lie in an immediate knowledge that itself contains the ultimate grounds for all judgments, i.e., for all derived knowledge. One such mode of immediate knowledge is intuition, both empirical intuition as the ground of all empirical judgments and mathematical intuition as the ground of all mathematical judgments. The unity and necessity, however, which we find as facts in our thinking and which we enunciate in the metaphysical principles, cannot find their source in intuition, for it is *only* through reflection that we become cognizant of them. But in so far as it is a *synthetic* unity, its origin cannot lie in reflection, since it is already a precondition for every reflective judgment. There exists, consequently, an immediate knowledge of a nonintuitive nature that is the ground of our metaphysical judgments. We call it the *immediate knowledge of pure reason.*

Judgment and Knowledge; Knowledge and Object

11. The ground of all thinking thus lies, in the last analysis, in immediate knowledge, and the truth of all judgments consists in their correspondence with this immediate knowledge. Reflection is not enough in itself; as such it is empty and can only repeat and clarify cognitions elsewhere provided. It does not extend, but simply *elucidates,* our knowledge. Accordingly, we can speak of error and truth in our thinking only in so far as a truth is presupposed that is independent of the thought in dispute. All dispute about truth and error, all doubt and uncertainty concerning reflective judgments arise from their being measured against the immediate knowledge they reiterate. There can be no dispute whatsoever about this immediate knowledge; its certainty can never be questioned or suspected of error, for error is nothing more or less than departure from immediate knowledge, a fallacious reiteration of immediate knowledge. Therefore, the possibility of error presupposes the existence of immediate knowledge, and he who calls immediate knowledge "wrong" simply contradicts himself; he does not know the meaning of the words "error" and "truth." All error and doubt pertain to reflection; they cannot touch immediate knowledge.

Efforts to verify our knowledge and disputes over truth and error cannot have any bearing on the relation of knowledge to the object of knowledge. Correspondence with the object can never be a criterion of the truth of our knowledge, because we should have to step outside our knowledge in order to compare it with the object; but this is impossible since it is only through knowledge that we achieve the object. We can thus never compare knowledge with the object, but only one mode of knowledge with another. A proposition is true when it is properly verified, i.e., when it coincides with the knowledge from which it was derived. *There can be no dispute about the truth of the immediate knowledge; there can be dispute only as to the question: Which is the immediate knowledge?*

We should be obliged to presuppose immediate knowledge

(in so far as it is immediate knowledge) in order to doubt its truth: doubt of immediate knowledge is a self-contradiction. All derived knowledge, on the other hand, is as such problematic and can be verified only by comparison with immediate knowledge. All the problems of philosophy can therefore be epitomized in the following: What is the immediate knowledge of pure reason? Every philosophical dispute can be decided by answering this question. The knowledge of our reason either corresponds with the object or it does not; and in neither case can we do anything about it. There is no vantage ground from which, standing as it were beyond or above our knowledge, we can make its validity the subject of a science. It cannot therefore be the task of philosophy to provide our knowledge with objective truth but only to certify consciousness as *knowing* consciousness, to assist consciousness to an unerring statement of knowledge.

Philosophy, then, concerns itself no more than any other human discipline with the question: Is our knowledge true, i.e., does it correspond to the object? It asks only: Is a proposition really knowledge, i.e., does it correspond to immediate knowledge? Is a judgment really an articulation of knowledge or is it no more than a factual occurrence in my consciousness? All error thus belongs in the realm of consciousness and cannot touch the immediate knowledge of reason.

Impossibility of a Theory of the Possibility of Knowledge

12. This can be elucidated in still another way. Every cognition is a thought, but not every thought is cognition; for there are also problematic thoughts, whereas it is an essential quality of cognition that it asserts the existence of that which is apprehended, that is, of the object of the thought. It might thus appear as if the concept of knowing could be derived from the general concept of thought; as if it might be possible to explain how assertion is joined to a notion, how a notion acquires objectivity; as if the possibility of knowing could be formulated in a theory. But the particular is by no means contained in the general and inferable from it. On the contrary, it is knowledge that makes problematic notions possible, and not vice versa. Knowledge is an im-

mediate quality of inner experience and not something compounded quantitatively, to be explained or constructed from simpler relations. All knowledge is as such already the knowledge of an object: the object is always in the cognition; it is not something that only later is added to it. The *relation of knowledge to the object* cannot be subjected to any mediate examination; it can only be immediately experienced as it exists as a fact in our knowledge. It is not a casual relation nor can it be delineated in concepts. Therefore, this relation cannot be the theme of any science: *there is no theory of the possibility of knowledge.*

Proof, Demonstration, and Deduction *

13. As we saw above (sec. 10), we verify the basic judgments of the empirical and mathematical sciences by pointing out the intuition on which they are grounded. We call this verification *demonstration.* (N.B., demonstration and proof are to be differentiated.) Such demonstration terminates the series of grounds for this sort of judgment by tracing these judgments back to immediate knowledge, to a ground that is independent of the arbitrariness of forming judgments. At this point there is no sense in searching for higher grounds, for all error consists only in a false repetition of truths otherwise arrived at. Now, where there is no further basic truth, it cannot be falsely stated; and where nothing is repeated, it cannot be falsely repeated. Also, when we speak of sensory illusion, it is, strictly speaking, not an illusion of the senses but one of our judgment, through which reflection attempts to explain and interpret the intuition of the senses.

But how are we to verify the *metaphysical* principles? We cannot prove them; else they would not be principles. No more can we demonstrate them; else they would not be metaphysical.

---

* *Deduction* is the anglicized form of *Deduktion,* a term established by Kant for the investigation of the proof of the reality of metaphysical principles: *quaestio juris.* ("The Deduction of the Pure Concepts of Understanding," *Critique of Pure Reason,* p. 120.) Fries and Nelson use the Kantian term for the same scientific undertaking although in the Fries school the character of the method of deduction has changed, as explained in subsequent chapters. All translators of Kant's *Critique of Pure Reason* have accepted this term and, because there are no English equivalents, we, likewise, retain the words used by Nelson—*Deduktion, deducieren, deducierbar* —though in anglicized form. The reader must constantly bear in mind that these words have a specific epistemological meaning and are not used in their usual logical sense.

We call the way of verifying them *deduction*. In what, then, will this deduction consist?

The only way to verify knowledge is through the authority of the immediate knowledge from which it is derived. The ultimate bases lie in the knowledge that is immediate as such. All derived knowledge, however, is knowledge through concepts, i.e., through forming judgments. Strictly speaking, then, we are not justified in demanding that all knowledge, but only that every judgment, must have a ground; so that all mediate judgments must be proved, and all immediate judgments either demonstrated or deduced. But this ground must under no circumstances be sought in the relation of the judgment to the object but only in its relation to immediate knowledge. Thus, it is all-important to differentiate between the relation of the judgment to knowledge and the relation of knowledge to the object.

Deduction and demonstration therefore coincide to this extent, that both methods serve to verify basic judgments. The function of both of them consists, accordingly, in the exposition of immediate knowledge in so far as the latter forms the grounds of the judgments in question. But, unlike the demonstrable judgments, the judgments that are only deducible are not rooted in intuition; that is to say, we become cognizant of the immediate knowledge that forms their basis, not immediately but *only* through the agency of reflection, *only* through the judgment.

This circumstance determines the essential difference between the two methods of precedure. In a demonstration we are able, for our comparison, to set intuition and judgment directly side by side; but in deduction we have only an indirect comparison at our disposal, since the criterion for the validity of the judgment is not immediately at hand (as it is for demonstration) but must first be subtly and circuitously searched out and thus made our own. But no matter how great the distinction between demonstrable truth, with its immediate evidentness, and the truth that is only deducible, we must nevertheless appreciate that this advantage is the result only of a different relation between the respective modes of knowledge and *consciousness;* for in neither case can the *object* be summoned as guarantor of the truth.

In order thus not to make too extravagant demands on deduction, let us state, as the most important result of our investigations so far, the finding that demonstration is only a subjective verification, and that consequently the certainty of even the most evident truths, for instance mathematical axioms, cannot (contrary to popular belief) rest on objective criteria.

Psychological Nature of Deduction

14. There are, then, three kinds of verification: proof, demonstration, and deduction. Verification by proof pertains only to mediate judgments and, in order even to be possible, presupposes principles. Consequently, the completeness of verification demands above all demonstration and deduction.

We are concerned here only with the most difficult sort of verification: deduction. We have found deduction to be the most important task of philosophical critique. We now assert that in this matter critique can proceed only *psychologically*, i.e., that it is itself a *science of inner experience*.

The proof of this assertion is easy in the light of what we have outlined above. We have just shown that in the case of demonstration we can juxtapose the cognitive ground and the judgment that is to be verified. However, in the verification of only deducible judgments such a direct comparison of the judgment with its cognitive ground is not possible, for we are not (as in the case of demonstration) immediately conscious of the cognitive ground but must first seek it out indirectly. We possess this cognitive ground of the judgments that are only deducible in the immediate knowledge of pure reason. Therefore, we must make the content of this immediate knowledge of pure reason itself the object of scientific investigation. But we can become acquainted with what cognitions we have only through inner experience. Consequently, the inquiry into the cognitive ground of the deducible judgments is the task of a science based on inner experience. Therefore, *the deduction of the metaphysical principles is the business of psychology*.

We must dwell on this proposition at greater length, for it is of decisive importance to all critical research. It will be further elucidated in the pages that follow.

III. THEORY OF DEDUCTION

Proof of the Possibility of Psychological Deduction

15. Every thought is a thought of an object, and the essential quality that distinguishes knowledge from the merely problematic thought is its assertion of the existence of the object. Knowledge must be differentiated both from the subject of the knowledge, the ego, and from the object of the knowledge. Whether the object be external or internal, knowledge is always different from it. The relation of knowledge to the object is not that of the mind to the body nor that of the ego to the external world. The ego, like the external world, can be the object of knowledge; but, although in the case of self-knowledge, *subject* and object are identical, *knowledge* and object are not.

No matter what the object of knowledge is, whether external or internal, knowledge is always an inner activity. As such it is itself an object, namely, the object of inner experience, and can be studied as an object. All cognitive activity, in so far as it belongs exclusively to the mind and is not merely the result of external impressions, is subject to the condition on which I discover introspectively my activities to be dependent. This original spontaneity, in contradistinction to the activity that is sensorily stimulated, is precisely that which distinguishes all knowledge of pure reason. I shall therefore be able to obtain for myself through inner experience a theory of reason that will contain the elements for the derivation of all the cognitions of pure reason.

Thus, it will be possible, without dealing *in abstracto* with the philosophical principles themselves, to deduce them empirically —a procedure with which skepticism cannot take issue since we shall be dealing entirely with *facts* which everyone can observe for himself and shall not become involved in any metaphysical considerations or hypotheses. This *psychological deduction* is at the same time independent of the establishment of the system of principles by the logical-regressive analysis of the judgments of our conscious thinking; and we possess the advantage of being able to compare the two afterward *and thus of being able to de-*

termine the "*quid juris*" of conscious thinking by the "*quid facti*" of reason.*

Position of This Task in Psychology

16. It is important, however, to notice that for this task we remain entirely within the limits of mental self-observation without becoming involved in comparisons with the material world; further, that we are dealing not with any sort of evolution, nor with concepts either inborn or acquired, nor with any comparisons of a historical or ethnologic nature. For we are seeking not the individual phenomena of mind but the universal form of inner life as a part of reason per se, as the basic norm of mental activities, and as it provides reflection with its laws. It will perhaps be objected that this is not a task of psychology; and, indeed, the name by which we call it is of no importance, whether we use the ambiguous term "theory of knowledge," or (in consideration of our purpose and interest) "transcendental psychology," or even "*philosophical anthropology*." In any case, whatever we call it, only inner experience will be adequate to the task.

Advantages of This Method: Certainty and Obviousness

17. No matter how great the difficulties may be that confront self-observation, this *subjective approach to all speculation* nevertheless possesses a twofold advantage. First, we remain entirely within the realm of observation, i.e., of knowledge through sensory intuition. We do not wander off into the field of abstract thought and do not get lost in the sophistries and subtleties of indirect procedures of proof where the danger of error is the greater the more indirect the proofs are and the more remote they are from intuition. The closer we stick to intuition (in our case, to self-observation), the less vulnerable we are to logical fallacies, and the more readily such fallacies as may occur can be discovered and corrected. We also avoid the danger of being satisfied with mere probabilities; all probability, like all error, pertains only to reflection and rests on incomplete conclusions. On

---

* Such deductions have been carried out in Fries's *Neue Kritik der Vernunft* and in Nelson's *Kritik der praktischen Vernunft* (translation in preparation).

the other hand, intuition, from which we do not depart and to which we may always return, is not subject to any uncertainty whatever and thus also not to various degrees of probability.

The second advantage is closely related to the first, namely, that the use of metaphysical principles, which no theory can circumvent, is in no field of our knowledge so limited as it is in psychology. The use of metaphysics in any science cannot be extended beyond the domain of mathematics since it is only through the medium of mathematical measurements that our observations can be subsumed under the metaphysical basic concepts. But the domain of mathematics is extremely limited in inner experience because of the total impossibility of extensive measurement. We are therefore almost exclusively here confined to the use of observation and thus evade (thanks to the nature of the object) the embarrassment of becoming involved in an exhaustive dispute over metaphysical universals.

To be sure, knowledge through empirical intuition is only assertoric and is not apodictic like the rational knowledge of philosophy; but it is not for that reason any less certain or less secure than the latter, which, on the contrary, is originally obscure and hence lacks the obviousness that distinguishes empirical knowledge. For it should be observed that the modal difference between assertoric and apodictic knowledge is not one of degree of certainty but one of source. Objective validity pertains in the same way to both sorts of knowledge, but their subjective relation to consciousness is different: the relation of the former is of immediate obviousness; the relation of the latter, on the other hand, is mediated by reflection.

It is precisely this original obscurity of their principles that makes all philosophical disciplines so extremely difficult; this complete absence of perspicuity and obviousness is the only reason why it is impossible by dogmatic means to assure universal recognition to a philosophical system. And for this reason criticism is really nothing but the suggestion that, instead of erecting philosophical abstractions systematically, it would be better to take a more circuitous road, which is illuminated by the evidence of concrete intuition and, though it requires more time and effort, leads all the more surely and unerringly to the goal.

The Logical Form of Deduction and the Principle of the Self-Confidence of Reason as Critical Maxim

18. Nothing is more important for an understanding of deduction than to differentiate it from every sort of proof. The critique of reason asks simply: *What* immediate knowledge does our reason possess? Just to ask this question, reason must have self-confidence in the truth of its immediate knowledge as the major premise of all deduction. Thus, although criticism deduces metaphysical principles from a theory of reason which itself can be attained through inner experience, i.e., only inductively, nevertheless the validity of the metaphysical principles is not grounded on experience or induction. For metaphysical principles are not proved by the theory of reason but are simply made manifest as such; and in this process the affirmation of their *quid juris* does not rest on the inductions of inner experience, which are used as the grounds of deduction, but on the self-confidence of reason. This self-confidence of reason is the universal principle that transforms the psychological conclusions of the theory of reason into critical deductions, i.e., that permits us to find in inner experience a guide to the systematic establishment of philosophy. The immediacy of knowledge, its origin in pure reason (in contrast to the derived knowledge of reflection, which is subject to arbitrariness and consequently to error), is the mediating concept of the whole critical train of thought so far as its logical form is concerned. It is precisely the psychological theory of reason which serves us as proof of the reality of this mediating concept.

Perhaps the following observations will help clarify the highly ingenious logical structure of deduction we have just outlined. Whereas we start by making the task of deduction the verification of principles, which are *unprovable* truths, we now discover that deduction actually contains a *proof*. This result will no longer seem paradoxical when we recall (cf. sec. 8, above) that critique is not concerned with the proof of a metaphysical principle, which is impossible, but with the proof that a proposition is really a metaphysical principle. In other words, critique proves the *psychological proposition* that the knowledge a particular metaphysical proposition enunciates is immediate knowledge from pure reason. *The proof of this psychological theorem is the deduction of that metaphysical principle.*

For example, critique proves the proposition: The principle of causality arises from the connection of the mathematical scheme (*Schema*) of change with the category of hypothetical synthesis in immediate knowledge. It does not prove the principle of causality itself. This principle is metaphysical; the proposition that critique proves is psychological. And this proof is drawn from a theory of reason gained through inner experience. Thus, critique, like every empirical discipline, presupposes among its premises metaphysical principles as preconditions of its possibility. However, it does so, not in order to prove them, since that is obviously circular reasoning, but in order to deduce them, i.e., to prove their source in pure reason. Thus, the law of causality is already presupposed among the bases of its above-mentioned deduction.

But how can the mere psychological ascertainment of the *source* of a metaphysical proposition become a *verification* of it? Only through reference to the fact of the self-confidence of reason. On the reference to this fact rests, in the last analysis, the possibility of deduction as a validation of a priori principles on the grounds of their possibility. The enunciation of this fact is thus the highest principle of critique; it is nothing more or less than the enunciation of the fundamental fact of cognition itself.

The *principle of the self-confidence of reason* deserves to be called a critical (or transcendental) principle only in so far as we understand under the term a proposition that, without itself being metaphysical, provides us with a criterion of the legitimacy of metaphysical propositions. For it entails the legitimation of all propositions that can demonstrate their origin in pure reason and hence can establish themselves as metaphysical principles. It is not able, however, to adjudicate *which* propositions arise from pure reason; it serves therefore only as major premise in the logical structure of deduction. We must assure ourselves of the minor premises in another way. This other way is the theory of reason or, to use a different terminology, the theory of "transcendental faculties of mind," by which Kant designates those faculties which contain the ground of the possibility of a priori principles.

Any allegedly critical maxim, other than the principle of the self-confidence of reason, is either too narrow, in that it arbitrarily restricts our metaphysical capacities, or too broad, in that it improperly inflates the pretensions of metaphysics.

An example will make this clearer. Kant still lacked such a unifying critical maxim; hence the lack of structure in his doctrine. He was not yet aware of the immediate knowledge of pure reason and contemplated metaphysical knowledge solely from the point of view of reflection. Thus, he could accord the metaphysical in our knowledge no immediate validity but only a derived validity, in so far as it could be logically connected with sensory intuition. Hence, his *principle of the possibility of experience* allowed him, to be sure, a justification of the categories as the logical preconditions of the possibility of experience, but this principle proved too narrow for the verification of the speculative ideas. He was thus obliged to call their objective validity a "transcendental illusion," though, as transcendental ideas, they have the ground of their possibility in reason. But since, on the other hand, he found them to be the preconditions of the possibility of morality, he had to introduce, in order to warrant their practical use, a new and critically unjustified principle, the principle of the primacy of practical reason. Thus, Kant's too narrow formulation of the critical principle mentioned above led to the uncritical restriction of our speculative capacities in the field of theory and consequently to a *critically* irreconcilable cleavage between speculative and practical reason.

Reflection and Reason, Error and Irrationality; the Problem of Universal Validity

19. We know that we can err; we know that we cannot be confident about even the most skillful proof or the most convincing conclusion in our scientific systems so long as we have not assured ourselves of their final principles and ultimate presuppositions. We therefore mistrust every judgment until its verification has been carried to its deepest roots. Every judgment is for us unfounded until we demonstrate its origin in the spontaneity of reason which is immune to arbitrary thinking. Reason is the highest court of all truth, invulnerable to any doubt, even though

we do not yet know what the genuine statement of its truth is—even though, indeed, it is just this that we are seeking. For what are we to trust, where are we to find the ground of our certainty —even if only in order to doubt—if not in reason? For it is through confidence in reason alone that we are able to think, and therefore also to doubt.

Philosophy is a science; *ergo*, it consists of thinking; *ergo*, it is itself possible only on the basis of confidence in reason. He who reproaches philosophy for this is simply confusing error and irrationality. Philosophy is as little able as any other science to create knowledge from nothing, to create truth where there is yet no truth on which to stand. Rather, in so far as it is not magic but science, it presupposes a properly organized faculty of reason for everyone who wishes to participate in it. Its task is simply to guide reflection to an infallible articulation of reason and not to submit reason itself to an examination of its fitness. He who does not trust his reason and would like to have its reliability certified for him should engage the services of a psychiatrist and leave the philosophers alone.

By discriminating between reflection (understanding) and immediate knowledge (reason), we dispose of an old but still recurrent suspicion, namely, that our method destroys the universal validity of the metaphysical principles since it is an unfounded *hypothesis* that what I find in my mind must be found in the minds of everyone else. It is rather surprising that those who raise this objection most persistently are precisely those who, in their next breath, demand that philosophy shall be established independently of all empiricism and psychology. For what is this assumed hypothesis if not a psychological proposition which simply has nothing at all to do with metaphysics? Are we not permitted, in our search for the metaphysical principles, to disregard ethnologic considerations of the mental structure of our fellow men? He whose confidence in his own reason does not assure him of the objective validity of his knowledge will hardly be persuaded of it by finding out how other people's reason is organized. But he who has this confidence in his reason and who is interested in philosophy *as a science* will be satisfied to acquaint

himself thoroughly with his reason, for precisely there will he
find philosophical truth.

The question whether or not all human minds are similarly
organized is not as philosophically important as it is credited with
being. What we can come to know empirically in other people is
always only their understanding. Understanding (reflection)
can err—others' as well as my own; and since a majority vote does
not decide truth and error, we shall have to determine philosophical truth by some method other than the statistical. But even if
the above-mentioned question referred not to the understanding
but to reason, it would still not be as important as is supposed.
Rather, it would then become trivial, an insignificant analytic
judgment. For since all the mind's knowledge is purely inner
knowledge, it is only by analogy with my own mind that I can
infer the existence and structure of the minds of others. And if I
decide that the reason of others is organized like mine, this is
neither deep speculative wisdom nor a psychological hypothesis
but the *concept* of man, more specifically, the only (psychological) concept of man I can form, viz., the concept of all the thinking beings whose reason is organized as mine is; for it is only because of my own mind that I conceive the existence of the minds
of others—otherwise I should have no idea of them at all.

But if this is so, then our method of deducing from our own
reason is doubly successful (and is, moreover, the only method
that could be); it not only demonstrates the validity, the *quid
juris* of the principles, but, in so doing and because of the unique
character of the method, it also demonstrates that *everyone* presupposes precisely these philosophical principles—*must* presuppose them, and *can* presuppose only these.

Our psychological differentiation between the arbitrariness of
reflection and the spontaneous activity of reason, and the corresponding logical differentiation between proof and deduction
have once and for all disposed of skepticism and have given us
the only possible evident approach to philosophy. Whoever,
now, is still in earnest about attacking the principles may bring
forth the proof, based on experience, that they have no place in

the deduced system of reason. But resistance to this *method* is merely the pastime of those who fear that once again philosophy as a clear discipline may put an end to the free play of their own speculative wisdom. They do not stop to consider that he who rebels against the sovereignty of reason thereby reduces himself to the mental stature of an idiot.

Criticism not a System of Philosophy but a Method of Philosophizing

20. Thus, criticism is the concept of a *method* and not of a philosophical system. Whoever adheres to this method is a criticist, no matter what conclusions he may reach with it; and whoever does not adhere to it and wants to establish philosophical knowledge as true through an objective verification, be it proof or comparison with the objects, is a dogmatist—even though he is induced by his ultimate realization of the futility of his undertaking to ascribe this futility to philosophical knowledge itself; and this is the whole game of skepticism. Therefore, skepticism, in so far as it preaches not the critical deferring of judgment but the impossibility of judgment, is also dogmatism.

This warning to think of criticism not in terms of results but in terms of method can help dispel many misunderstandings. Thus, for instance, it has often been thought that criticism, because it does not seek the truth through a comparison with the objects, denies their existence, and that criticism is synonymous with idealism and thus the antithesis of materialism. The fact is that criticism is neither idealism nor materialism because it is not a Weltanschauung at all, but a method.

Application of Criticism to Logic and Mathematics (Critical Logic and Critical Mathematics)

21. Although we have explained the *necessity* of this method only for metaphysics, we have nevertheless proved its *possibility* from certain unique characteristics of *rational science as such*, and it can easily be seen that its results must be just as applicable to the analytic principles of *logic* as to the synthetic a priori judgments of metaphysics. (The task of the *critique of the prin-*

ciples of logic herewith postulated has hitherto, as a result of the confusion of deduction with proof, been mistaken by almost all logicians in that either they have attempted to make logic as a whole a psychological discipline or, in order to escape this danger, they have tried to proceed strictly dogmatically and have declared a special elaboration of psychological criticism to be superfluous. In practice this has most often meant that they have intermixed scattered fragments of psychological criticism in the system of philosophical logic without recognizing their psychological nature.)

Further, since the field of synthetic a priori judgments embraces not only metaphysics but pure mathematics as well, it follows that the field of the deducible in our knowledge does not end with philosophy. *Critical deduction of the axioms of mathematics* in their entirety must also be possible, quite aside from verification by demonstration, which is at once clear and consequently satisfies by itself the needs of the mathematician. This application of criticism to the axiom systems of mathematics constitutes a separate scientific discipline: the philosophy of mathematics or, to use a better designation, *critical mathematics*.[4]

IV. THE RELATION OF CRITIQUE TO SYSTEM; THE PREJUDICE OF THE TRANSCENDENTAL

Interdependence of Induction and Criticism

22. Criticism, in the sense in which it is here presented, was first called for and practiced with complete precision by Fries; but in the widest sense of the concept it was already a part of Greek philosophy. Socrates insisted that the rules of truth be sought in the *unwritten laws* of one's own reason, as a rejoinder both to those who believed they could find these rules elsewhere and to those who denied such rules any validity at all. But only recently has this method been successfully introduced, thus providing philosophy with a solid scientific foundation; and this

4. A summary of the problems and methods of this discipline is to be found in G. Hessenberg, "Über die kritische Mathematik," *Sitzungsberichte der Berliner Mathematischen Gesellschaft*, III (1904), No. 2. [See the subsequent essay, "Critical Philosophy and Mathematical Axiomatics."]

has happened as a result of the discovery of empirical methods in natural science. Induction, too, searches for the universal, which it attempts to derive from observed particulars, but it does so only on the basis of the preassumption of something even more universal: the highest laws of nature, in which all experience is grounded; and these laws, as the ultimate major premises of all conclusions, can be derived neither inductively nor by any process of proof. Accordingly, as soon as the empirical method was carried out with clarity, the question of these ultimate leading principles of all inductions was bound to arise, and speculation had to lead back to the general question of the necessary truths in these unwritten laws. In other words, induction demands speculation even in order to be possible. The problems this fact presents were solved by Kant in his critique of reason.

Objections to the Critical Procedure

23. Kant's method of having a critique of reason precede the metaphysical system very early met with many objections based in part on the fact that Kant himself was not entirely clear about the relation of critique to metaphysics as he still confounded deduction and proof. Thus, Herbart imagined that he had refuted Kant with his question whether it is easier to know reason than to know other things. This depends on what one means by "other things." If one means, as Kant does, the objects of metaphysics, then, of course, it is easier to know reason, because knowing reason is a matter of inner observation whereas the "other things" are a matter of abstract thinking. Thus, Hegel raised the objection, often repeated, that critique is an attempt to swim before one is in the water. To be sure, I shall be obliged to apply to inner experience, too, certain principles that I must still deduce; but deduction is not proof, and what would be circular reasoning for proof is not necessarily circular reasoning for deduction.

Confusion of Deduction with Proof

24. If one holds critical deduction to be a sort of proof, i.e., if one holds the relation of critique to the philosophical system to be a relation of logical ground to its consequence, then one reaches,

because of the contradiction implicit in this assumption, two anti-thetical opinions depending on whether one draws a conclusion from the consequence to the ground or vice versa,[5] to wit, either one can conclude:

Philosophy is a rational science. A rational science can, how-ever, not be derived from empirical grounds. Therefore, critique cannot be empirical-psychological, but only rational.

Or one concludes:

Critique is a science from inner experience, i.e., empirical psy-chology. But only empirical-psychological consequences can be derived from empirical-psychological grounds. Therefore, there is no such thing as philosophy as a rational science but only phil-osophy as empirical psychology.

The first is the point of view of the adherents of [Fichte's] "theory of science" (*Wissenschaftslehre*), the second, the point of view of the adherents of psychologism. But the opposing points of view are based on the assumption—consciously or uncon-sciously held by both—that the relation of critique to the phil-osophical system is the logical relation of the ground to the conse-quence. This logical prejudice leads necessarily to the confusion of the psychological principles of critique with the ultimate phil-osophical principles of science. This assumption makes the con-tradiction between these two factions inevitable and irreconcil-able. But once we have recognized the fallacy in their common prejudice, we have knocked the foundation out from under their quarrel. Both parties misunderstand the relation of psychology to philosophy: the first mistakes as philosophical what is actually only psychological; the second mistakes as psychological what is actually philosophical.

5. According to the principle: "The ground of a cognition must be homologous to the cognition itself." This is a logical proposition that is extremely important for the critique of reason. Its proof is essentially as follows: The ground of a cognition is always itself a cognition, either immediate or derived. If it is a derived cognition, it consists of a judgment and it is verified by a proof. In this case the proposition follows from the logical nature of syllogisms as *analytic* hypothetical judgments. Nothing can be asserted in the conclusion that is not already contained in the premises. But if the ground is an immediate cognition, then it is this cognition itself that is enunciated in the judgment. In this case the proposition follows from the principle of identity.

The Prejudice of the Transcendental

25. Kant himself could not find his way to an exact determination of this relation, nor could he clearly establish the logical quality of his "transcendental" knowledge, no matter how masterfully he was able to employ it in practice. The vagueness lies in his concept of *transcendental philosophy*. The ambiguity of this term induced all those who, without *methodological* training, took over the new *results* to revive the dogmatism that had scarcely been laid to rest and to return, depending on their predilections, either to Leibniz' logical dogmatism or to the inductive prejudices of the English philosophers—thus transforming philosophy into either logic or empiricism and so condemning it to death.

This can be very well demonstrated historically. Kant used the term "transcendental" to denote the investigation of the grounds of possibility of synthetic a priori judgments. A priori knowledge is therefore the object of transcendental investigation, which forms the content of critique. We apprehend knowledge in no other way but through inner experience. The transcendental knowledge of critique is therefore obviously knowledge from inner experience. Although transcendental critique has a priori knowledge as its object, it is itself nevertheless an empirical science. Now, he who does not discriminate sharply enough between the content and the object of transcendental critique and who confuses transcendental knowledge (the content of critique) with philosophical knowledge (the object of critique) will easily overlook the disparity between the two, will not recognize the psychological nature of the former, and will hold it to be philosophical, i.e., a sort of a priori knowledge.[6]

Reinhold, in search of the system of transcendental philosophy that was lacking in Kant, allowed himself to be seduced by this misunderstanding of the transcendental into attempting to treat philosophy as a "theory of the faculty of perception." Fichte seized on this lamentable notion and was led by it in his "theory of science" to the "ego as the principle of philosophy," whereas

6. Cf. Kant, *Critique of Pure Reason*, p. 96.

Schulze, Beneke, and others developed from it the antithetical psychological consequences. Since then this confusion of psychological and philosophical principles has dominated the history of philosophy; even today it is the fundamental error committed by all those who pursue the phantom of a pure "theory of knowledge."

Fries pointed out long ago that this confusion of psychological and philosophical principles, inherent in the concept of the transcendental, which he called the *prejudice of the transcendental*, was the basic error of all post-Kantian dogmatism and corrected the mistake by elucidating the difference between proof and deduction.

Metaphysics not Psychological, Critique not Metaphysical

26. The relation of psychology to metaphysics is apparent from this differentiation between the content and the object of critique. It is implicit in the very concept of metaphysics that it is not an empirical science, i.e., it is not psychological; and in the same way it is implicit in the concept of critique that it is not metaphysical. For critique, as propaedeutic, as investigation of the ground of possibility of metaphysics, must precede it. To call the critique of reason metaphysical is therefore a *contradictio in adjecto*. But what again and again leads Kuno Fischer and so many others astray in this simple and obvious relation is nothing but the confusion of deduction with proof. To be sure, apodictic conclusions cannot be derived from empirical premises. Consequently, critique, if it were proof, could not be of an empirical, and therefore also not of a psychological, nature; otherwise metaphysics itself would have to sacrifice its a priori and apodictic nature, which cannot be denied it without contradiction. Thus, regarded from the point of view of this prejudice, the great accomplishments of Fries's deductions appear to be no more than a relapse into Locke's empiricism. But since this prejudice leads to the consequence that critique must be metaphysical, it loses sight of the basic idea of the critique of reason, annuls *eo ipso* the concept of criticism, and leads directly back to dogmatism.

Breakdown of "Neo-Kantianism" on the Transcendental Prejudice

27. This same prejudice prevents the so-called neo-Kantian school from getting back to pure criticism. One neo-Kantian states: "If one could describe transcendental deduction as an investigation that 'belongs' to psychology, then the metaphysical discipline as a whole would disappear in the psychological." [7] This is true only for him who regards transcendental deduction as a proof, but this contradicts the concept of deduction as the verification of basic principles. Thus, even today it is the prejudice of the transcendental that stands in the way of the correct understanding and healthy continuation of critical philosophy.

And, indeed, we read in the same work: "If the investigation of the mode of knowledge is called transcendental in so far as the latter is a priori possible, the *a priori* itself is thereby declared possible only in that it is apprehended in transcendental knowledge. And this is actually the case." [8] Here we find the clearest sort of statement of the confusion of the psychological grounds of critique with the logical grounds of the system: the transcendental investigation of the ground of possibility of a priori cognitions is itself designated as the ground of their possibility. *In that case* certainly transcendental investigation could not be regarded as a psychological investigation, for by what logical means could one succeed in deriving a priori cognitions from empirical grounds? So then, if transcendental investigation cannot be empirical, it must be a priori knowledge. But how can it be a priori knowledge if it is first to make a priori knowledge possible?

Once this demand for a transcendental knowledge that is first to make a priori knowledge possible has been postulated, one must hit on the idea of a science that stands logically above the principles and first derives them from an "ultimate principle"— a science that, to be sure, could not be empirical psychology unless one wishes again to find the origins of philosophy in experience. Thus, we find ourselves once more committed to the hopeless task of deriving metaphysics *from mere logic*, that is, we have

7. H. Cohen, *Kants Theorie der Erfahrung* (2d ed. Berlin, 1885), p. 294.
8. *Ibid.*, p. 134.

reached Fichte's idea of "theory of science." But others have marked this trend better than Cohen; and nowadays we hear, as a sequel to the recent lively battle cry, "Back to Kant!" the new, "Forward to Fichte!" That, at least, is consistent; and the sooner we get back again to Hegel in this familiar routine, the sooner this false philosophical structure will again destroy itself.

To be sure, the seeds of this misunderstanding of the transcendental, which has been fatal to post-Kantian philosophy, were planted by Kant himself. This defect remained without serious consequences in the background of Kant's investigations; but later it was seized upon and an effort was made to draw conclusions from it and to develop them into a system. Thus, Kant is really the underlying cause of the fact that those who try to pursue his work further inevitably fall prey, if they have not corrected this error, to the old fallacies, and this is why the entire neo-Kantian movement, not relinquishing this prejudice, depends for its ephemeral existence on a crude inconsistency. For this reason an appeal to Kant will not assist us but will only drive us in circles; and until we free ourselves of this prejudice, criticism will remain merely a word, and philosophy as a lucid science, which Kantian critique promised, will remain a dream.

V. THE CONSTITUTIVE PRINCIPLE OF METAPHYSICS. THE GENERALIZED HUMEAN PROBLEM AND ITS CRITICAL SOLUTION

Constitutive and Methodic Principles

28. Science is distinguished from mere knowing by the logical form of the synthetic unity in the arrangement and verification of the judgments that contain the knowledge. Every science has, from the logical point of view, a unique systematic form that is different from the knowledge it contains. The rule by which one establishes this logical form of a science I call its *methodic principle*. Whether the crude and disordered raw materials of the knowledge that is scattered about in our minds are to become a science depends on the discovery of the correct methodic principle of the science. Now, the method of a science is obviously

conditioned by the source of the knowledge contained in its judgments. This source of the knowledge contained in the judgments of a science I call the *constitutive principle* of the science. Accordingly, it is possible to make a science of any branch of learning only if we achieve insight into the constitutive principle of the science.

Thus, mathematics gives credit for the justly famous rigor of its scientific development to the early recognition that its concepts can be constructed in pure intuition; for it is the nature of just this constitutive principle that alone makes possible the strict application of the dogmatic method of progressive proof. Thus, also, the successful scientific development of modern natural science rests on the realization that it must find its constitutive principle in observation. This realization permitted the introduction of the inductive method of regressive proof. And, on the other hand, the hitherto very unhappy fate of metaphysics is solely the result of the fact that there is as yet no unanimity regarding its constitutive principle—that, indeed, the question of its constitutive principle has not even received general attention.[9]

9. Any general rule, in so far as the development of a science depends on it, can be called a *principle*. There are therefore just as many kinds of principles as there are kinds of dependence of the development of a science on general rules. Accordingly, we must discriminate primarily between three kinds of principles. The development of a science depends (1) on the immediate knowledge that is reiterated in the judgments of the science and that constitutes the criterion of the validity of the basic judgments of this science—from this we derive the concept of the constitutive principle of the science; (2) on the universal rule *according* to which its systematic development takes place—from this we derive the concept of the methodic principle of the science; (3) on the universal basic premises *from* which its system is evolved by logical inferences. These last universal premises of a science have thus also a right to the name of principle; and one might call this principle, to distinguish it from the constitutive and the methodic principle, the *logical principle* of the science—although it must be kept in mind that in this case the adjective "logical" denotes only how the development of the science depends on the principle; it does not designate the sort of knowledge to which the principle itself belongs.

Thus, this classification of principles must carefully be kept separate from the differentiation between principles according to the kinds of knowledge to which they belong. From the latter point of view only the principles of logic can be called logical principles, whereas in the other meaning of the word the basic principles of metaphysics, mathematics, and logic are the logical principles of these sciences. Common usage generally employs the word "principle" to designate the sort of knowledge; for this reason we inquired above as to the correct verification of the "metaphysical principles" and accordingly discriminated between "psychological" and "metaphysical" principles.

Let me remark further, in order to prevent a possible misunderstanding, that in

The Constitutive Principle of Metaphysics

29. However, that there must be in our knowledge a special constitutive principle of metaphysics is proved by the undeniable fact of metaphysical judgments.[10] Consequently, it must also be possible to determine this principle from the unique characteristics of the judgments that arise from it. And it must be possible to ascertain the desired methodic principle from the character of the constitutive principle that is thus determined.

This is, in fact, the path we pursued in our investigations above and followed to our goal. We established at the very beginning (sec. 2, above) that metaphysics is precarious and uncertain, not as to the fund of knowledge contained in it but only as to the

---

the Kantian school the expression "constitutive principle" is used in still another sense, one which does not fit the definition we have just given. In the differentiation between constitutive and regulative principles that is to be found in the *Critique of Pure Reason* (which does not embrace in the scope of its investigations the relation of the immediate knowledge of reason to the derived knowledge of reflection), constitutive principles are to be understood as those universal laws which are susceptible of an immediate theoretical development by the progressive method, whereas regulative principles are those which, as the guiding maxims of induction, first of all make possible the discovery of the constitutive principles. Thus, Robert Mayer and Helmholtz were led by the principle of the conservation of energy to the discovery of the mechanical equivalent of heat and thence to the first law of thermodynamics. However, the basic laws of thermodynamics themselves form the constitutive principles (or, in the terminology of the physicists, the major premises) of the mechanical theory of heat.

10. The word "metaphysics" is, to be sure, somewhat out of fashion as a result of the assertion that there is no such thing as metaphysics. But this assertion rests on a mere logomachy and has no bearing on the scientific meaning that Kant gave the word and that we accept. On the contrary, in our sense of the word all empirical science is founded on metaphysical preassumptions—indeed, as Kant lucidly and incontrovertibly proved, every empirical *judgment* demands, aside from the logical possibility of concepts and aside from the intuitive apprehension of its object, a form of its synthetic unity that can only be in our thinking. Consequently, either there is no science at all or there is also metaphysics.

For example, Ostwald (*Annalen der Naturphilosophie*, I (1902), 51 f., 61) asserts, in rebuttal to Kant's doctrine of the metaphysical primary grounds of natural science: "There is for the modern scientist no a priori knowledge and therefore no apodictic learning. . . . One is permitted only to assume a probability of $\frac{1}{\infty} = 0$ that an assumption, extended to infinity or absolute, is true." This empirical proposition is self-contradictory, since in itself it is an apodictic assertion; the probability that it is a statement of the truth is $\frac{1}{\infty} = 0$. But if, in order to avoid this contradiction, one qualifies it by saying that every *other* apodictic proposition but this one is true with a probability of zero, then one has broken out of the limits of empiricism, since there is then at least *one* apodictic proposition.

problem of isolating this knowledge that is scattered about in the various fields of thought and of reducing it to a scientific form. In order to find the method for solving this problem, we undertook an investigation of the constitutive principle of the metaphysical judgments. We found this constitutive principle in the immediate knowledge of pure reason; and the unique nature of the latter led us finally to the theory of deduction as the correct methodic principle of metaphysics. Since the immediate knowledge of pure reason, as nonintuitive knowledge, cannot be compared directly with the judgments that arise from it, we had to find a way to effect this comparison indirectly. This proved to be possible only if we subjected the fact of the existence of the cognitions of the immediate knowledge of pure reason itself to scientific scrutiny in order to deduce the judgments in question by establishing their ground in immediate knowledge. Now, since we apprehend the factual content of cognitions only through inner experience, deduction showed itself to be a task of psychology. Consequently, the methodic principle of metaphysics leads to the task of deducing its judgments by establishing their source in the immediate knowledge of pure reason through a theory of reason.

It is at once apparent that the heart of our methodological findings is our determination of the constitutive principle of metaphysics. Now, this determination may seem simple and obvious once we have correctly formulated the inquiry into this principle; but the history of philosophy teaches us how diverse are the misconstructions and confusions to which this principle is exposed. Every methodological error in the realm of metaphysics, and consequently the miscarriage of every previous attempt to elevate metaphysics to the rank of science, can be traced back to the misapprehension of its constitutive principle. So far we have dealt only with the *consequences* of this misapprehension; now we shall pursue back to its source the methodological dispute with which we were last concerned and shall inquire into how the possible ways of arbitrating it depend on the correct or incorrect determination of the constitutive principle of metaphysics.

Prejudice of Logical Dogmatism

30. So far we have met the prejudice that logical dogmatism cherishes in favor of the omnipotence of proof by pointing out the contradiction that is contained in it. But this contradiction is so patent that the question arises: What motive can be so deeply rooted that it is able to assert unlimited sway despite the obvious contradiction to which it leads? We must go still further and search out the ground of this prejudice in order to cut at the very root of it.

Now, this ground lies in nothing more or less than the fallacy we have uncritically taken over from an age of scanty scientific development and have enthroned as dogma, namely, that all immediate knowledge is intuition and that all that is not intuitive in our knowledge belongs to the derived knowledge of reflection. For if all immediate knowledge is intuitive, then obviously metaphysical knowledge, since it is not intuitive, must have its ground in reflection; that is to say, it rests on proof.

Consciousness and Knowledge; Psychology of Association and Theory of Knowledge

31. Intuition is that knowledge of which we are conscious immediately (that is, without the mediation of concepts, independently of reflection). Now it may sound somewhat paradoxical to speak of knowledge that is not intuitive and yet is immediate; but the immediacy that is the essence of the concept of intuition is not the immediacy of knowledge but the immediacy of the consciousness of the knowledge. The seemingly paradoxical element in the concept of nonintuitive immediate knowledge thus vanishes as soon as we distinguish between immediate consciousness and immediate knowledge. What is most confusing in this matter is the following: intuitive knowledge obviously appears earlier in our consciousness than the knowledge that consciousness possesses only by reflection. But it does not follow from this temporal priority of intuitive knowledge over reflective knowledge that intuition is the sole ground of the possibility of reflective knowledge. For we must discriminate sharply between the question of the source of knowledge and the genetic question of the temporal

development of consciousness. The significance of the difference
between these two questions has been stubbornly misunderstood
by psychologists up to the present day. The neglect of this elementary difference is perhaps the one mistake that has prevented
a general understanding of the psychological foundations of criticism; and it is because of it that the constitutive principle of metaphysics and even of logic is still so vigorously disputed.

To be sure, an examination of these matters belongs entirely in
the field of psychology, but our logical purpose makes it impossible for us—the state of this science being what it is today—to
avoid it. Modern trends in logic, disunited and multifarious as
they are, nevertheless have this in common, that they know of no
other means of verifying judgments than demonstration and
proof; and in the same way it would seem to be a generally accepted psychological fact that we possess no other immediate
knowledge than intuition. Thus, to almost all the modern investigators in psychology it is axiomatic that the task of psychology is
to explain all our knowledge solely by the senses and by association.* What does not fall within the boundaries of the genetic
point of view is regarded as not pertaining to psychology at all
and is relegated to another—ostensibly nonpsychological—discipline, the so-called *theory of knowledge*. It goes without saying that such treatment of psychology affords philosophy little
enlightenment, and he who nevertheless hopes that it will must
finally come to doubt the possibility of all philosophical knowledge.

Incompleteness of the Disjunction of Intuition and Thinking

32. In view of this, our task must be to show that if psychology is not to evade, but to deal competently with the facts of
inner experience, the question as to the ground of possibility of
metaphysical judgments (i.e., our old question regarding a
unique source of the metaphysical in our knowledge, which is
neither intuitive nor logical) becomes unavoidably a psychological problem. We must furthermore show that only by a
thorough empirical-psychological treatment of this problem can

* This refers to the state of psychology at the beginning of the twentieth century.

the ever recurrent fallacies be avoided that hitherto have made clear and consistent scientific work in the field of metaphysics impossible.

Accordingly, we assert that, unless we admit the *fact* of a nonintuitive immediate knowledge, not only will all paths be closed to a psychological explanation of the facts of cognition but any agreement in matters of metaphysics will be forever hopeless. Indeed, we assert further—little as we are permitted to hope that our efforts will bring about a lasting contribution to the development of metaphysics—that the general acceptance of this psychological discovery will alone be sufficient to overcome philosophical anarchy and to arbitrate once and for all the quarrels of the various schools.

It can easily be demonstrated that almost every original speculative thinker in the history of philosophy was more or less clearly on the track of this discovery but was prevented from following it up by the dogmatic prejudice that dominated his age. Plato's "divine intuition of the ideas," Aristotle's "*νοῦς*"; in modern philosophy, Jacobi's "revelation," Kant's "transcendental apperception," Reinhold's "immediate consciousness," Fichte's "pure ego," Schelling's "intellectual intuition," and so on to Windelband's "normal consciousness" and Rickert's "moral imperative as transcendental minimum"—all these are simply more or less clumsy attempts to effect a transition from mere reflection to the immediate knowledge of pure reason.

Consequences of This Psychological Fallacy

33. Despite the fact that this immediate knowledge has hitherto been so generally misunderstood, the search for it has nevertheless been the guiding motive and main purpose of all endeavor in the history of philosophy. A moment's deliberation will suffice to orient us in this matter.

A point of view that does not recognize the immediate knowledge of pure reason and that attempts to derive all knowledge solely from intuition and reflection leaves no room for knowledge other than intuition and such knowledge as can be derived from intuition by the methods of reflection, i.e., by the logical forms of definition and proof. Such a point of view can do justice to pure mathematics and empirical knowledge but not to the metaphysical in our knowledge. Hence, the ever recurrent disputes in all those fields in which metaphysics plays a part: the dispute over the principles of theoretical physics, over the basis of ethics and politics, and over the establishment of religious ideas; hence, the fact that metaphysics, in unhappy contrast to the high development of our mathematical and empirical sciences, has remained a battlefield of hypotheses. Thus, the previously uncovered prejudice is seen to be the sole ground of all dogmatism and hence, likewise, of all skepticism in philosophy. The reason is this: the dogmatic method of proof was pursued whenever a verification of metaphysical truths was attempted. But the realization that, where intuition is the only immediate knowledge at hand, no procedure of proof can achieve cognitions that extend beyond intuition—in other words, the realization that the vacuity and mediacy of reflection make it impossible to create metaphysics from mere logic—this realization of the merely analytic nature of reflection necessarily conduced to the denial of the possibility of all metaphysical knowledge and thus to empiricism. Those who wished nevertheless to assert a metaphysical cognition, without entrusting themselves to the methods of reflection, had to take refuge in the mystical fiction of a nonsensory and intellectual intuition. Thus, this prejudice led unavoidably to the dispute between the followers of Plato and the followers of Aristotle, which has dominated the entire history of philosophy.[11]

11. Kant once asked the question: "Would it be possible to draw a priori a diagram of the history of philosophy, with which the eras of the various theories that philosophers have held (on the basis of the available data) would correspond as though they had had this very diagram before them and had proceeded in the knowledge of it?" And he answers: "Yes, if the idea of a metaphysics inevitably occurs to human reason, and if human reason feels the need to develop it; but such a science reposes entirely in the spirit, although embryonically sketched out. . . . The history of philosophy is not the history of the theories that crop up fortuitously here and there but the history of reason as it develops from concepts. . . . A philosophical history of philosophy is neither historical nor empirical but rational, i.e., a priori, possible. For although it presents rational facts, it does not derive them from the chronicle of history; it extracts them as a philosophical archeology from the nature of human reason." (*Lose Blätter aus Kants Nachlass*, Zweites Heft [Königsberg, 1895], pp. 286, 278.)

Our discussion above confirms its value by making it immediately possible for us to draw the diagram of this "philosophical archeology."

Scientific interest in the history of philosophy is directed solely toward progress in the development of methods, not toward the results of individual philosophers

Origin of the Dispute between Plato and Aristotle

34. The basic fallacy of all previous dogmatic logic—the prejudice that all judgments are either demonstrable or provable —rests, therefore, on an insufficient knowledge of the *facts* of knowing. We took over this prejudice of traditional logic from the Greeks. Their lack of knowledge is to be explained by the inadequate development of their natural science. Greek spiritual life moved only in the sphere of intuition and the esthetically beautiful; theoretical natural science was alien to it. The merely *ethical* motives that moved Socrates to his endorsement of "unwritten laws"—in which Plato recognized an ἀνυπόθετον (the unprovable) that was different from πίστις (experience) and διάνοια (mathematics) and the ground for which he sought in intellectual intuition (though it is lost at birth)—these merely ethical motives were not strong enough to prevent Aristotle's scientific mind from rejecting Socrates' discovery because of its foundation in myth.

The mystical in the Platonic conception, on the one hand, and the obviousness of sensory intuition, on the other, necessarily gave the Aristotelians a superiority in science. But as theoretical science developed sufficiently, even superficial self-observation had to lead back to the recognition of the indisputable *reality* of metaphysical preassumptions and thus to revive the question of the ground of their possibility.

This is borne out by the development of modern philosophy.

The Humean Problem

35. If we assume the fallacious psychological disjunction that all knowledge rests either on intuition or on reflection, the reality

—or at any rate it is directed toward these results only so far as they are dependent on the method followed. A law of the development of ideas can be formulated only in respect to method; and this law is rendered manifest by our diagram. This diagram is modeled on the organization of reason itself. The psychological point of view according to which it is constructed guarantees, on the one hand, that it shows completely the heterogeneity of all the possible historical forms and, on the other hand, that in all its subdivisions it is independent of standards that are either historically conditioned or arbitrarily assumed. Thus, it affords us a secure prescript by which we can peruse, in the light of principles, all the methodologically significant advances and errors in the history of the philosophical disciplines, in order to trace them back to their origin in reason itself.

Use and application of the chart (p. 146) are readily seen by reference to the deliberations that follow.

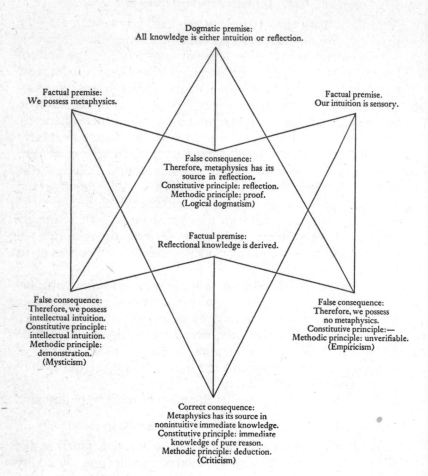

Dogmatic premise:
All knowledge is either intuition or reflection.

Factual premise:
We possess metaphysics.

Factual premise.
Our intuition is sensory.

False consequence:
Therefore, metaphysics has its
source in reflection.
Constitutive principle: reflection.
Methodic principle: proof.
(Logical dogmatism)

Factual premise:
Reflectional knowledge is derived.

False consequence:
Therefore, we possess
intellectual intuition.
Constitutive principle:
intellectual intuition.
Methodic principle:
demonstration.
(Mysticism)

False consequence:
Therefore, we possess
no metaphysics.
Constitutive principle:—
Methodic principle: unverifiable.
(Empiricism)

Correct consequence:
Metaphysics has its source in
nonintuitive immediate knowledge.
Constitutive principle: immediate
knowledge of pure reason.
Methodic principle: deduction.
(Criticism)

of metaphysical judgments remains—in view of the actually sensory nature of our intuition and the actually analytic nature of reflection—an inscrutable paradox. On the basis of that assumption the fact of metaphysical judgments is inexplicable; indeed, it is impossible. For, unless one is willing to deny either the sensory nature of our intuition or the merely analytic nature of reflection, that assumption and the fact of metaphysical judgments are simply irreconcilable.

The paradoxical nature of this relation became a bone of contention between the rationalists and the empiricists. Rationalism correctly asserts that the necessary truths of metaphysics cannot be grounded on sensory intuition; but empiricism maintains with as much justification that they cannot possibly have their source in reflection, for reflection is in itself empty and without content and can only derive or prove consequences from *given* truths in obedience to the analytic laws of logic. This dilemma is the theme of Hume's skepticism. Hume ingenuously started from the same prejudice. He demonstrated that the principle of causality is already presupposed a priori whenever we conclude the effect from the cause or the cause from the effect and showed with great perspicuity by this example that apodictic knowledge cannot arise from the senses since, if it did, it would not be apodictic. But reflection, in its turn, can only deal with concepts analytically. In the matter of causality, however, we reach beyond the concept in question and assert its necessary connection with another concept, which is not contained in it. Consequently, causality also cannot have its source in reflection. Therefore, on the basis of this prejudice apodictic knowledge is impossible and, inasmuch as the senses are the only source of knowledge, it is a deception on empirical grounds.

Thus, Hume's skepticism was not directed immediately against the objective validity of metaphysical knowledge but primarily only against its source, i.e., against the subjective ground of its possibility. Its psychological possibility had to be made comprehensible before we would be justified in treating of its objective validity.[12] If, then, Hume's skepticism rests not only on a legiti-

12. Thus Kant himself says: "The question was not whether the concept of cause was right, useful, and even indispensable for our knowledge of nature, for this

mate but also on an unavoidable psychological problem, it follows that it can be resolved only by an appeal to psychology.

Refutation of Empiricism

36. Now, without attacking the basic prejudice with sufficient precision, Kant refuted Hume's result *de facto* by the example of mathematics. The mathematical judgments are, as Hume saw, apodictic; but, as he failed to see, they are also synthetic. Therefore, there exists apodictic synthesis.[13]

The possibility of synthetic a priori judgments is, then, proved by *fact*. Hence, there can remain only the question *how* they are possible.

Hume himself, when he denied universal validity to the presupposition of causality by finding its origin in the habitual expectancy for similar cases, became entangled in contradictions of his own clear demonstration that causality is the presupposition for every explanation: in attempting to explain causality by habit he makes habit its cause and thus has already presupposed the validity of the law of causality.

But, aside from this contradiction, this explanation—still popular in psychology—is also *psychologically* inadequate. The expectancy for similar cases not only rests on association but itself presupposes for its possibility (although it is originally obscure) the idea of a causal relation. Association can explain how a sensory impression can recall to mind a previous impression but it cannot explain the expectation that this impression will ac-

---

Hume had never doubted; but whether that concept could be thought by reason a priori, and consequently whether it possessed an inner truth, independent of all experience, implying a wider application than merely to the objects of experience. This was Hume's problem. It was a question concerning the *origin*, not concerning the *indispensable need* of the concept. Were the former decided, the conditions of the use and the sphere of its valid application would have been determined as a matter of course." *Prolegomena to Any Future Metaphysics,* edited in English by Paul Carus (Chicago, 1902), Introduction, p. 5.

13. This question regarding the analytic or synthetic nature of the mathematical judgments, which even today is still disputed by many philosophers, can be said to have been settled—if not by Kant himself, then by the critical investigations of modern mathematics, which have proved conclusively the correctness of Kant's discovery of the nonlogical origin of the mathematical axioms. Cf. the abovementioned (p. 131, n. 4) study by G. Hessenberg as to this matter and for a discussion of the question of the a priori.

tually occur again. Association can in itself explain only the connection between the apprehensions of objects, never the apprehension of the connection between objects.

An impartial observation of facts, which rigorously excludes overhasty attempts at explanation, clearly exposes Hume's empirical result as fallacious. But the *ground* of his skepticism has not thereby been removed. On the contrary, this skepticism now asserts itself all the more insistently with the question: How can metaphysics be real if neither the senses nor reflection offer a ground of its possibility? This question is crucial to the interests both of any metaphysics that lays claim to the title of science and of a valid *empirical* psychology that is not guilty of overhasty theorizing.

Kant's Transcendental Proofs. Failure to Recognize the Mediacy and Emptiness of Reflection

37. In his introduction to the *Critique of Pure Reason* and in the "universal questions" of his *Prolegomena* Kant correctly generalized the Humean problem and gave it its classic formulation. Nevertheless, his treatment of it strayed further and further from the psychological attitude toward this inquiry and slipped back gradually from empirical-psychological criticism into logical formalism. Although he demonstrated negatively how inadequate the logical forms of reflection are for metaphysics by proving the impossibility of a logical criterion of material truth, he himself did not go beyond reflection and then too attempted again a proof of the metaphysical principles that he called transcendental—with this result: as soon as one inquired into the principles of these transcendental proofs, one found oneself thrown back again on intuition. And thus it happened once more: his successors split into two schools, a school of empiricism and a school of intellectual intuition.

But Kant's so-called transcendental proofs of the metaphysical principles through the principle of the possibility of experience are actually not proofs at all but merely regressive ascertainments. We ascertain by logical analysis of the given experience that the categories and principles are the preconditions of its possibility. Hence, if experience is grounded on the metaphysical principles as the logical preconditions of its possibility, it would be circular reasoning to try to prove these principles to be "ultimate" by the principle of the possibility of experience. The use and application of metaphysical principles in experience may therefore serve to ascertain them as facts in our knowledge but not to make them possible as such nor to prove their validity.

Kant overestimated the independence of reflection. It is both logically and psychologically impossible that thinking can beget its own synthetic principles. Just as a judgment cannot provide itself with its content, neither can it provide the rule by which this content is made a unity. The norm by which reflection must unify the content provided it by the senses, in order not just to think but rather to know, must originally be provided it by reason. Reflection, therefore, can afford us only a consciousness that repeats the unity and necessity of our knowledge; it cannot give us the knowledge itself of this unity and necessity. But this original knowledge of reason, which is already preassumed by the derived knowledge of reflection, is not intuition since it reaches our consciousness *only* indirectly, *only* through reflection. There exists, therefore, an immediate knowledge of reason, which is in itself obscure and can only be illumined by reflection, and which is the ground of the fact that our judgments are apodictic: it is that hidden "*x* on which understanding is founded" and which forms the ground of the possibility of synthetic a priori judgments evolved through mere concepts.

Thus, the primary basis of truth in our knowledge is missing in Kant. The ground of the possibility of experience lies in the metaphysical principles, and they in turn, according to Kant, should find their validity in the fact that they make experience possible. He was unable to find the immediate knowledge of pure reason and tried instead to have reflection guarantee its own truthfulness through the analytic relation between experience and its principles. He had found in the *fact* of experience a stout defense against skepticism; and he was able to restore to the a priori, by relating it to the *actual experience*, the reality that Hume had denied it in relation to things. In the same way he es-

tablished the truth of faith as the precondition of the reality of
the *moral imperative*—the truth he denied faith as independent
conviction. But, on the other hand, he was unable to find an objective principle of the esthetic—at least not in reflection, which
was the only place he looked for it.

Such a presentation, however, is obviously only a makeshift
protection against empiricism, which demands that all truths
must be proved that cannot demonstrate their objects in experience; and Kant did not advance beyond this demand. It is an altogether provisional standpoint, to be explained by his position
vis-à-vis Hume, which is on the one hand polemic and on the
other hand quite dependent. He thereby showed only that the
possibility of the fact of the actual experience and of the moral
imperative postulates a system of metaphysical principles, which
he established in its entirety but without being able to follow
through to the real ground of the possibility of its principles. According to him, these metaphysical principles are not innate ideas.
But what else are they? He did not delve to the bottom of this
question, although here also he made a certain beginning by
showing (in his doctrine of the identity of apperceptions) that
all analytic unity of consciousness already presupposes a synthetic unity of some sort. Despite his great effort to differentiate
this "subjective deduction" from "objective deduction," he mis-
conceived its psychological nature because of his misunderstanding of the transcendental and gave it a misleading objective cast
for fear of becoming entangled in "physiological derivation."
Thus, his work left us a problem, a riddle in the history of philosophy, the solution of which was not vouchsafed him.

Renewal of the Dispute between the Platonists and Aristotelians as a Consequence of This Error

38. This lacuna perforce soon made itself felt. It has been
pointed out that the solution of the riddle requires that we reach
beyond reflection, which is in itself without content, and search
for a ground of the apodictic that is independent of the mediacy
of reflection. But the basic prejudice that all immediate knowl-

edge is intuition transformed the above essentially correct demand into a spurious demand, namely, that we must abandon reflection as unsuitable to philosophy and must attain philosophy through intuition, which, then, to be sure, could not be sensory intuition. But since we possess no such intellectual intuition, philosophers engaged in this undertaking were obliged to resort secretly to the logical forms of reflection: these forms were taken for more than they are, and so it happened that imperceptibly the error of trying to squeeze metaphysical content out of empty logical forms was again committed, and thus precisely the mistake that had to be avoided was brought to its culmination.

In the other camp, in contrast to this relapse into Platonism, Hume's prejudice, which Kant had not overcome—or at least had refuted only by an *argumentum ad hominem*—asserted itself as a matter of course. It was concluded, from the really sensory nature of our intuition and the really empty and derived nature of reflection, that metaphysical knowledge is impossible. Thus it happened that psychology bogged down in Hume's empiricism, disdained the evidence of facts, and held fast to the fundamental dogmatic prejudice. This hypothesis was changed into an axiom, and thus the fact of metaphysical knowledge, which had given rise to the Humean problem, was removed from the sphere of psychology altogether. Because modern psychology closes its eyes to this fact, it has also lost sight of the most prominent task that its founder set it.

Thus, this prejudice, common to both parties, led to a renewal of the dispute between the Platonists and the Aristotelians. Where scientific interest predominated, empiricism naturally triumphed over Platonism. He who today wishes to defend the rights of philosophy finds himself with no weapon save mere reflection. The active principle of reflection, however, is the will. In confounding the arbitrary nature of reflection with the spontaneity of cognition, one is seduced into an endorsement of the *will* as highest principle. Since the determining motives of the will are purposes, the attempt was made to verify the philosophical principles teleologically, as means for achieving the purpose of science, or as "postulates of the striving for complete knowledge." But the question remains unanswerable [14] whence reflection, in itself empty, acquires this purpose, or—if the purpose be conceded to it—whence it acquires the means for its achievement.

The Critical Solution of the Humean Problem

39. The result that Hume derived from the presuppositions of Aristotelian logic is correct in that metaphysical judgments are impossible on the ground of these presuppositions. Now, instead of trying to prove them, as Kant does, we conclude differently: the reality of metaphysical judgments proves their possibility. Consequently, the presupposition of Aristotelian logic must be false. *There exists an immediate knowledge of a nonsensory nature.*

At the same time that we make this concession to Platonism, we must join the Aristotelians in saying this against it: We do not possess intellectual intuition; we cannot dispense with reflection. The immediate knowledge of pure reason is not intuition; *it reaches our consciousness solely through reflection.*

Only in this way is it possible to correct Aristotle's error without committing Plato's. Their otherwise irreconcilable quarrel is settled as soon as we relinquish their common prejudice, viz., that we possess no immediate knowledge other than intuition. The discovery of this nonintuitive immediate knowledge of pure reason is the guiding beacon that alone can preserve us from the Scylla of empiricism and the Charybdis of neo-Platonic mysticism.

Metaphysics as science can consist solely of an elucidation

14. Unanswerable, unless one leaves the critical path of the comparison of the cognitions with one another and embraces a theory of the relation of knowledge to the object. [See the subsequent essay, "The Impossibility of the 'Theory of Knowledge.'"] Thus, this point of view too strives beyond mere reflection, but its prejudice allows it to reach beyond reflection only in that it reaches beyond knowledge as such. Unfortunately, a theory of the possibility of knowledge lies outside the province of any possible science; and so this point of view, too, simply points backward to mysticism. The representatives of this teleology, therefore, have no right at all to claim descent from Kant, since they are not faithful to the highest precept of the Socratic-Kantian scientific method, which states that the law of truth is not to be found outside knowledge but within it. It bespeaks a better understanding of history that the more modern students of this doctrine turn back to Plato and Fichte. Criticism finds its origins solely in Socrates and Kant; Plato and Fichte, on the other hand, have already deviated from the rigorous basic idea of criticism.

of this immediate knowledge of pure reason. The critique of reason is the tool for this elucidation. Its function is to deduce the principles, i.e., to establish them by demonstrating the ground of their possibility in the immediate knowledge of pure reason.

In the dogmatic assumption that all immediate knowledge is intuition also lies the deepest source of the empiricism that vitiates all philosophy. Reflection is not able by any manner of proof to create new knowledge; it can only elucidate given knowledge. Hence, we can acquire no knowledge through it that was not already contained in the immediate knowledge from which we started. But if this immediate knowledge is intuition, it follows indisputably that metaphysical knowledge must be impossible for us.

The impotence of existing philosophy in the face of the destructive force of empiricism is therefore caused solely by the fact that its own structure is also built on this fundamental dogma of empiricism. This is why empiricism is able to assert itself against even the most cogent of rebuttals; for until it is deprived of this foundation, it can be accused at most only of inconsistency. The entire struggle against empiricism is hopeless, and any success in this struggle is specious, so long as this foundation is not destroyed. If we are to succeed in a convincing refutation of empiricism, we must make up our minds to abandon its basic dogma.

Philosophy as Science

40. Hence, we come to the following conclusion: If we accept the dogmatic assumption that all knowledge is either intuition or reflection, then the maxim that we can elucidate metaphysics through reflection—which, as thus stated, is correct—inevitably assumes the fallacious form of logical dogmatism, according to which reflection itself begets metaphysical knowledge and thus proves it—as if the capacity to elucidate could itself generate the truth to be elucidated. This is a procedure that must necessarily be frustrated by its own inconsistency and must surrender the entire field of metaphysical legislation to skepticism. The miscarriage of this undertaking leads to this alternative: Either we must renounce (with empiricism) all metaphysical truth or we must desert (with mysticism) the scientific path of enlighten-

ment, renouncing reflection as a means unfit for metaphysics and then seeking the truth through intellectual intuition. Thus, the failure of logical dogmatism fathered the dispute between empirical skepticism and neo-Platonic mysticism.

The prejudice that the method of verifying judgments is either demonstration or proof still rules over logic today because of the ignorance of the constitutive principle of metaphysics; as a result, enlightenment is impracticable and metaphysics as science remains an insoluble problem.

The solution of this problem lies in the discovery of the non-intuitive immediate knowledge of pure reason, which, together with the consequent definitive resolution of the Humean problem, was the achievement of Fries. This discovery first made clear and comprehensible how and why Socrates could combine a mistrust of his own knowledge with a confidence in truth. The fund of truth that the dogmatist demands belongs to reason but not on that account to consciousness, which, as the skeptic realizes, is in itself empty. But it is possible for consciousness, through reflection, to make itself master of the knowledge of reason and to articulate it in judgments. Only this discovery can enthrone philosophy as a clear science and usher in a lasting philosophical peace. This is the accomplishment of the critical method, that it attains this enlightenment and in so doing triumphs over it; for it shows that reflection cannot, to be sure, guarantee the necessary truths, but at the same time it points out the way by which reflection can overcome this insufficiency of reflection.

APPENDIX

The Relation of So-called Neo-Kantianism to Fries's New Critique of Reason: *Excerpts*

[Nelson introduces the Appendix with the following paragraphs:]

Let us, in order to establish our point of view historically, summarize the results of our investigations. We have ascertained that Kant's discovery, the critique of reason, is the only proper procedure in philosophizing. But the critique of reason must, we found out, be treated according to a psychological method; and so we turn back to the pattern that Fries gave scientific philosophizing. I say: We turn back. For our demand for psychological criticism stands in sharpest opposition to the predominant trends today as they are most energetically represented by precisely those who link their teachings to the name of Kant. A respected modern school of thinkers calls for and is attempting a return to Kant, but one hears nothing about following in Fries's footsteps, although it was Fries, and no other, who as much as a century ago readopted the method of a critique of reason and with its help undertook a further development of philosophy.

How is it to be explained that those who avow their devotion to a revival of Kantianism pay Fries no scientific attention, neither recognition, nor refutation, nor even a *historical* evaluation—Fries, the first and only philosopher so far to undertake once more the critique of reason and thus to fashion a new basis for Kantian philosophy? The explanation must be that they, as we have seen, misconceive the psychological nature of critique; and we found the ultimate reason for this error in their misunderstanding of the concept of the transcendental. But Fries founded his reform of criticism on an examination of just this concept and on a clarification of what is ambiguous in it. Why, then, have not the "neo-Kantians" allowed Fries to instruct them in this matter? Only because, as a comparison of their writings shows, they have preferred not to study his critique of reason but to parrot the traditional fable of Fries's "psychologism."

[Nelson now points out in a lengthy footnote that the circumstance of Fries's being misinterpreted or even forgotten so quickly was greatly influenced by the fact that his most important pupil, Ernst Friedrich Apelt, died in 1859, surviving his teacher by only sixteen years. Apelt's memory, either through neglect or intention, was completely obliterated by the historians of German philosophy. Ernst Hallier deserves the credit for having rescued Apelt's scientific work from the general disregard of contemporary philosophers and for having handed it down to posterity.[15]

In subsequent parts of the appendix Nelson quotes and analyzes excerpts from German philosophers—W. Windelband, A. Riehl, and Hermann Cohen—dealing with Fries, and refutes their assertions, proving that these writers completely misunderstood Fries's philos-

15. Cf. *Kulturgeschichte des Neunzehnten Jahrhunderts* (Stuttgart, 1889), 12. Abschnitt, "Die mathematisch-naturwissenschaftliche Schule," §2, "Ernst Friedrich Apelt und die Theorie der Induktion."

ophy. The specialist interested in these discussions and in other literature quoted on the Fries problem is referred to the German original. Nelson devotes the most space to Cohen, probably the most prominent neo-Kantian, and shows that Cohen, in his arguments and protestations against Fries's assumed psychologism, himself uses unclear *psychological* explanations based on inner experience where he does not substitute empty analytic propositions.

To clarify Fries's and Apelt's theory Nelson cites the following interesting sentences from Apelt's *Metaphysik* (par. 45)*:]

"Because there is no intuitive form of arrangement in inner experience, nothing analogous to space, there is also no intuitive locating of the simultaneously existent activities within my inner self, and consequently there are no empty spaces for the obscure activities of apprehending and knowing. This explains the impossibility of indicating a location of the obscurity within my inner self."

[In conclusion, Nelson asks the reader not to fall into the usual misunderstanding of Fries and cites this passage from him:]

"The uniqueness of my demand for deductions and my appeal to psychological anthropology, which shall make these deductions possible, have been repeatedly misunderstood, even by the most acute; and consequently my philosophy has unjustifiably been classed with the empirical systems. The source of this misunderstanding seems to me to lie in the fact that in academic logic the doctrine of the verification of judgments was not treated thoroughly enough, and therefore my verification of philosophical principles was confounded with proof of them. He who now studies my exhaustive elucidation of this matter will not again be able to commit this error." [16]

* Ernst Friedrich Apelt, *Metaphysik* (new ed. Halle, 1910), p. 210.
16. *System der Metaphysik* (Heidelberg, 1824), par. 23, pp. 117 f.

VI

CRITICAL PHILOSOPHY
AND MATHEMATICAL AXIOMATICS *

All earnest endeavor to exalt philosophy to the rank of an exact science
has always laid the greatest stress on a mathematical orientation; and of
the various fields of mathematics the study of its fundamental principles
holds the deepest interest for philosophers. Throughout his life Leonard
Nelson followed the development of these principles with profound attention. Ever conscientious in his search for truth, he turned the entire
acuity of his thought to furthering an understanding between philosophy and mathematics, for he was thoroughly convinced of the profound
scientific connection between his philosophy and the results of axiomatics. His address, "Critical Philosophy and Mathematical Axiomatics,"
bears eloquent witness to this fact.

An inexorable fate decreed that this eminent savant was not to finish
his most important work. The world of science has suffered a grave loss
in his untimely death. May his friends and disciples remain faithful to
the lofty goals he set himself; may they carry to fruition the ideas em-
bodied in his work.

David Hilbert †

IF we are to devote ourselves, within the modest time granted
us at this meeting of the mathematics and physics departments, to the relation of these fields of knowledge to philosophy, and if we are not to allow our treatment of this task to consist in a few casual generalities, we shall do best to scrutinize a
limited complex of questions that can, because of their particular
pertinence and universal significance, shed as bright a light as
possible on the deeper connection between the so-called exact
sciences and philosophy. From the wealth of examples that this
intent brings to mind I choose the one that strikes me as the most

---

* An address, "Kritische Philosophie und mathematische Axiomatik," delivered at
Göttingen on September 28, 1927, at the fifty-sixth convention of the teachers' so-
ciety, *Deutsche Philologen und Schulmänner*. Published in *Unterrichtsblätter für
Mathematik und Naturwissenschaften*, XXXIV (Berlin, 1928).

† Nelson's monumental work, *Critique of Practical Reason*, is dedicated to David
Hilbert.

appropriate to the locality and time of our meeting—I refer to the modern elaboration of mathematical axiomatics as it has been developed and brought close to a sort of culmination by Hilbert and his followers. The decisive innovation, which alone made this culmination possible, is still little known and indeed not even recognized as such, and its great philosophical importance is entirely unknown—a circumstance, to be sure, that is not amazing when one considers the fact that philosophy today lacks any solid and generally accepted foundation that might provide a basis from which to approach these matters. I shall therefore have to go back somewhat in order to pick up the thread of scientific philosophy at that point in its history where it was broken and where, as a consequence, the progress already made by philosophy was sacrificed in the chaos of dilettante philosophy *à la mode*.

I

First of all I must direct your attention to a revolutionary intellectual achievement of Kant's which, although it is highly praised, is very little understood today.

Philosophy before Kant was dominated by the prejudice that all knowledge of apodictic certainty, since it obviously could not arise from experience (from observation and experiment), must be of a logical nature, that is, must be derived from mere concepts or, in Kant's more precise terminology, must be enunciated in analytic judgments. If this were so, the distinction would be valid that judgments must be either analytic or empirical. Influenced by this assumption, philosophers have tried to solve the metaphysical problems that are so important to them by tracing metaphysical judgments back to purely logical principles, in order thus to establish metaphysics as an apodictic science—an approach to the subject that leads one to seek the criterion of the truth of an apodictic judgment in the fact of the contradictoriness of its opposite.

The prejudice in favor of the omnipotence of logic was first successfully shaken by Kant—as it happens, precisely in the field of mathematics. Indeed, it was here that he broke it once for all;

he destroyed the delusion that the so-called mathematical method, i.e., the syllogistic procedure of proof, can unlock the real secret of mathematical knowledge.

This delusion of the so-called "mathematical method" provided by its example a perpetual temptation to develop metaphysics according to the same logicizing ideal, and mathematics seemed to assure the success of this approach. Kant destroyed this concept with his demonstration that the ground of the certainty of mathematical knowledge does not at all lie in its use of the logical method but that, conversely, this method can be effectively applied to mathematics only because mathematics possesses a fund of knowledge that has certainty independent of all logic. The discovery of such a fund of knowledge in mathematics, one that reaches beyond the competence of logic, forms the real cornerstone of Kant's reform of philosophy.

Once in possession of this discovery, Kant was able also to explain why the mathematical method must fail in the field of metaphysics. The assured fund of knowledge that makes possible a rewarding application of mathematical method lies clearly at hand in the principles of mathematics, so that the science can be erected on them without further ado. But metaphysical principles altogether lack such clarity; although logically the first and simplest, they are the very last and the most difficult for our consciousness to grasp; and thus the success of metaphysics as a science depends entirely on our shedding light on—indeed, on our discovering—its principles in all their abstractness.

It was this fact that induced Kant to choose the very opposite of the method that was at that time usual, but unsuccessful, in metaphysics. Instead of starting, as the mathematical method does, from principles as general as possible, in order to extract from them through logical conclusions the content of the science, Kant does the converse: he starts from the *individual* content, as that which is given, and progresses from it to the general principles. It was this inversion of method that led him to the critique of reason and through which he became the reformer of philosophy.

Of all Kant's successors only Fries held fast to these great and decisive discoveries; and he not only held fast to them but brought them in all their implications to fruition and elaborated them in detail.

What particularly interests us here is Fries's demonstration that the nonanalytic character of mathematical knowledge, which Kant discovered, forms the basis of a distinct and theretofore wholly unknown science, namely, what he called the "philosophy of mathematics." He not only drew up a program for this science but also put it into execution by developing the new science systematically. This he did by carrying over the critical method to mathematics in all its branches, so far as they were then known.

The problem of this science is simply this: to determine in its entirety the content of mathematics, which extends beyond the limits of logic, and to systematize it according to its principles. The solution of this problem obviously makes necessary a sharp distinction within each mathematical discipline between that which is logically provable and that which intuition provides as preassumption for such proof. In short, that method of abstraction is needed which analyzes the proofs of given judgments in order to expose their preassumptions and trace them back to their ultimate principles. The task demands, on the one hand, that the number of axioms shall be reduced to a minimum, namely, to those preassumptions that are *necessary* to the logical construction of the theory in question, and that the others that are provable shall really be proved; and, on the other hand, that the number of axioms shall be increased (contrary to the usual procedure in mathematics), since the total number of axioms must be *sufficient* for a purely logical development of the whole theory from them, without the assistance of additional preassumptions. And indeed, if as this task requires we formulate as special preassumptions (preassumptions that are usually tacitly admitted) everything that has been borrowed from intuition in the course of a proof, we discover new axioms.

We see that this "critical mathematics" or "philosophy of mathematics" is nothing more nor less than the axiomatics so familiar to the modern mathematician. Thus Fries is really the true founder of modern mathematical axiomatics, for he was not only the first to give the problems of this science a universal formulation but also the first to elaborate them systematically. For decades after Fries created this science, mathematicians were familiar with the task that confronted them only from the point of view of a single, partial problem, namely, the problem of the parallel postulate. It was only much later that they discovered, independently of Fries, the possibility and necessity of generalizing this problem; and thus they discovered the proper field of modern axiomatics.

This modern axiomatics verifies in all its aspects the correctness of the path Fries chose, for it has taken exactly the direction he prescribed for it. What is more, it also verifies, in a wealth of important and still pertinent detail, the correctness of the results that Fries had already elaborated.

To be sure, the refinement of its methods has carried modern axiomatics far beyond the stage that Fries reached in this science. It is the more significant how completely the doctrines he had already developed have been verified.

II

The decisive refinement of methods, which we must now delineate and which is the real triumph of modern axiomatics, consists in the fact that it was possible to develop *logic itself* as an instrument by which could be determined the *independence* from logic of certain mathematical cognitions. This was an advance that, curiously enough, followed from certain discoveries that were made at the same time that Fries made his. I refer to the discoveries of Gauss, Lobachevski, and Bolyai, which were independent not only of Fries's discoveries but of one another, and which made possible a solution of the problem of the parallel postulate.

We are dealing here with a question that is interesting in precisely the matter with which we are now concerned: Is there a criterion for determining the axiomatic character of a proposition, i.e., its logical independence of the other propositions of the system? This is the general problem, of which the so-called parallel postulate is only the first case to become known. This postulate states that in a plane only *one* straight line can pass through a point outside another straight line without crossing it. The question then is: Is it possible to prove the parallel postulate, which is introduced in Euclidean geometry as an axiom, from the other axioms of Euclidean geometry? For centuries men have striven to find such proof, but all they could find were pseudo-proofs. Since, however, one could not be absolutely certain from the previous failures to develop this proof that the problem was really insoluble, it remained a problem but an unsolved one. Not until Gauss, Lobachevski, and Bolyai turned their attention to it was it solved. They succeeded in their solution of the problem by inverting it; instead of searching further for proof of the parallel postulate, they attempted to prove its unprovability. Now, what was the criterion they used to determine the unprovability and thus the logical independence of the axiom? The criterion of the provability of a proposition from certain premises is the fact that the contrary of the proposition to be proved leads to a contradiction with one of the consequences of these premises. If we can show that the denial of a proposition does not contradict the consequences of certain other propositions, we have then found a criterion of the logical independence of the proposition in question. In other words, the logical independence of this Euclidean axiom of the other axioms would be proved if it could be proved that a geometry free of contradictions could be erected which differed from Euclidean geometry in the fact, and only in the fact, that in the place of the parallel axiom there stood its negation. That is just what Gauss, Lobachevski, and Bolyai established: the possibility of erecting such a noncontradictory geometry which is different from the Euclidean.

We see at once that this problem has further implications. For herewith the question of the logical independence of a proposition is reduced to the other question of the consistent nature of a a system of propositions, and we are confronted with the question: Is there in turn a criterion for this consistency? For the fact that Gauss, Lobachevski, and Bolyai were able to develop the so-called non-Euclidean geometry without contradictions is not exact proof that a contradiction may not be discovered at some time in the future, after the consequences of this system have been pursued far enough. Here, then, was another important task for science to undertake. This task entailed finding a strict criterion for the consistency of a system of propositions, i.e., a criterion which makes certain that no consequence of that system can ever lead to a contradiction. This problem, too, has been largely solved by modern axiomatics; in the case we are considering, it was solved by the successful proof that if a contradiction should ever turn up in the non-Euclidean geometry of Gauss, Lobachevski, and Bolyai it would necessarily involve a contradiction in ordinary Euclidean geometry as well. In this way the uncontradictory nature of non-Euclidean geometry has been associated with that of Euclidean geometry; and in the same way the consistency of Euclidean geometry has been associated with that of arithmetic.

What is important to us here is this: The results of modern axiomatics are a completely clear and compelling corroboration of Kant's and Fries's assertion of the limits of logic in the field of mathematical knowledge, and they are conclusive proof of the doctrine of the "synthetic" character of the mathematical axioms. For if it is proved that the negation of one axiom can lead to no contradiction even when the other axioms are introduced, it is certainly proved that the axiom leads to no contradiction when the other axioms are not introduced. And this was just the criterion that Kant had already specified for the synthetic character of a judgment: the uncontradictory character of its negation.

III

But what is much more important for us is how modern axiomatics has confirmed the characteristic basic thought of Fries's method, that characteristic sharp distinction between the content and object of critical knowledge which is to be found in no other philosopher. The uniqueness of the critique of reason lies, in Fries's modification of it, in the fact that the same knowledge that forms the content of the system of metaphysics is the object of that knowledge which forms the content of the critique of reason. On this thought alone rests the solution of all the objections that again and again have been raised against Fries's method of critique. What is the axiomatic method, so familiar to every mathematician today, if not Fries's regressive method for the disclosure of principles? What is being done here if not this: The propositions that make up the content of the system of mathematics have become the object of those propositions that make up the content of axiomatics and therefore of the critique of mathematics.

Take for instance the parallel axiom. Here we have the proposition which we shall call *A:*

A. *On a plane surface only one straight line can pass through a point outside another straight line without crossing it.*

This is the parallel axiom, a proposition from the system of geometry. Now this proposition *A* becomes the object of a proposition of the critique of geometry, which we shall call proposition *A':*

A'. *A is unprovable.*

This proposition of the critique of geometry has the former proposition from the system of geometry as its object, as is clearly evident simply in the statement of it. It has nothing to do with the *validity* of this geometric proposition. We are not at all concerned here with the question of the validity of the geometric proposition but only with the question of its provability; and this question is answered by the proof of proposition A'. Not proposition *A* but proposition *A'* is proved here. This very example clearly illustrates the fact that critique cannot attempt to prove axioms, for what *A'* asserts is exactly the *unprovability* of *A.*

We find a similar relation between metaphysics and the critique of its principles in what Fries called "deduction." * This "deduction" of metaphysical principles does not mean, as might be supposed, proof of these principles but verification of them. This verification is a highly complex and ingenious procedure, on which I cannot expatiate at this time. In brief, it consists in tracing back the principle in question to an immediate cognition, in a manner analogous to that in which one justifies the introduction of axioms in mathematics by referring them to intuition. The difference is only—and this is the reason for all the profound diffi-

---

* Regarding the use of the word "deduction," see p. 119, n.

culties in this procedure—that the immediate cognition to which we must trace the principles back is not of an intuitive nature and therefore does not lie clearly at hand but must first be ingeniously sought out through a theory of reason.

Let us take as an example the metaphysical proposition which we shall call *B:*

B. *Every change has a cause.*

This proposition is the principle of causality. In the critique of reason it becomes the object of proposition *B′:*

B′. *B is the rendering of an immediate cognition.*

This proposition *B′* is then proved, and the proof of *B′* is the deduction of *B.*

Thus modern axiomatics presents us with a relation which is altogether analogous to that between Fries's critique of reason and the metaphysical system, since the principles of the system are made the object of the critique; since, further, critique, particularly "deduction," has in view something quite different from a proof of the principles in question; and since, finally, the proposition that has the proposition from the system as its object is proved.

Moreover, critique is introduced into mathematics and metaphysics for quite similar purposes. The purpose of axiomatics is not, as I have already said, to guarantee the validity of mathematical knowledge but to guarantee the abstract system of the mathematical principles—just as the purpose of the critique of reason is not to guarantee the validity of metaphysical knowledge but to guarantee the abstract system of metaphysical principles. In other words, in both cases the purpose is not to guarantee the knowledge in question, as such, but to reduce this knowledge to scientific form. Scientific form demands systematic unity and therefore the reduction to principles.

IV

What has already been said has by no means exhausted the remarkable analogy that we find here, nor have we said all we could about the corroboration, indicated thereby, of Fries's discoveries; the implications extend much further. Modern critical mathematics, in its most recent phase, has elaborated a striking parallel to what is most characteristic of Fries's method of deduction. The crowning achievement of modern axiomatics is the proof of the consistency of arithmetic, long held to be impossible but finally furnished by Hilbert. The affinity of the method that has produced this proof with Fries's method of deduction is so close that we may confidently assert: If there is even the slightest justification to the well-known and oft-raised objections to Fries's method of deduction, then for the same reasons Hilbert's proof of the consistency of arithmetic must irremediably collapse—so true is it that the basic methodic thought which made this proof possible is a reanimation of that profound methodic achievement of Fries's philosophy, which a century's lack of comprehension has buried in obscurity.

The similarity of methods that we are here delineating is not a freak of chance but stems from the affinity of the problems themselves. The problem of the consistency of arithmetic was so pressing because certain apparently insurmountable difficulties and accumulating paradoxes had begun to turn up in the highly abstract concepts and syllogisms of the theory of transfinite numbers—similar to the well-known difficulties and antinomies in the abstractions of metaphysics, which are characterized by a total absence of obviousness.

And so the dexterity with which Hilbert attacked and solved this recondite problem is altogether analogous to that of Fries's deduction. The procedure is as follows: The problems of the theory of transfinite numbers, which are so abstract as to be impalpable, are replaced by corresponding problems of the theory of elementary numbers, which is founded on intuition; in this way it is possible to solve the former without propounding them as such at all. This is the same procedure as the one by which Fries's deduction, which deals only with psychological problems, nevertheless approaches the solution of the problems of metaphysical principles without ever propounding them *in abstracto*. The analogy here is complete. The propositions and syllogisms of the theory of transfinite numbers are here made the object of mathematical critique—of "metamathematics," as Hilbert also calls it. More precisely, what here becomes the object of critical investigation is in reality not even the judgments and conclusions of transfinite arithmetic but the *symbols* in which these judgments and conclusions are expressed—the mere symbols, without consideration of their meaning; these are simply finite, intuitively perceptible forms which, as such, constitute the object of concrete and demonstrable knowledge. What is thereby achieved is not a *logical derivation* of the propositions of the theory of transfinite numbers from those of the theory of elementary numbers but rather a logical "mapping" of the propositions of the one system on those of the other. That is to say, every proposition from the one system is here made to correspond to one from the other system in such a way that if a contradiction appears in one, an equivalent, precisely definable relation must be traceable and *demonstrable* in the other, namely, the appearance of a certain combination of symbols, for instance, a formula such as $0 \neq 0$ which can be determined intuitively.

In just the same way Fries's deduction examines not the universal metaphysical truths, which are the object of abstract judgments, but the concrete fact of the *knowledge* of these truths; and it does so without taking into consideration the objective meaning of this knowledge—that is to say, without considering what it allows one to know about the object; it examines this knowledge only to discover where it originates in human reason. This knowledge thus becomes the object of a knowledge that is not, to be sure, purely intuitive (as it is in the case of mathematics) but is empirical, and for that reason the knowledge of which it becomes the object is in its turn the content not of abstract but of concrete judgments; and hence it is free of the difficulties to which we are helplessly exposed if we attempt to erect the system of abstract metaphysical judgments without taking this roundabout course. Thus the analogy is indeed complete; and I should like to mention in passing the remarkable fact that to some extent the operations in Fries's deduction can be carried out with fruitful results if one uses symbols and combinations of symbols to designate the various metaphysical concepts.

There is, nevertheless, a difference between the two procedures; it manifests itself most clearly in the fact that, as I have just said, Fries's deduction does not deal with purely intuitive but with empirical, i.e., psychological, modes of knowledge. This difference is deeply rooted and not accidental. It finds its source in the different purposes of the respective investigations: whereas mathematical axiomatics is concerned with the proof of consistency, Fries's deduction is concerned with true verification. It is understandable that a logical problem, such as that of proving something consistent, demands methods for its solution that are different from those demanded by the psychological problem of proving the existence of an immediate cognition.

The development of the philosophy of mathematics gives us also the solution to an ancient riddle; it affords the answer to a question first raised by Plato. Here we find a continuity between thinkers such as we have found elsewhere. It is a fact that Plato already applies the idea of the critical method, which is to be found, symbolically formulated, in his doctrine of "reminiscence," to mathematical knowledge and in this way succeeds in presenting with complete clarity the problem of critical mathematics, namely, the problem of critically investigating proofs in order to discover axioms.

V

I should be unwilling to conclude my remarks without at least mentioning how far what I have said here is from exhausting the wealth of points of contact between critical philosophy and mathematical axiomatics, even if we confine ourselves to the problem of the principles of *pure* mathematics.

It is my contention that we can find in this axiomatics that firm point of departure from which we can approach even the most disputed theory of the critical philosophy of mathematics and from which we can already clearly see how the decision must inevitably fall. I refer to the doctrine of the a priori nature of mathematical knowledge, i.e., the doctrine of its independence of experience.

This is a matter that has not been decided, or even touched on, by the determination of the synthetic character of the mathematical judgments, for this determination only assures us of the nonlogical source of the principles in question. After logic has been excluded as a possible source of knowledge, we must still make the positive decision whether the principles in question could have their source in experience, or whether they require a third source of knowledge. We are directly confronted with this question by Kant's demonstration of the logical incompleteness of the disjunction between the various sources of knowledge, which was the curse of pre-Kantian philosophy.

One conviction that guides every serious mathematician in his research and gives him the strength to persevere in an investigation despite all disappointments—a conviction that, because of Hilbert's accomplishments in axiomatics, has come more and more to occupy a prominent place in our attention—is this: that every mathematical problem must be *resolvable* in the sense that we must be able to decide the truth or falsity of every mathematical proposition by pure thought, with no help from outside; or in short, as Hilbert states it, paraphrasing a familiar saying of Emil du Bois-Reymond's: that we can have no *ignorabimus* in mathematics.

If we subscribe to this assertion, then experience (that is, observation and experiment) is eliminated as a source of the knowledge necessary to decide any mathematical problem. For what we are asserting here is just this, that for the solution of mathematical problems we are not thrown on the mercies of any circumstances that make possible for us a particular experience; that on the contrary we need take no consideration of such circumstances, since we are already *in possession* of the data that are necessary and sufficient to prove or disprove any mathematical assertion whatsoever.

"We are in possession": every mathematician who understands himself endorses this saying of Delambre's.

Mathematical knowledge must be such that we dispose over it *independently* of the circumstances, and such that it *needs no extension whatsoever* in order that it shall enable us to decide a problem purely logically.

We might wish to limit the meaning of the assertion that all mathematical problems can be decided, namely, by saying that a system of axioms can be assigned arbitrarily to every mathematical problem, which will suffice for an unequivocal logical solution of the problem. But if it is taken in this sense, our assertion becomes simply trivial and loses all meaning for just that process of cognition which is distinctive of *pure mathematics*. For in this sense every *non*-mathematical problem can also be decided: in every case in which the decision would otherwise be impossible, it could always be managed by the addition of a new axiom.

Another attempted subterfuge is also unavailing, namely, calling only those problems "mathematical" that prove to be solvable. This interpretation really robs the above assertion of all importance and meaning, since the importance and meaning of our conviction lie precisely in the fact that we are confident, *before* we attempt a real solution, of being able to force a solution by pure thinking—in the fact, namely, that it gives us the courage to attack the problem with the confidence that we shall succeed.

VI

Time does not permit me to dilate on the circumstance that metaphysical knowledge, if we possess such, is also a priori knowledge, although it cannot pride itself, as mathematical knowledge can, that it knows no *ignorabimus*. I mention this, however, because it may call to our attention the fact that the quality of being a priori is in itself not *sufficient* to explain the impossibility of the *ignorabimus* and that therefore mathematical cognition is marked by a special superiority over metaphysical cognition.

It will be found that it is the connection of the a priori quality with *intuitiveness* which is peculiar to mathematical cognition, that gives it its superiority over metaphysical cognition.

Thus, step by step, a dispassionate examination of the modern development of mathematical axiomatics sheds a bright light on the discoveries with which the creators of critical philosophy had already illuminated the mysterious nature and the unique power of mathematical cognition, and which had enabled them at long last to infuse philosophy too with the essence of true science. The understanding and the gratitude that have been denied them for a century will be accorded them automatically as soon as this century's achievements in the field of mathematical axiomatics are grasped in their true significance.

Here, and only here, is the "place to stand"—which Archimedes demanded if he were to move the earth—from which it will be possible once more to elevate philosophy to the rank of science.

Let Leonardo da Vinci speak to those mathematicians who, paying homage to the philosophical fashion of the day, despise their own science:

"He who slanders the highest wisdom of mathematics nourishes himself on chaos and will never silence the sophistic sciences, from which one gains nothing but an eternal vociferation."

REPLY
TO THE OBJECTIONS RAISED BY MESSRS. C. AND B.[1]

The remarks I made in my address were based on the assumption that mathematics is a system of cognitions and that consequently its theorems contain *solutions* and are not simply the objects of *problems*. All objections raised in the discussion entail, in the last analysis, an abandonment of this assumption. It is not surprising that under these circumstances the inferences I drew did not seem to hold up.

Mr. C. objected that the usual concept of truth or validity must be limited to metamathematics: we may attribute truth not to the mathematical propositions themselves but only to the interrelations of mathematical propositions with one another. Thus also the general claim of determinability can be maintained only for the problems of metamathematics.

Mr. B. carried this thought further. His exposition was roughly as follows:

That the mathematical axioms lay no claim to being knowledge is already indicated by the effort to prove the consistency of a system of axioms. If the axioms, as the rendering of immedi-

1. This reply is an extension of the remarks I made in the discussion that followed my address.

ate cognition, were themselves cognition, proof that they were consistent would be entirely superfluous since true propositions can always be brought into relation with one another without contradiction. When a mathematician demands that his basic system of axioms be proved consistent, he thereby renounces any vindication of his axioms that might be possible by relating them to a pure intuition of space or time. To be sure, the mathematician cannot get along without any intuition whatever since metamathematics must start from intuitively surveyable symbols and combinations of symbols. If, then, one modifies Kant's doctrine of pure intuition in such a way that it asserts only the existence of that intuition which is the ground of metamathematics, it can stand; but the doctrine of the establishment of mathematical axioms through the pure intuition of space and time is untenable.

I

Let us turn our attention first to the argument that is here directed against Kant's doctrine of the verification of mathematical axioms. Is the proof of consistency really nonsensical if one has preassumed that a system of axioms is correct?

The problem of proving a system of axioms uncontradictory first arises, as we have seen, with the development of non–Euclidean geometry; then the proof, precisely if one assumes Euclidean geometry to be valid, becomes very important for two reasons: (1) the proof that non-Euclidean geometry is not contradictory is at the same time proof of the synthetic character of the Euclidean axioms and hence proof of the presence of a source of knowledge of geometric judgments that is different from mere logic; (2) but the *indirect method* of proof, i.e., the demonstration of the consistency of non-Euclidean geometry through the consistency of Euclidean geometry, rests entirely on the independently—intuitively—given security of the latter.

Once the problem of proving a system of axioms free of contradiction has arisen, it awakens systematic scientific interest in another, that of finding this proof for every system of axioms that is the basis of a mathematical discipline. To be sure, if we know that a system of axioms reiterates immediate knowledge, then we are already certain that it is not contradictory; we need not prove it consistent in order to justify our reliance on it. But, as we know, it is no simple matter to reduce even an immediately obvious cognition to an unobjectionable conceptual formulation. The more abstract mathematical assertions are and the more remote they become from that which is at once intuitively discernible, the easier it is to commit errors in formulating them. The paradoxes in the theory of sets are sufficient proof of the difficulties one may encounter in abstract mathematics through overhasty or uncritical formulations. And so the problem of the proof of consistency becomes once more a live issue. Furthermore, the interests of scientific systematics and completeness make it desirable to prove a system of axioms consistent even if the cognitional character of this system of axioms is already established.

II

We shall better discern the untenability of this argument against the cognitional character of the mathematical axioms if we ask ourselves what significance mathematics still retains in the light of it. According to Mr. B., the individual axioms are not cognitions. But mathematics as a science must be a system of cognitions. We cannot seek these cognitions in the theorems of mathematics, for these theorems rest on the axioms, and their cognitional character is sacrificed with that of the axioms. Consequently, according to Mr. C., the cognitional value of mathematics lies only in the *interconnection* among mathematical propositions. Hence statements about the logical relations between the mathematical theorems and the axioms of mathematics are the only propositions in the field of mathematics in which the question of validity really makes any sense.

But, as Mr. C. himself states, these assertions no longer belong in the system of mathematics proper; rather, they are propositions in metamathematics. An example will make this clear. The parallel axiom is a proposition of Euclidean geometry. According to the objection brought forward here, the question of the truth of this axiom has no meaning. Hence the axiom as such is, rather, an arbitrary statement and, standing by itself, has of course no scientific meaning. Only those propositions have scientific meaning that tell us what new theorems can be proved by adding this axiom to the other Euclidean axioms, and also those that tell us whether the axiom is not only necessary but adequate for the derivation of these theorems, and so on. But these are propositions from metamathematics. According to the objection that has been raised, therefore, mathematics becomes a system of merely arbitrary statements that can have no scientific significance. If we ask whether a plane is divided into an inner and an outer section by a closed curve having no double points, whether a regular septagon can be constructed with ruler and compass, whether every continuous function can be differentiated, whether 7 is a prime number—all these questions either become meaningless or at least lose the character of mathematical problems and become problems in experimental physics. One can thus no more demand that they be decided than one can make such a demand of the problem of a definite weather forecast or the problem of finding a way to visit the inhabitants of Mars. Only metamathematics, in which the logical relations among these arbitrary assertions are investigated, is science; and thus mathematics as a science is supplanted by metamathematics.

But it is easy to see that such an interpretation completely distorts the meaning that Hilbert gave metamathematics—indeed, it perverts it to its opposite. Hilbert was stimulated to his studies by the well-known difficulties that confronted mathematics in the field of the theory of sets. In opposition to the growing skeptical inclination to capitulate in the face of these difficulties and to surrender whole departments of the science, Hilbert's metamathematics was directed toward securing the fruitful results of the science against the dangers that threatened it in the paradoxes of the theory of sets. The protection of mathematical results, not the abandonment of mathematics, is thus the significance of metamathematics. He who makes metamathematics an end in itself by allowing it to usurp the position of mathematics is doing it the worst possible service and certainly may not appeal to the creator of metamathematics in his defense. Even Brouwer's and Weyl's skepticism, against which Hilbert directs his attacks, goes only as far as a "mutilation" of mathematics; but the nihilism of the two speakers in this discussion is not satisfied even with that: it *destroys* mathematics.

But we must go even a step further. Metamathematics—and with it the problem of the consistency of a system of axioms—is supposed, even after the destruction of mathematics, to retain scientific meaning; more, the solution of this problem is supposed to be the way by which the scientific value of a system of axioms is first determined. A consistent application of this criterion thus compels us to undertake an investigation of the possibility of metamathematics, now severed from mathematics, before we attempt to erect it. What becomes of metamathematics after the destruction of mathematics? The concept of this science relates it to mathematics. Its task is to investigate the logical relation between the axioms of the mathematical disciplines; therefore, it has mathematics as its object. But what problem is metamathematics to work out if mathematics is nothing but a system of arbitrary assertions of no scientific significance and is distinguished only by the fact that it has been traditionally inherited from century to century? At best, such a mathematics could be of interest to the historian but not to the metamathematician. The historian can ask himself how it was possible for generations of mathematicians to embrace the egregious fallacy of holding arbitrary assertions to be knowledge; but what reason has the metamathematician, who long ago freed himself from the silly misconceptions of his predecessors, to make just these misconceptions the object of scientific study?

Could he be induced to do so perhaps by an interest in the applicability of these arbitrary assertions to the hypotheses of physics? No, for if he were, he would have to exclude from his investigations those mathematical disciplines whose concepts extend far beyond that which is observable in nature. From this point of view metamathematical investigation of the axioms of transfinite arithmetic would be a senseless waste of time—but just this investigation is the main problem of Hilbert's metamathematics.

If, then, the mathematical axioms are distinguished neither by their own scientific importance nor by their applicability to other sciences, it is simply the current fashion that makes precisely them the object of a proper science. But why should the metamathematician commit himself to so arbitrary an occupation as this? Supposedly, there is no scientific principle that prescribes to him the object of his investigations; hence the choice of the system of axioms that is to be the basis of his investigations is left entirely to his discretion. At best, he can be guided in his choice only by the precept that he should choose those axioms whose logical relations are the least discernible so that the metamathematical investigations will be as interesting as possible.

The research to which one might be induced by such arbitrary inclinations might certainly be quite diverting, but it would have no more scientific value than any other pastime; for a pastime differs from a scientifically significant theory in that one busies oneself with the former because it is diverting, whereas the treatment of scientific problems is of interest only because here serious questions call for an answer.

We become acutely aware of how metamathematics degenerates to mere trifling if divorced from mathematics when we take into consideration the fact that the arbitrary axioms from which the metamathematical inquiry seems to start themselves do not appear in the inquiry at all. The object of this inquiry is rather the system of symbols that is made to correspond with the system of axioms. Now, if we presuppose the arbitrariness of mathematical axioms, the system of axioms interests us only in so far as a treatment of it promises to entertain us. But in this treatment we are not even concerned with the axioms themselves but only with the symbols that stand for them. Hence not only shall we formulate the problem of metamathematics more concisely and more clearly if we entirely relinquish the connection with the system of axioms, but it is only in this way that we can really do justice to the actual situation. It is then the task of metamathematics to demonstrate that operations conducted in accordance with certain rules can never lead us to a certain combination of symbols, namely, the formula $0 \neq 0$.

But here the question arises anew: Why is the metamathematician so interested in just this formula? The original meaning of the formula has been entirely lost—in truth, there can be no question here of a proof of consistency, for the appearance of the formula o ╪ o is not itself a contradiction; there simply corresponds to it (a fact, however, which in this case we must entirely ignore!) a contradiction in the consequences of a system of axioms. If we examine the symbols alone, with no reference to the axioms they represent, the formula o ╪ o is no more remarkable than any other, for example, the formula o = o.

The effort to demonstrate the impossibility of the symbol o ╪ o, of all problems, is therefore, as is the predilection for the axioms of the mathematical disciplines, merely a question of current fashion; there is no scientific principle at all that distinguishes the rules of the game followed here from any other conceivable rules. Are we with Weyl to place our reliance in the "reasonableness of history" and to believe that the axioms and methods that tradition has handed down to us will lead us, although they lack all scientific meaning, "in a process of vital spiritual development" [2] to scientifically meaningful results?

No, this hope, too, must be frustrated by the facts. If the success with which axioms and methods have been crowned in the course of history is the criterion for the necessity of making them the basis of a metamathematics, the discerning mathematician today must devote himself, before turning his attention to other problems—no matter how important or interesting they may be —to the development of a new metamathematics that is the exact antithesis of Hilbert's, one the main problem of which is not to demonstrate the impossibility of the formula o ╪ o but to prove the possibility of the equation 1 = 3. I refer to that metamathematics which, as Bismarck [3] says, feels justified in claiming to be persecuted wherever it does not reign supreme; for this metamathematics has, through its statistically demonstrable successes, legitimated itself as the only rightful metamathematics for those who allow their confidence in the "reasonableness of history" to dictate their axioms and methods.

2. H. Weyl, "Diskussionsbemerkungen zu dem zweiten Hilbertschen Vortrag über die Grundlagen der Mathematik" in *Hamburger Mathematische Einzelschriften*, V (Leipzig, 1928).

3. Otto von Bismarck, *Gedanken und Erinnerungen* (Stuttgart, 1898), II, chap. xxiv, sec. 1, p. 125.

III

But we can say even more. Whoever denies that mathematical axioms are knowledge, thereby denies the existence of pure intuition as the source of knowledge for mathematical judgments. It is then immaterial whether one disputes pure intuition as such or admits the possibility of it but, as Mr. B. said, "prefers to disregard it" for the erection of mathematics. But if pure intuition is not to be utilized for the establishment of axioms, on what then is the certainty of metamathematics founded, which (as we saw) replaces mathematics in this approach to the problem and for which the question of the validity of its propositions should admittedly still make sense? We are dealing in metamathematics with intuitive symbols which appear in an intuitively perspicuous arrangement. Therefore, we are helpless in metamathematics without intuition, as Mr. B. specifically admitted in the discussion. But with what sort of intuition, then, are we here concerned? The symbols that are perceived in metamathematics are extended, that is to say, spatially extended, forms which are given in spatial arrangements. The intuition, therefore, on which metamathematics is based is *spatial* intuition. This spatial intuition is either a priori knowledge or it is empirical knowledge. Whoever holds it to be a priori knowledge thereby admits that we possess a pure spatial intuition and that this pure spatial intuition is the ground of knowledge of the science that has here replaced mathematics. But whoever admits this cannot on the other hand deny that the geometric axioms are knowledge simply because a pure spatial intuition is necessary for their establishment.

Those who deny that pure spatial intuition is the source of knowledge of mathematical judgments must consequently, if they are to be consistent, turn to empirical intuition as the ground of metamathematics. The symbols with which he operates—and that means in this context *experiments*—are therefore the chalk marks on the blackboard or the ink lines on the paper, which appear to sensory perception. But metamathematics, if it is to arrive at universally valid conclusions, must make certain preassumptions regarding the constancy of its symbols and the possibility of creating these symbols; and these preassumptions must themselves be apodictically valid. If the chalk marks on the blackboard are the objects of metamathematics, metamathematics needs an apodictically certain axiom according to which these chalk marks possess permanence and according to which it is possible to produce them on any part of the blackboard; and this axiom, as an apodictic judgment, would have to refer back to a priori knowledge. N.B., a priori knowledge of the imperishability of the chalk! Whoever, therefore, supposes he can do without pure spatial intuition for the establishment of mathematics must entrust himself instead to a priori knowledge of the destiny of blackboard and chalk. This fantastic admission is the least to which our skeptics, under penalty of contradicting themselves, must accommodate themselves—not to mention the fact that the a priori knowledge which they need has the disadvantage of contradicting the most obvious facts of *experience*, which precisely they prize so highly.

Thus mathematical empiricism turns everything upside down. For fear of becoming involved in a priori knowledge in the only place where it belongs, they let it in through a back door, where it has no business to be—where, rather, its interference would destroy all confidence in observation and experiment. After the loss of *pure mathematics* which, as a priori knowledge, provided us with the preconditions for all significant experimentation, we find ourselves at the mercy of the *metaphysics of chalk*, which makes any experiment a mockery.

The attempt to sustain mathematics ultimately with presuppositions regarding the nature of the writing material has actually and in all seriousness been made. No less a person than E. Schröder, the well-known founder of the algebra of logic, introduces in his *Lehrbuch der Arithmetik und Algebra* [4] as the "single axiom" the "axiom of the inherence of the symbols." This axiom, he declares, "gives us the certainty that in all our calculations and conclusions the symbols are fixed in our memory—but are fixed even more firmly on the paper," a dubious assumption in view of the fact (as Schröder himself must admit) that it "possesses, depending on the memory of the calculator

4. (Leipzig, 1873), I, 16 f.

and the nature of the material he uses, only a greater or lesser degree of *probability*." "For instance, the assumption would be impossible, or at least its probability would be very slight, if one wrote with disappearing ink." But nevertheless—and Schröder sets his mind at rest with this assertion—"this confidence is in general so great that we base on it our conviction of the *absolute certainty* of mathematical truths." Thus the absolute certainty of mathematical judgments rests on a precondition that possesses no absolute certainty but merely a degree of probability!

He who denies pure intuition as the source of knowledge and still holds metamathematics to be a system of cognitions must perforce, if he is to be consistent, take refuge in the absurdity of fabricating a knowledge of the nature of his working material that not only is independent of experience but actually contradicts it. In the proof of the consistency of mathematical axioms through metamathematics the claim of these axioms to being knowledge is not by any means abandoned, nor is reference to pure intuition in order to vindicate the axioms shown to be unnecessary or even absurd; on the contrary, this very proof presupposes for its possibility pure intuition as the source of knowledge. It rests on precisely that knowledge which some have supposed, in the name of metamathematics, that they could do without.

IV

These reflections give us insight into the significance of another parallel—one I did not mention in my address—between Hilbert's axiomatics and the methods of the critique of reason. Metamathematics, one of whose functions it is to prove the consistency of systems of geometric axioms, itself uses pure spatial intuition and hence geometric cognitions! We find something quite analogous in Fries's deductions of metaphysical principles. These deductions rest on a psychological theory which, like all empirical theories, itself already presupposes metaphysical principles.

This relation of deductions to metaphysical principles, according to which on the one hand the deductions serve to verify the principles and on the other hand these principles are already the logical preassumptions of the deductions, has often given rise to attacks on the methods of the critique of reason, since it would appear that the deduction is based on circular reasoning: it seems to presuppose what it first wishes to prove.

If this attack is justified, then the critique of reason draws Hilbert's metamathematics with it in its downfall; for metamathematics, as a theory about the intuitive relation of intuitive symbols, applies geometric cognitions to prove the consistency of systems of geometric axioms. Does not this proof then become circular reasoning?

This question leads us back to our starting point, namely, to the assertion made during the discussion that the mathematical axioms are not knowledge and that only for this reason the proof of their consistency is meaningful and requisite; and that only through the proof of its uncontradictoriness can a system of axioms be established as serviceable for the erection of a mathematical discipline. If this is so, then the objection is definitely legitimate that Hilbert's proof, because it uses geometric preassumptions, becomes circular reasoning. For if the use of the axioms presupposes for its legitimacy the proof of their consistency, this proof of consistency loses its logical integrity if it itself rests on these axioms. If the proof of the impossibility of the formula $o \neq o$ makes use of principles whose freedom from contradiction has not yet been determined, it would not be beyond the realm of the possible that the formula $o \neq o$ could be proved with the same principles. The proof of consistency thus becomes circular reasoning when it is regarded as the only justification of the system of axioms.

But the situation is quite different if we admit pure intuition to be the source of knowledge for mathematical axioms. Then the function of the proof of consistency is not to vindicate a system of axioms as the basis of a mathematical discipline—the axioms are vindicated by an appeal to pure intuition. Its function is rather the critical clarification of a logical relation between the axioms of a mathematical discipline, and thus at the same time the frustration of skepticism, which sustains itself on the difficulties present in the abstract fields of mathematics. In the proof of consistency it is not the mathematical axioms that are proved but only assertions that have these axioms as their object. Thus it is not circular reasoning if this proof itself makes use of geometric presuppositions.

An analogous situation exists for the deductions of metaphysical principles. If these deductions were *proofs* of the principles, it would be quite impermissible to apply in them the principles in question. But in the deductions only psychological propositions are proved, which in their turn have the metaphysical principles as their object. Fries's deductions are therefore just as free from circular reasoning as Hilbert's proof of the consistency of arithmetic.

V

I have not been able and have not wished, either in my address or in this reply, to treat exhaustively the problem of the source of mathematical knowledge.* I have limited myself to a few conclusions of philosophical importance, starting from a point of view that, as it seemed to me, was suitable and congenial to the mathematician. This point of view which holds mathematics to be a science is the conviction, outlined above, that all mathematical problems can be solved. It is, as I have already said, not surprising that if this point of view (in one word, the *mathematical* point of view) is abandoned, the concomitant conclusions which I have drawn do not hold up; and consequently I have, of course, not the slightest objection to the statement of this circumstance. The only thing that is surprising here is this: that it is *mathematicians* who, by their own blunt confession, wish to have nothing to do with the mathematical point of view. Such a measure of self-abnegation is indeed striking and requires our special consideration. The candid admission that one must turn one's back on mathematics in order to escape the philosophically unpalatable inferences of my address is a real step forward in the clarification of our old controversy. I record it as a welcome corroboration of

* See Nelson's "Bemerkungen über die Nicht-Euklidische Geometrie und den Ursprung der mathematischen Gewissheit," *Abhandlungen der Fries'schen Schule*, I (Göttingen, 1906).

the only fact that appears essential to me, namely, that from the mathematical point of view my inferences are conclusive.

The self-abnegation to which we were witness is, moreover, an appalling example of the sinister force with which a compulsive metaphysical notion can cast its spell over human minds, and at the same time testimony to the earnest need of exorcising these obscure forces—just such a need as *critical* philosophy can meet. A mathematical nihilism of the sort embraced by such eminent mathematicians as the participants in today's discussion might indeed disconcert us were it not for our knowledge that it is their *philosophical* viewpoint that has made them renounce their mathematical knowledge. For this mathematical knowledge does not, as they recognize very clearly, fit into the *metaphysical pattern* that is the point of departure of their philosophizing—that metaphysical pattern which, curiously enough, is dictated to them (as my analysis demonstrates) precisely by their *fear of a priori knowledge* and which crystallizes in their "*ceterum censeo*": *mathematicam esse delendam.*

For the sake of this pattern, which is based on *no knowledge whatsoever* but on a mere compulsive notion, they unhesitatingly sacrifice the clearest and most lucid knowledge that we possess —indeed, the *only* knowledge that is clear and lucid per se.

I prefer to strike the opposite course. If a philosophy, no matter how attractive or plausible or ingenious it may be, brings me into conflict with mathematics, I conclude that not mathematics but my philosophy is on the wrong track.

VII

THE IMPOSSIBILITY OF THE "THEORY OF KNOWLEDGE" *

IF we review the activity of this Congress so far, we become aware of two facts—facts of which other sources might have informed us but which it is good to find here corroborated. One of them is heartening, the other must sadden us. What is gratifying is that the mere existence of this Congress bears witness to a belief in the possibility of philosophy as science. That an international congress for philosophy is possible presupposes the conviction that there can be common philosophical endeavor; and such endeavor is possible only if we believe in philosophy as science. But this conviction is manifested even more clearly and strikingly in the unusually close connection, at this Congress, between philosophy and the exact sciences; and the union of science and philosophy in the personality of our honored president is a special symbolic expression of our faith that such union is possible.

As you know, there are many who ridicule a congress for philosophy, who feel that attendance at such a congress is beneath the true dignity of a philosopher. Such an opinion is necessary and natural to all those who regard philosophy as a matter of personal experience, as something that cannot be molded to precise, communicable forms—all those, in short, to whom philosophy is not a science. Those, however, who do not share this opinion must welcome the lively interest this Congress has aroused and the special emphasis its program lays on the relations of philosophy to the exact sciences, as refreshing testimony to the belief in philosophy as science.

But even though we who have convened here believe in the

* An address, "Die Unmöglichkeit der Erkenntnistheorie," published in *Abhandlungen der Fries'schen Schule*, III (Göttingen, 1912), No. 4; also in *Die Reformation der Philosophie* (Leipzig, 1918), delivered on April 11, 1911, before the Fourth International Congress for Philosophy at Bologna.

possibility of a scientific philosophy, we must ask ourselves whether we really possess such a philosophical science; and we must in all honesty confess—and this is the second, saddening fact of which this Congress makes us aware—that at present the state of philosophy is not that of a science. We have observed, and the discussions have borne it in upon us, that there is no unanimity among those present on even the most elementary philosophical questions. The more we are concerned with achieving the goal of philosophy as a science, the more important it must be to us not to gloss over this fact, that philosophy is not now a science, but rather to bring it out as clearly as possible. Thus we shall find occasion all the sooner to scrutinize the reasons *why* we have not yet succeeded in making a science of philosophy and to inquire in what way we may hope to put an end to this unseemly state of affairs.

This is the problem to the solution of which my address will attempt to make a contribution.

The nature of this task obliges me to deal primarily with the formulation of our problem and with questions of method. In so doing, I am undertaking nothing new: our age is strikingly rich in such methodological research. Indeed, it has been regarded as a failing, as a sort of morbid symptom, that current philosophy is preponderantly concerned with the question of its proper method. I cannot share that point of view. Whatever the case may be in other sciences, in philosophy it is not a sign of decline but a sign of convalescence, when attention is paid above all to the correct method. In other sciences the cognitive material that is to be reduced to scientific form is accessible to us through relatively simple procedures, and we do not require a special preliminary investigation to find out how we can make it our own; but in philosophy everything is based on just such a methodological preliminary study. For the sum total of the cognitions that are to form the content of philosophical science are not available to us without special effort, and everything turns on how we go about getting hold of them. Consequently, the trustworthiness of our results depends altogether on our choice of method. Difficult though it may be to achieve unanimity regarding this method, it is futile to enter into a discussion of specific results until this has been achieved. Even though the many methodological efforts of recent times have not yet led to the desired goal, we may not on that account conclude that it would be better to abandon such methodological research in order finally to turn from the method to the real matter at hand. On the contrary, it is my opinion that if methodological work has not hitherto met with the hoped-for success, that is only because it has not attacked its task vigorously *enough*. If only this work is carried on with the necessary earnestness and energy, the correct way will soon be found to escape from philosophical anarchy to a harmonious and planned scientific endeavor.

It must strike a dispassionate observer of the development of philosophy in recent times as particularly remarkable that the contention and variety of philosophical opinions is greatest in just that discipline whose specific intention it has been to put an end to the fruitless quarrels of the earlier academic metaphysics, namely, in the studies on the "theory of knowledge" (*Erkenntnistheorie*).* These studies were originally undertaken with the sole purpose of making the philosophical problems, which without them appeared unsolvable, accessible to scientific treatment, either by establishing thus a scientific metaphysics or by ascertaining once and for all through a "theory of knowledge" the impossibility of such a scientific metaphysics. How is it to be explained that this apparently highly justified hope for a peaceful scientific form of philosophy has not only not been realized but on the contrary has immeasurably widened the dissension among the schools? I shall show that this curious phenomenon has a very simple cause, and that the problem of the "theory of knowledge" is similar to many allied problems in other sciences. We very often find that a problem we have disputed at great length, without getting a step nearer its solution, finally turns out to be one that simply permits of no solution or one whose solution (if we can call it that) is not the hoped-for positive finding but rather the proof of its unsolvability.

---

* A comprehensive history of *Erkenntnistheorie* since Kant can be found in Nelson's "Über das sogenannte Erkenntnisproblem," *Abhandlungen der Fries'-schen Schule*, II (Göttingen, 1908).

I shall, therefore, prove the impossibility of the "theory of knowledge," but in order not to conclude with a negative, unconstructive result, I shall enter into the question as to what positive consequences can perhaps be drawn from this fact—the question whether we are thus obliged to abandon the search for philosophy as science, whether, in other words, we must relapse into dogmatic metaphysics, or whether perhaps there is a third path, which really leads to our goal. I believe I can show you that this last is the case, and I hope that my address itself will provide you with an illustration that we can follow this path.

First of all, I shall say as much regarding the *method* I shall employ as is necessary to an understanding of my exposition.

When we concern ourselves with philosophy as science, it is natural for us to take the example of the exact sciences as a model, though we know, or at least we should know from Kant, that we cannot blindly transfer to philosophy a method that is appropriate to the mathematical sciences. Pre-Kantian metaphysics made precisely this mistake of trying to imitate in philosophy the usual dogmatic method of mathematics. Kant proved definitively the faultiness of this undertaking. But the relation of the two sciences, philosophy and mathematics, has changed in a curious way since Kant's time: during the last century modern mathematics has developed in what is called *axiomatics* a method that corresponds exactly to the one Kant demanded for philosophy. This is the *regressive* method, the importance of which does not lie in extending our knowledge, adding new truths to the fund of those already known, elaborating their consequences, but rather in examining the known truths with regard to their preassumptions. It serves as a means of investigating the conditions of the solvability of a problem before we attack the problem itself; it assures us whether or not the problem is solvable at all and what presuppositions are already implicit in the mere setting of the problem; it determines what presuppositions are necessary and sufficient for a definite solution of a problem.

I wish to apply this method to the problem of the "theory of knowledge," also called the problem of knowledge. This problem is that of the objective validity of our knowledge. It is the task of a "theory of knowledge" to test the truth or objective validity of our knowledge. I maintain that a solution of this problem is *impossible*, and I prove this as follows:

In order to solve this problem, we should have to have a criterion by the application of which we could decide whether or not a cognition is true; I shall call it briefly the "validity criterion." This criterion would itself either be or not be a cognition. If it be a cognition, it would fall within the area of what is problematic, the validity of which is first to be solved with the aid of our criterion. Accordingly, it cannot itself be a cognition. But if the criterion be not a cognition, it would nevertheless, in order to be applicable, have to be known, i.e., we should have to know that it is a criterion of the truth. But in order to gain this knowledge of the criterion, we should already have had to apply it. In both cases, therefore, we encounter a contradiction. A "validity criterion" is consequently impossible, and hence there can be no "theory of knowledge."

One need only take any example in order to make the content of this proof clearer. For instance, someone might assert that *agreement of thinking subjects with one another* is the criterion in question. To be able to apply this criterion, we should have to *know* that agreement of various subjects is a criterion of the truth of their knowledge. But in order to know this, we should have to apply this criterion itself to the assumption that agreement is the criterion in question. We should have to convince ourselves that all subjects agree on the assertion that agreement is a criterion of the truth of their assertions. But in order to realize from this the truth of this assumption, we should already have had to presuppose that it is correct, i.e., that agreement is a "validity criterion." Thus the possibility of achieving this knowledge would involve an inner contradiction.

Or someone might claim that *obviousness* is the criterion in question. In order for this criterion to be applicable, it would have to be known to us as such, i.e., we should have to *know* that the obvious cognitions are the true ones. But we could only know this if it were *obvious* that the obvious cognitions are true; however, in order to deduce the truth of this assumption from its obviousness, we should already have had to *presuppose* that obviousness is a criterion of truth. It is therefore impossible to achieve the knowledge in question.

Or let us take pragmatism. If the usefulness of a notion is to be the sought-after criterion of truth, we should have to *know*, in order to be able to apply this criterion, that usefulness is the criterion of truth. We should therefore have to know that it is *useful* to think that useful thinking is the true thinking, and thus we should have to presuppose that the usefulness of thinking is a criterion of its truth. So here, too, we meet the same contradiction; and it is the same in every other case.

Now, what is the *preassumption* that we make in setting the problem of a "theory of knowledge" and that involves the contradiction we have observed? It is important, first of all, to realize that such a preassumption is really implicit in the problem, and that the alleged absence of preassumptions, proudly proclaimed by the "theory of knowledge," is simply a chimera. If one asks whether one possesses objectively valid cognitions at all, one thereby presupposes that the objectivity of cognition is questionable at first, and that we can assure ourselves of this objectivity only indirectly, namely, through the process of the "theory of knowledge." What can be said about this preassumption, which is indispensable to the "theory of knowledge"?

Let us begin by drawing up a clearer picture of the meaning and content of this preassumption. It seems at first to be nothing more than an application of the logical principle of sufficient reason, according to which every assertion needs a *verification*. And indeed, the "theory of knowledge" stands or falls with the preassumption of the necessity of verifying every cognition; for the task of this discipline is none other than to verify our cognition. Although this very preassumption seems to aim at the elimination of all prejudgments, the contradiction it leads to, demonstrated above, makes us aware that some error must lie concealed here and that consequently the preassumption is itself a prejudgment.

This contradiction really lies in the following: If every cognition needs a verification, that is equivalent to saying that it presupposes another cognition as its ground, to which it must be traced back if it is to be asserted as truth. The contradiction lies in the proposition, here implied, of the *mediacy* of all knowledge. For if every cognition were possible only on the ground of another, we should have to execute an infinite regression in order to reach any true cognition, and hence no verification of cognitions would be possible.

We can phrase this result in another way. If one asserts the mediacy of all knowledge in the manner just outlined, one therewith asserts that every cognition is a *judgment*. The word "judgment" is here used in its usual sense to mean the assertion of a thought that is in itself problematic. Every judgment presupposes a notion that is not in itself assertoric but to which the assertion is only mediately added. However, this preassumption that every cognition is a judgment involves also another, namely, that the verification of a cognition can only be a *proof*. A proof is the tracing back of one judgment to another that contains the logical ground of the first. But if there is no other verification of judgments except proof, no verification of judgments is possible at all; for all proof consists only in the tracing back of the judgment to be proved to unproved and unprovable judgments. Therefore, either there is another means of verifying judgments besides proof, or no verification of them is possible at all.

The above-demonstrated preassumption in the "theory of knowledge"—and on this point I should like to lay particular stress—involves not only the logical contradiction we have discussed; it also contradicts psychological facts. It contains, as we have seen, the psychological conclusion that every cognition is a judgment; but this statement contradicts the facts of inner experience. To convince ourselves of the existence of cognitions that are not judgments, we need only consider any intuition at all, such as an ordinary sensory perception. For example, I have a sensory perception of the sheet of paper that lies here on the table before me. This perception is, first of all, a cognition, not merely a problematic notion. The existential assertion that is an element of this cognition is, however, not a judgment. To be sure, I can also render in a judgment the same circumstances that I here cognize through the perception; but when I judge that a piece of paper is lying before me on the table, that is an altogether different sort of cognition from the perception of this situation. I need concepts for the judgment, e.g., the concept "table," the concept "paper," etc. I connect these concepts in a certain manner and assert that objective reality pertains to this combination of concepts. Perception, on the other hand, has no need of any concepts nor of any problematic notion of its objects whatsoever; rather, it is itself an originally assertoric notion—is, in other words, an *immediate* cognition.

Thus we find that problematic notions are not that which is original, to which objectivity would have to be contributed from some other source, but that it is cognition itself that is original. It is correct that judgments are possible only on the basis of concepts, which are problematic notions; nevertheless, this does not apply to cognition as such. With this ascertainment the problem of the "theory of knowledge" disappears: the possibility of cognition is not a problem but a fact.

We must now scrutinize this *factual* character of cognition. Once one is clear in one's mind about it, one will see a problem not in the possibility of cognition but rather in the possibility of *error*. For if we originally have only cognitions, the question presents itself how error can arise at all. To solve this problem, we need only inquire into the relation of judgments to immediate knowledge. In and of itself a judgment is not yet a cognition; it is such only under the condition that it reiterates an immediate cognition. Judgments are acts of reflection, and to that extent arbitrary. The combination of concepts in judgments is arbitrary and hence depends on a factor that is foreign to cognition. The truth of *judgments*, namely, their correspondence with immediate knowledge, *is not an original fact*; it is rather a task that we arbitrarily set ourselves so far as our interest in truth motivates us; and in the choice of the means for the accomplishment of this task we can be mistaken.

Before I proceed to develop the consequences of my previous observations, I should like to illuminate the impossibility of the "theory of knowledge" from another angle. The impossibility of such theory can be proved also in the following manner. Since for this discipline knowledge is not a fact but a problem, the "theory of knowledge," in order to solve this problem, cannot assume any knowledge as given; rather, it must begin solely with problematic notions, that is, mere concepts. Now, only analytic judgments can be developed from mere concepts, and they never provide a new cognition, which can only consist in synthetic judgments. Thus our task amounts to deriving synthetic from merely analytic judgments.

That this task, however, is incapable of execution can be proved as follows. If we assume that it is possible to derive synthetic from merely analytic judgments, then there must appear somewhere in the series of syllogisms a syllogism both of whose premises are still analytic while the conclusion is already synthetic. But if both the premises of this syllogism, major as well as minor, are analytic, this means that, on the one hand, the major term of the syllogism is already contained in the middle term and, on the other hand, the middle term is already contained in the minor term. But with major term thus contained in middle, as well as middle in minor term, then the major term is also already contained in the minor term, i.e., the conclusion must also be analytic, contrary to our assumption. Thus it is impossible ever to derive a synthetic judgment from merely analytic judgments, and the task of the "theory of knowledge," to show how knowledge can arise from purely problematic notions, consequently cannot be accomplished.

I presuppose for this second proof of the impossibility of the "theory of knowledge" that one concedes my distinction between analytic and synthetic judgments. I shall therefore briefly consider the principal objection that is raised against this distinction. It has been held that this distinction is variable and unprecise, so that one and the same judgment can at different times and for different people be now analytic, now synthetic; consequently, a mutation of a judgment from the one type to the other is possible. This objection vanishes when we discriminate between judgments and their linguistic expression. What varies and is unprecise is only the co-ordination between the expression and the thought it stands for. The same words can, at different times and for different people, have different meanings, and for this reason, to be sure, one and the same sentence can stand here for an analytic, there for a synthetic, judgment. Whoever concludes from this that the division of judgments into analytic and synthetic is unprecise thereby confounds [fixed] concepts and [changing] word significations.

It is only through this same confusion that the dialectical illusion arises in attempts to solve the problem of the "theory of knowledge." All these endeavors tend toward a renewal of the old, logicizing metaphysics and accordingly can be no more than a repetition of the same old errors in new guise. The apparent success of attempts to create metaphysics from mere logic rests only on the ambiguity of words. This alone makes it possible, in "theories of knowledge," unconsciously to foist off an analytic judgment as a synthetic one by expressing them both in the same sentence.

I should like to adduce two examples of what I have just said, which at the same time will serve to clarify the importance of the basic thought I have presented and to distinguish it from other views with which it might perhaps be confused.

The answer to the question whether or not we possess valid knowledge—no matter what this answer may be—can only be sought in a synthetic judgment, since it is concerned with a fact. And yet it would appear as if we could prove our possession of knowledge purely logically by demonstrating a contradiction in the opposite assumption. This contradiction, with which absolute skepticism has time and again been reproached since Plato, is well known. It is said: Whoever asserts his inability to know anything is contradicting himself, for he claims to *know* what he is asserting, namely, his inability to know anything; and it follows from this contradiction that he knows something. This reasoning is not sound. It is, to be sure, contradictory if someone claims to know that he knows nothing; but it does not follow, by any means, from this contradiction that he knows something; it follows only that he does *not* know what he claims to know, namely, that he knows nothing. The contradiction lies not in the skeptical assumption that we know *nothing* but in the other assumption that we can *know* this. It is not judgment *A*, "I know nothing," but judgment *B*, "I know that I know nothing," that leads to a logical contradiction; hence it follows only that judgment *B* is false, not judgment *A*. The refutation of skepticism by such a theory rests only on the confusion of these two judgments.

This result, viz., insight into the impossibility of a positive validation of knowledge, might induce us to make the opposite attempt to decide the problem *negatively*. If no verification of the validity of our knowledge is possible, it seems to follow that we can know nothing about the validity of our knowledge, that we shall therefore have to regard it skeptically. But this skeptical conclusion from the impossibility of verifying knowledge is just as erroneous. It makes the tacit assumption that we can assert only that to be valid which can be verified; and this is precisely the same prejudice of the "theory of knowledge" on the basis of which we were, at the outset, led to the contradictory demand for a verification of knowledge.

I mention this last particularly because it might be objected that my proof of the impossibility of the "theory of knowledge" simply reiterates an old idea, often enunciated by the skeptics. It can be seen from what has been said that the skeptical arguments in question prove too little. *I do not assert the impossibility of the "theory of knowledge" in order to conclude that knowledge is impossible; rather, I assert that this skeptical conclusion, that knowledge is impossible, is itself merely a consequence of the prejudice held by the proponents of a "theory of knowledge."* The contradiction I have pointed out is characteristic not only of the positive solution of the problem of the "theory of knowledge" but indeed of every supposed solution, and hence also of the skeptical.

The opposite mistake from this skeptical reasoning is to be found in certain other arguments to which one might wish to call my attention in order to trace back my proof of the impossibility of a "theory of knowledge" to ideas that have long been known. I am thinking of the attacks on the "theory of knowledge" initiated by Hegel and Herbart and especially championed by Lotze and Busse; they all have in common the fact that they were launched in favor of dogmatism. Where the skeptical attacks prove too little, these prove too much in that they postulate the necessity of a dogmatic metaphysics—*a consequence that cannot be derived from the proofs I have offered.* Moreover, nothing can be decided by such vague arguments as, for example, the argument that one cannot swim before going into the water, or that cognition cannot cognize itself. In this way one could just as well prove the impossibility of philology with the assertion that one cannot use language with reference to language.

The alternatives of the "theory of knowledge" and dogmatism, i.e., of the necessity of verifying every cognition and the necessity of positing some judgments without any verification, are, to be sure, inevitable as long as one adheres to the already refuted presupposition that all cognitions are judgments. For on this presupposition one must necessarily extend the application of the principle of sufficient reason to *all cognitions whatsoever* and, on the other hand, confuse the obvious impossibility of verifying every cognition with the postulation of unverifiable *judgments*. If, however, one abandons the presupposition that every cognition is a judgment, the choice between a "theory of knowledge" and dogmatism disappears. The possibility then opens up of satisfying the postulate of the verification of all judgments without falling victim to the infinite regress of the "theory of knowledge."

The criterion of truth that we here use does not give rise to the contradiction that we have found in the concept of the "validity criterion." Indeed, the criterion of the truth of judgments cannot itself be a judgment, but it does not for that reason have to lie outside cognition; instead, it lies in immediate knowledge, which in its turn does not consist of judgments.

If philosophy wishes to be a science, it, like every science, will have to confine itself to this one task, the task of verifying judgments. It will only then assert its own scientific existence or, rather, will first be able to achieve it when, instead of setting itself above the competence of science and sitting in judgment on the rights and qualifications of the various sciences, it is satisfied to take over for treatment a particular field of knowledge alongside the other individual disciplines.

That this is possible and how we shall easily see if we call to mind the purpose the misinterpretation of which originally created the problem of the "theory of knowledge." If we disregard *proofs*, which only serve to trace judgments back to other judgments, and consider only the basic judgments, we find that these —unless they are analytic and have their ground in mere *concepts*—are verified by being traced back to *intuition* in accordance with the universal procedure in all special sciences. But, as Hume first pointed out, there are judgments where this means of verification fails, judgments that do not have their ground in intuition although they are not analytic: these are all the judgments through which we conceive a necessary connection between things. One such judgment is, for instance, the principle of causality. The verification of these judgments, which Kant called the "synthetic judgments evolved through mere concepts," is, indeed, the task to which metaphysicians have always, more or less gropingly, devoted their efforts but which Kant, through his generalization of the Humean problem, was the first to formulate scientifically. It is readily understandable that once the nature of these "metaphysical" judgments was clearly recognized, once the impossibility of tracing them back to the only recognized sources of knowledge—concept and intuition—was grasped, it was tempting (for lack of an immediate knowledge on which to ground them) to try to verify them through comparison with the object, i.e., through the "theory of knowledge."

Our rejection of this cast to the problem as an inadmissible misconstruction exposes Hume's original problem in its true significance. The possibility of verifying metaphysical judgments, and therewith the life or death of metaphysics as a science, depends on the solution of this problem. But it can easily be demonstrated that its solution can only be sought in *psychology*. We cannot develop the metaphysical judgments immediately from their source of knowledge in the way that geometry, for instance, can be developed from the intuition of space, for the nature and even the existence of this source of knowledge are precisely what are being questioned: this source is not readily at our disposal; rather, we must first *search* for it. The problem at hand, correctly understood, thus concerns the existence of a certain kind of cognition, namely, immediate metaphysical knowledge. This is first of all a *question of facts,* and consequently a question that can only be decided by way of *experience.* Secondly, the object whose factuality is in question is a *cognition;* and cognitions, whatever their object may be, are themselves only the object of *inner* experience. Therefore, the Hume-Kant problem can only be resolved through psychology, i.e., through the science of inner experience.

Now, what are the possible, that is, a priori conceivable, solutions of this problem?

Initially, the opinion is conceivable that the difficulty that gives rise to the problem only *seems* to exist, and that the so-called "metaphysical" judgments can actually, as the metaphysicians before Hume endeavored, be traced back to the then recognized sources of knowledge, i.e., mere reflection or intuition. Indeed, if we presuppose the completeness of the disjunction between reflection and intuition as sources of knowledge, any other way to verify the judgments in question is logically inconceivable.

If one chooses reflection as the source of knowledge of the metaphysical judgments, one arrives at metaphysical *logicism;* if intuition, metaphysical *mysticism.* If, however, one rejects both sources of knowledge for the metaphysical judgments, holding still to the exclusiveness of these two sources of knowledge, there remains only the conclusion that no source of knowledge exists as basis for the metaphysical judgments, that they are therefore altogether unverifiable, and hence are fraudulent assertions. This is the consequence of metaphysical *empiricism.*

These attempts at solution through metaphysical logicism, mysticism, and empiricism exhaust the logical possibilities available under the presupposition of the completeness of the disjunction between reflection and intuition as sources of knowledge. It has been generally assumed heretofore that therewith *all* the logically possible solutions of the problem have been exhausted. This would indeed be the case if the completeness of the disjunction between reflection and intuition as sources of knowledge were logically assured.

Now, it seems to be logically self-evident that a cognition that is not intuitive must arise from concepts and therefore from reflection, and vice versa, that a cognition we possess independently of reflection must pertain to intuition. This is true, to be sure, if we *define* intuition as nonreflective knowledge, but such a definition does not correspond to linguistic usage. According to general usage we understand "intuition" to mean a knowledge of which we are immediately conscious. But not every immediate cognition is necessarily a cognition of which we are immediately *conscious*. There is no contradiction in the assumption that a cognition that does not arise from reflection reaches our consciousness only through the mediation of reflection. Immediacy of cognition and immediacy of consciousness of the cognition are logically two different things. The illusion of the logical completeness of the disjunction between reflection and intuition as sources of knowledge arises only as a result of the confusion of these two concepts, in other words, as a result of the false conclusion of the immediacy of consciousness from the immediacy of cognition.

The demonstration of the logical incompleteness of this disjunction reveals to us a fourth possible solution of our problem. It consists in tracing back the metaphysical judgments to a cognition that belongs neither to reflection nor to intuition, that is, to a nonintuitive immediate cognition. I denote this solution, which follows from the criticism of the dogmatic disjunction of the sources of knowledge, as metaphysical *criticism*.

The disjunction, expanded by our indication of the possibility of a nonintuitive immediate cognition, is in its turn *logically* secured. Since thereby the completeness of the above-considered possibilities of solution is now guaranteed, we can turn to the further question of how we are to decide between these various attempts at solution, i.e., which of the various logically possible theories is psychologically correct. With this question we leave the realm of purely logical criticism and turn to the testimony of inner experience. And here we can avail ourselves of work done long ago.

Both the positive solutions possible under the dogmatic assumption of the completeness of the disjunction—metaphysical logicism and metaphysical mysticism—have already been refuted by Hume.

Logicism, such as formed the basis of scholastic metaphysics and which has been revived in the "theory of knowledge," breaks down on the psychological fact of the indirectness and emptiness of reflection. Reflection can analyze and elucidate cognitions elsewhere provided but cannot of itself creatively beget new cognitions, that is to say, it is a source only of analytic, but not of synthetic, judgments.

Metaphysical *mysticism*, such as forms the basis for neo-Platonic mysticism in its old and new forms, breaks down on the psychological fact of the original obscurity of metaphysical knowledge. There is no immediate obviousness in metaphysical truths; we cannot derive these cognitions from an "intellectual intuition"; they reach our consciousness only through thinking (reflection), through abstracting from the intuitively given content of empirical judgments.

If, then, we are not permitted to seek the source of the metaphysical judgments either in intuition or reflection, two ways are still open to us: either we can dispute altogether the existence of metaphysical knowledge; or we can abandon the assumption of the exclusiveness of reflection and intuition as sources of knowledge and assert the existence of nonintuitive immediate cognition.

Hume sought the basic fallacy of the theories he refuted in their assumption that we possess metaphysical cognition at all; in this way he was led to his negative attempt at solution and hence to metaphysical *empiricism*. His task then became not that of verifying the metaphysical judgments but that of explaining psychologically the illusion that calls forth these judgments, i.e., of explaining how the claim to knowledge asserted in these judgments is possible without presupposing an actual source of knowledge, merely as a product of the blind mechanism of the association of ideas. The question now arises whether this task is capable of fulfillment.

Hume believed that he could find the basis for the judgments that were the object of his problem in the psychological principle of the expectancy of similar cases. But he was not unaware of the difficulty to be encountered in basing this principle on the laws of association. Association explains only that event A reminds me of a previous event *B* connected with it, but not that I expect the reoccurrence of *B*. The remembered thought, as such, is only problematic, whereas expectation comprises an assertion which —whether it be one of certainty or only of probability—cannot be explained by association alone. Hume tried to overcome this difficulty by presenting the difference between problematic and assertoric notions as merely one of degree, basing *this* difference on a difference in the intensity of the clarity of the notions. On this supposition our recollection would, indeed, after sufficiently frequent reproduction, be able to pass over into an expectation merely through the effectiveness of the association. But this Humean hypothesis, that the difference between problematic and assertoric notions is only one of degree, contradicts the facts of self-observation. This is generally admitted today; and so Hume's attempted solution collapses.

It is easy so to generalize this criticism of Hume's theory that through it any empirical attempt at solution, whatever its nature, is excluded. The problem lies in the actual existence of certain judgments through which we conceive a necessary connection of things. What is important here is not the assertion that the merely problematic thought of a necessary connection, which is to be found in these judgments, cannot be explained through association. To be sure, every *connection of ideas* must be explicable by the laws of association. What we must explain here, however, is not a connection of ideas but the *idea of connection*. This is in its content an entirely new conception vis-à-vis the ideas of that which, in this idea, is thought of as connected; accordingly, it can never arise from these other ideas through mere association but presupposes a source of knowledge of its own.

The critical analysis of metaphysical logicism and mysticism shows us that this source of knowledge can lie neither in reflection nor in intuition. If we now consider the above psychological analysis of empiricism together with the critical analysis of both these other theories, we have proof of the correctness of the fourth theory, the only one that still remains, viz., *criticism*. The mere exclusion of the first two theories permitted us only the conclusion that, *if* we possess metaphysical knowledge at all, the existence of nonintuitive immediate knowledge must be assumed. But we were not yet able to claim that this condition is valid; rather, the possibility was still open to us of following Hume in the opposite direction and concluding, from the dogmatic disjunction of the sources of knowledge, that metaphysical knowledge is impossible. It is only after we have also refuted this empiristic consequence that we are able, in connection with the exclusion of metaphysical logicism and mysticism, to conclude the existence of nonintuitive immediate knowledge. We thus can, at the same time, supplement the proof of the logical incompleteness of the dogmatic disjunction with the proof of its psychological falsity.

At this juncture we perceive what we have gained from our previous logical analysis of the several possible solutions of the problem. In addition to the fact that this analysis at once precludes us from the contradictory attempt to find in the "theory of knowledge" a solution of the problem, it also prevented us from too hastily excluding from our range of choices what at first sight appeared to be a logically impossible course. The service that this analysis rendered us is all the more important since in our case the course that, by and large, has not even been considered heretofore is precisely the only one that really leads to a solution. Without this preparation through such a logical criticism one continually runs the danger of blinding oneself, through the deceptive illusion of the dogmatic disjunction, to the most obvious facts of self-observation. On the supposition of the completeness of this disjunction, as we have seen, the facts of the emptiness of reflection, the nonintuitive nature of metaphysical knowledge and the actual existence of metaphysical knowledge cannot be logically reconciled with one another because one of these facts always contradicts the consequences of the other two. And so—as, moreover, the history of philosophy bears in on us—without that critical analysis we are constantly driven hither and thither between these three equally necessary, but mutually contradictory, consequences. But the antinomy in which we thus become entangled is immediately resolved once we become aware of the prejudice that lies behind it, set aside all dogmatic suppositions, and look only the facts themselves in the eye.

We can accordingly epitomize the results of these critical observations as follows:

On the assumption of the exclusiveness of reflection and intuition as sources of knowledge, we have a choice only between metaphysical logicism, mysticism, and empiricism; that is to say, we have only the choice of contesting either the fact of the emptiness of reflection, or the fact of the nonintuitive nature of metaphysical knowledge, or the fact of the existence of metaphysical knowledge—or, finally, we may conclude from these three facts that nonintuitive immediate knowledge exists.

In conclusion, let us consider what we have gained in all this compared to the "theory of knowledge."

If we must admit the possibility of metaphysics, we still need a criterion by which to distinguish between legitimate and spurious metaphysical assertions. But here we are exposed to the difficulty that this criterion must itself be metaphysical in nature since we know it can lie neither in reflection nor in intuition.

The wish to escape this difficulty is the real reason why recourse had to be taken to the "theory of knowledge." For, since metaphysics can obviously no more contain in itself the basis of the validity of its judgments than can any other discipline, this basis had to be sought in another, higher discipline, which, however, in its turn could no more derive its content from mere reflection or intuition than metaphysics itself could. It is therefore not surprising that so far no one who has gone into this higher discipline has been able to disclose its origins.

But the embarrassment of which this enigmatic science is to relieve us is merely a consequence of the confusion of knowledge with judgment. If we discriminate between judgment and immediate knowledge, the fact that the ground of the validity of metaphysical judgments must itself be metaphysical in nature will not lead us to conclude that this ground itself must lie in metaphysical judgments, but we shall seek it in immediate cognition. In this immediate cognition, not in a higher discipline, lies the basis of metaphysical judgments.

To be sure, this immediate cognition is not intuition. And precisely here we see the really decisive reason why psychological critique is so fruitful for metaphysics. For even though we find the basis of metaphysical judgments in an immediate cognition, we do not become immediately conscious of this cognition in such a way as would enable us to compare it directly with the metaphysical judgments in order to verify them. Rather, in order to execute this verification, i.e., to trace back the metaphysical judgments to the immediate knowledge that forms their ground, we must first ingeniously bring this immediate knowledge to light and therefore make it the object of psychological investigation.

Hence we need a special science to verify metaphysical judgments. But this science is no "theory of knowledge": it does not itself contain the basis of metaphysical judgments but only serves to bring it to light. For this very reason, also, the empirical and psychological character of this science is entirely compatible with the rational and metaphysical nature of the propositions it is to verify. For the basis of the metaphysical propositions does not lie in the assertions of this psychological critique but in immediate metaphysical knowledge.

Perhaps we can best clarify this relation by drawing an analogy from critical mathematics. In geometric axiomatics is to be found the proposition of the unprovability of the parallel postulate. Here, then, we must distinguish between two propositions: proposition A, the parallel postulate, and proposition B, which states that proposition A cannot be proved. Now, proposition B can be proved. There is nothing paradoxical in this, because A is a proposition from the system of geometry, whereas B belongs only to critique. B does not contain the ground of A but simply has A as its object. The situation in the critique of the metaphysical propositions is altogether analogous. Let us take, for example, the principle of causality, which we shall call C. Then psychological critique proves proposition D: There exists a non-intuitive immediate cognition which contains the ground of C. C is a proposition from the system of metaphysics and as such is rational; D is a proposition from psychological critique and as such is empirical. D does not contain the ground of C but simply has C as its object.

Of course, this positive importance of psychology for the verification of metaphysics can only be asserted from the viewpoint of criticism. A logicistic or mystic metaphysics has no need of psychology. Nevertheless—and this should no longer be overlooked—psychology has a *negative* importance for every sort of metaphysics (and anti-metaphysics!), which manifests itself in the fact that every metaphysics—consciously or unconsciously—comprises a psychological preassumption regarding its source of knowledge, in view of which every metaphysics must submit to criticism through comparison with the psychological facts. In this general psychological criticism we are provided with a limiting principle, by the help of which, over and beyond logical criticism, we can at least exclude all those metaphysical doctrines, consistent in themselves, which stand from the very start in contradiction to psychological facts.

Herewith, also, the dispute is transferred to a field more accessible to scientific treatment, and in which it is possible to work on common problems according to a common method. Only after we have succeeded in making truly manifest the importance of the general logical and psychological criticism that we have been considering, can we hope to launch a program of cooperative and fruitful scientific endeavor in philosophy in the place of divisive and barren dogmatic quarrels.

INDEX

Explanation of certain terms is indicated by italicized figures.

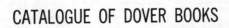

CATALOGUE OF DOVER BOOKS

Psychology

YOGA: A SCIENTIFIC EVALUATION, Kovoor T. Behanan. A complete reprinting of the book that for the first time gave Western readers a sane, scientific explanation and analysis of yoga. The author draws on controlled laboratory experiments and personal records of a year as a disciple of a yoga, to investigate yoga psychology, concepts of knowledge, physiology, "supernatural" phenomena, and the ability to tap the deepest human powers. In this study under the auspices of Yale University Institute of Human Relations, the strictest principles of physiological and psychological inquiry are followed throughout. Foreword by W. A. Miles, Yale University. 17 photographs. Glossary. Index. xx + 270pp. 5⅜ x 8. T505 Paperbound **$1.75**

CONDITIONED REFLEXES: AN INVESTIGATION OF THE PHYSIOLOGICAL ACTIVITIES OF THE CEREBRAL CORTEX, I. P. Pavlov. Full, authorized translation of Pavlov's own survey of his work in experimental psychology reviews entire course of experiments, summarizes conclusions, outlines psychological system based on famous "conditioned reflex" concept. Details of technical means used in experiments, observations on formation of conditioned reflexes, function of cerebral hemispheres, results of damage, nature of sleep, typology of nervous system, significance of experiments for human psychology. Trans. by Dr. G. V. Anrep, Cambridge Univ. 235-item bibliography. 18 figures. 445pp. 5⅜ x 8. S614 Paperbound **$2.25**

EXPLANATION OF HUMAN BEHAVIOUR, F. V. Smith. A major intermediate-level introduction to and criticism of 8 complete systems of the psychology of human behavior, with unusual emphasis on theory of investigation and methodology. Part I is an illuminating analysis of the problems involved in the explanation of observed phenomena, and the differing viewpoints on the nature of causality. Parts II and III are a closely detailed survey of the systems of McDougall, Gordon Allport, Lewin, the Gestalt group, Freud, Watson, Hull, and Tolman. Biographical notes. Bibliography of over 800 items. 2 indexes. 38 figures. xii + 460pp. 5½ x 8¾. T253 Clothbound **$6.00**

SEX IN PSYCHO-ANALYSIS (formerly CONTRIBUTIONS TO PSYCHO-ANALYSIS), S. Ferenczi. Written by an associate of Freud, this volume presents countless insights on such topics as impotence, transference, analysis and children, dreams, symbols, obscene words, masturbation and male homosexuality, paranoia and psycho-analysis, the sense of reality, hypnotism and therapy, and many others. Also includes full text of THE DEVELOPMENT OF PSYCHO-ANALYSIS by Ferenczi and Otto Rank. Two books bound as one. Total of 406pp. 5⅜ x 8. T324 Paperbound **$1.85**

BEYOND PSYCHOLOGY, Otto Rank. One of Rank's most mature contributions, focussing on the irrational basis of human behavior as a basic fact of our lives. The psychoanalytic techniques of myth analysis trace to their source the ultimates of human existence: fear of death, personality, the social organization, the need for love and creativity, etc. Dr. Rank finds them stemming from a common irrational source, man's fear of final destruction. A seminal work in modern psychology, this work sheds light on areas ranging from the concept of immortal soul to the sources of state power. 291pp. 5⅜ x 8. T485 Paperbound **$2.00**

ILLUSIONS AND DELUSIONS OF THE SUPERNATURAL AND THE OCCULT, D. H. Rawcliffe. Holds up to rational examination hundreds of persistent delusions including crystal gazing, automatic writing, table turning, mediumistic trances, mental healing, stigmata, lycanthropy, live burial, the Indian Rope Trick, spiritualism, dowsing, telepathy, clairvoyance, ghosts, ESP, etc. The author explains and exposes the mental and physical deceptions involved, making this not only an exposé of supernatural phenomena, but a valuable exposition of characteristic types of abnormal psychology. Originally titled "The Psychology of the Occult." 14 illustrations. Index. 551pp. 5⅜ x 8. T503 Paperbound **$2.00**

THE PRINCIPLES OF PSYCHOLOGY, William James. The full long-course, unabridged, of one of the great classics of Western literature and science. Wonderfully lucid descriptions of human mental activity, the stream of thought, consciousness, time perception, memory, imagination, emotions, reason, abnormal phenomena, and similar topics. Original contributions are integrated with the work of such men as Berkeley, Binet, Mills, Darwin, Hume, Kant, Royce, Schopenhauer, Spinoza, Locke, Descartes, Galton, Wundt, Lotze, Herbart, Fechner, and scores of others. All contrasting interpretations of mental phenomena are examined in detail — introspective analysis, philosophical interpretation, and experimental research. "A classic," JOURNAL OF CONSULTING PSYCHOLOGY. "The main lines are as valid as ever," PSYCHO-ANALYTICAL QUARTERLY. "Standard reading . . . a classic of interpretation," PSYCHIATRIC QUARTERLY. 94 illustrations. 1408pp. 2 volumes. 5⅜ x 8. Vol. 1, T381 Paperbound **$2.50** Vol. 2, T382 Paperbound **$2.50**

THE DYNAMICS OF THERAPY IN A CONTROLLED RELATIONSHIP, Jessie Taft. One of the most important works in literature of child psychology, out of print for 25 years. Outstanding disciple of Rank describes all aspects of relationship or Rankian therapy through concise, simple elucidation of theory underlying her actual contacts with two seven-year olds. Therapists, social caseworkers, psychologists, counselors, and laymen who work with children will all find this important work an invaluable summation of method, theory of child psychology. xix + 296pp. 5⅜ x 8. T325 Paperbound **$1.75**

The more difficult books are indicated by an asterisk (*)

Books Explaining Science and Mathematics

WHAT IS SCIENCE?, N. Campbell. The role of experiment and measurement, the function of mathematics, the nature of scientific laws, the difference between laws and theories, the limitations of science, and many similarly provocative topics are treated clearly and without technicalities by an eminent scientist. "Still an excellent introduction to scientific philosophy," H. Margenau in PHYSICS TODAY. "A first-rate primer . . . deserves a wide audience," SCIENTIFIC AMERICAN. 192pp. 5⅜ x 8.   S43 Paperbound **$1.25**

THE NATURE OF PHYSICAL THEORY, P. W. Bridgman. A Nobel Laureate's clear, non-technical lectures on difficulties and paradoxes connected with frontier research on the physical sciences. Concerned with such central concepts as thought, logic, mathematics, relativity, probability, wave mechanics, etc. he analyzes the contributions of such men as Newton, Einstein, Bohr, Heisenberg, and many others. "Lucid and entertaining . . . recommended to anyone who wants to get some insight into current philosophies of science," THE NEW PHILOSOPHY. Index. xi + 138pp. 5⅜ x 8.   S33 Paperbound **$1.25**

EXPERIMENT AND THEORY IN PHYSICS, Max Born. A Nobel Laureate examines the nature of experiment and theory in theoretical physics and analyzes the advances made by the great physicists of our day: Heisenberg, Einstein, Bohr, Planck, Dirac, and others. The actual process of creation is detailed step-by-step by one who participated. A fine examination of the scientific method at work. 44pp. 5⅜ x 8.   S308 Paperbound **75¢**

THE PSYCHOLOGY OF INVENTION IN THE MATHEMATICAL FIELD, J. Hadamard. The reports of such men as Descartes, Pascal, Einstein, Poincaré, and others are considered in this investigation of the method of idea-creation in mathematics and other sciences and the thinking process in general. How do ideas originate? What is the role of the unconscious? What is Poincaré's forgetting hypothesis? are some of the fascinating questions treated. A penetrating analysis of Einstein's thought processes concludes the book. xiii + 145pp. 5⅜ x 8.   T107 Paperbound **$1.25**

THE NATURE OF LIGHT AND COLOUR IN THE OPEN AIR, M. Minnaert. Why are shadows sometimes blue, sometimes green, or other colors depending on the light and surroundings? What causes mirages? Why do multiple suns and moons appear in the sky? Professor Minnaert explains these unusual phenomena and hundreds of others in simple, easy-to-understand terms based on optical laws and the properties of light and color. No mathematics is required but artists, scientists, students, and everyone fascinated by these "tricks" of nature will find thousands of useful and amazing pieces of information. Hundreds of observational experiments are suggested which require no special equipment. 200 illustrations; 42 photos. xvi + 362pp. 5⅜ x 8.   T196 Paperbound **$1.95**

THE UNIVERSE OF LIGHT, W. Bragg. Sir William Bragg, Nobel Laureate and great modern physicist, is also well known for his powers of clear exposition. Here he analyzes all aspects of light for the layman: lenses, reflection, refraction, the optics of vision, x-rays, the photoelectric effect, etc. He tells you what causes the color of spectra, rainbows, and soap bubbles, how magic mirrors work, and much more. Dozens of simple experiments are described. Preface. Index. 199 line drawings and photographs, including 2 full-page color plates. x + 283pp. 5⅜ x 8.   T538 Paperbound **$1.85**

SOAP-BUBBLES: THEIR COLOURS AND THE FORCES THAT MOULD THEM, C. V. Boys. For continuing popularity and validity as scientific primer, few books can match this volume of easily-followed experiments, explanations. Lucid exposition of complexities of liquid films, surface tension and related phenomena, bubbles' reaction to heat, motion, music, magnetic fields. Experiments with capillary attraction, soap bubbles on frames, composite bubbles, liquid cylinders and jets, bubbles other than soap, etc. Wonderful introduction to scientific method, natural laws that have many ramifications in areas of modern physics. Only complete edition in print. New Introduction by S. Z. Lewin, New York University. 83 illustrations; 1 full-page color plate. xii + 190pp. 5⅜ x 8½.   T542 Paperbound **95¢**

CATALOGUE OF DOVER BOOKS

THE STORY OF X-RAYS FROM RONTGEN TO ISOTOPES, A. R. Bleich, M.D. This book, by a member of the American College of Radiology, gives the scientific explanation of x-rays, their applications in medicine, industry and art, and their danger (and that of atmospheric radiation) to the individual and the species. You learn how radiation therapy is applied against cancer, how x-rays diagnose heart disease and other ailments, how they are used to examine mummies for information on diseases of early societies, and industrial materials for hidden weaknesses. 54 illustrations show x-rays of flowers, bones, stomach, gears with flaws, etc. 1st publication. Index. xix + 186pp. 5⅜ x 8.　　　　　　　　　　　　**T622 Paperbound $1.35**

SPINNING TOPS AND GYROSCOPIC MOTION, John Perry. A classic elementary text of the dynamics of rotation — the behavior and use of rotating bodies such as gyroscopes and tops. In simple, everyday English you are shown how quasi-rigidity is induced in discs of paper, smoke rings, chains, etc., by rapid motions; why a gyrostat falls and why a top rises; precession; how the earth's motion affects climate; and many other phenomena. Appendix on practical use of gyroscopes. 62 figures. 128pp. 5⅜ x 8.　　　　　　　**T416 Paperbound $1.00**

SNOW CRYSTALS, W. A. Bentley, M. J. Humphreys. For almost 50 years W. A. Bentley photographed snow flakes in his laboratory in Jericho, Vermont; in 1931 the American Meteorological Society gathered together the best of his work, some 2400 photographs of snow flakes, plus a few ice flowers, windowpane frosts, dew, frozen rain, and other ice formations. Pictures were selected for beauty and scientific value. A very valuable work to anyone in meteorology, cryology; most interesting to layman; extremely useful for artist who wants beautiful, crystalline designs. All copyright free. Unabridged reprint of 1931 edition. 2453 illustrations. 227pp. 8 x 10½.　　　　　　　　　　　　　　　**T287 Paperbound $3.00**

A DOVER SCIENCE SAMPLER, edited by George Barkin. A collection of brief, non-technical passages from 44 Dover Books Explaining Science for the enjoyment of the science-minded browser. Includes work of Bertrand Russell, Poincaré, Laplace, Max Born, Galileo, Newton; material on physics, mathematics, metallurgy, anatomy, astronomy, chemistry, etc. You will be fascinated by Martin Gardner's analysis of the sincere pseudo-scientist, Moritz's account of Newton's absentmindedness, Bernard's examples of human vivisection, etc. Illustrations from the Diderot Pictorial Encyclopedia and De Re Metallica. 64 pages.　　　　**FREE**

THE STORY OF ATOMIC THEORY AND ATOMIC ENERGY, J. G. Feinberg. A broader approach to subject of nuclear energy and its cultural implications than any other similar source. Very readable, informal, completely non-technical text. Begins with first atomic theory, 600 B.C. and carries you through the work of Mendelejeff, Röntgen, Madame Curie, to Einstein's equation and the A-bomb. New chapter goes through thermonuclear fission, binding energy, other events up to 1959. Radioactive decay and radiation hazards, future benefits, work of Bohr, moderns, hundreds more topics. "Deserves special mention . . . not only authoritative but thoroughly popular in the best sense of the word," Saturday Review. Formerly, "The Atom Story." Expanded with new chapter. Three appendixes. Index. 34 illustrations. vii + 243pp. 5⅜ x 8.　　　　　　　　　　　　　　　　　　　**T625 Paperbound $1.45**

THE STRANGE STORY OF THE QUANTUM, AN ACCOUNT FOR THE GENERAL READER OF THE GROWTH OF IDEAS UNDERLYING OUR PRESENT ATOMIC KNOWLEDGE, B. Hoffmann. Presents lucidly and expertly, with barest amount of mathematics, the problems and theories which led to modern quantum physics. Dr. Hoffmann begins with the closing years of the 19th century, when certain trifling discrepancies were noticed, and with illuminating analogies and examples takes you through the brilliant concepts of Planck, Einstein, Pauli, Broglie, Bohr, Schroedinger, Heisenberg, Dirac, Sommerfeld, Feynman, etc. This edition includes a new, long postscript carrying the story through 1958. "Of the books attempting an account of the history and contents of our modern atomic physics which have come to my attention, this is the best," H. Margenau, Yale University, in "American Journal of Physics." 32 tables and line illustrations. Index. 275pp. 5⅜ x 8.　　　　　　　　　　　　　　**T518 Paperbound $1.50**

SPACE AND TIME, E. Borel. Written by a versatile mathematician of world renown with his customary lucidity and precision, this introduction to relativity for the layman presents scores of examples, analogies, and illustrations that open up new ways of thinking about space and time. It covers abstract geometry and geographical maps, continuity and topology, the propagation of light, the special theory of relativity, the general theory of relativity, theoretical researches, and much more. Mathematical notes. 2 Indexes. 4 Appendices. 15 figures. xvi + 243pp. 5⅜ x 8.　　　　　　　　　　　　　　　　　　**T592 Paperbound $1.45**

FROM EUCLID TO EDDINGTON: A STUDY OF THE CONCEPTIONS OF THE EXTERNAL WORLD, Sir Edmund Whittaker. A foremost British scientist traces the development of theories of natural philosophy from the western rediscovery of Euclid to Eddington, Einstein, Dirac, etc. The inadequacy of classical physics is contrasted with present day attempts to understand the physical world through relativity, non-Euclidean geometry, space curvature, wave mechanics, etc. 5 major divisions of examination: Space; Time and Movement; the Concepts of Classical Physics; the Concepts of Quantum Mechanics; the Eddington Universe. 212pp. 5⅜ x 8.　　　　　　　　　　　　　　　　　　　　　　　　　**T491 Paperbound $1.35**

CATALOGUE OF DOVER BOOKS

*THE EVOLUTION OF SCIENTIFIC THOUGHT FROM NEWTON TO EINSTEIN, A. d'Abro. A detailed account of the evolution of classical physics into modern relativistic theory and the concomitant changes in scientific methodology. The breakdown of classical physics in the face of non-Euclidean geometry and the electromagnetic equations is carefully discussed and then an exhaustive analysis of Einstein's special and general theories of relativity and their implications is given. Newton, Riemann, Weyl, Lorentz, Planck, Maxwell, and many others are considered. A non-technical explanation of space, time, electromagnetic waves, etc. as understood today. "Model of semi-popular exposition," NEW REPUBLIC. 21 diagrams. 482pp. 5⅜ x 8.
T2 Paperbound $2.00

EINSTEIN'S THEORY OF RELATIVITY, Max Born. Nobel Laureate explains Einstein's special and general theories of relativity, beginning with a thorough review of classical physics in simple, non-technical language. Exposition of Einstein's work discusses concept of simultaneity, kinematics, relativity of arbitrary motions, the space-time continuum, geometry of curved surfaces, etc., steering middle course between vague popularizations and complex scientific presentations. 1962 edition revised by author takes into account latest findings, predictions of theory and implications for cosmology, indicates what is being sought in unified field theory. Mathematics very elementary, illustrative diagrams and experiments informative but simple. Revised 1962 edition. Revised by Max Born, assisted by Gunther Leibfried and Walter Biem. Index. 143 illustrations. vii + 376pp. 5⅜ x 8.
S769 Paperbound $2.00

PHILOSOPHY AND THE PHYSICISTS, L. Susan Stebbing. A philosopher examines the philosophical aspects of modern science, in terms of a lively critical attack on the ideas of Jeans and Eddington. Such basic questions are treated as the task of science, causality, determinism, probability, consciousness, the relation of the world of physics to the world of everyday experience. The author probes the concepts of man's smallness before an inscrutable universe, the tendency to idealize mathematical construction, unpredictability theorems and human freedom, the supposed opposition between 19th century determinism and modern science, and many others. Introduces many thought-stimulating ideas about the implications of modern physical concepts. xvi + 295pp. 5⅜ x 8.
T480 Paperbound $1.65

THE RESTLESS UNIVERSE, Max Born. A remarkably lucid account by a Nobel Laureate of recent theories of wave mechanics, behavior of gases, electrons and ions, waves and particles, electronic structure of the atom, nuclear physics, and similar topics. "Much more thorough and deeper than most attempts . . . easy and delightful," CHEMICAL AND ENGINEERING NEWS. Special feature: 7 animated sequences of 60 figures each showing such phenomena as gas molecules in motion, the scattering of alpha particles, etc. 11 full-page plates of photographs. Total of nearly 600 illustrations. 351pp. 6⅛ x 9¼.
T412 Paperbound $2.00

THE COMMON SENSE OF THE EXACT SCIENCES, W. K. Clifford. For 70 years a guide to the basic concepts of scientific and mathematical thought. Acclaimed by scientists and laymen alike, it offers a wonderful insight into concepts such as the extension of meaning of symbols, characteristics of surface boundaries, properties of plane figures, measurement of quantities, vectors, the nature of position, bending of space, motion, mass and force, and many others. Prefaces by Bertrand Russell and Karl Pearson. Critical introduction by James Newman. 130 figures. 249pp. 5⅜ x 8.
T61 Paperbound $1.60

MATTER AND LIGHT, THE NEW PHYSICS, Louis de Broglie. Non-technical explanations by a Nobel laureate of electro-magnetic theory, relativity, matter, light and radiation, wave mechanics, quantum physics, philosophy of science, and similar topics. This is one of the simplest yet most accurate introductions to the work of men like Planck, Einstein, Bohr, and others. Only 2 of the 21 chapters require a knowledge of mathematics. 300pp. 5⅜ x 8.
T35 Paperbound $1.75

SCIENCE, THEORY AND MAN, Erwin Schrödinger. This is a complete and unabridged reissue of SCIENCE AND THE HUMAN TEMPERAMENT plus an additional essay: "What Is an Elementary Particle?" Nobel Laureate Schrödinger discusses such topics as nature of scientific method, the nature of science, chance and determinism, science and society, conceptual models for physical entities, elementary particles and wave mechanics. Presentation is popular and may be followed by most people with little or no scientific training. "Fine practical preparation for a time when laws of nature, human institutions . . . are undergoing a critical examination without parallel," Waldemar Kaempffert, N. Y. TIMES. 192pp. 5⅜ x 8.
T428 Paperbound $1.35

CONCERNING THE NATURE OF THINGS, Sir William Bragg. The Nobel Laureate physicist in his Royal Institute Christmas Lectures explains such diverse phenomena as the formation of crystals, how uranium is transmuted to lead, the way X-rays work, why a spinning ball travels in a curved path, the reason why bubbles bounce from each other, and many other scientific topics that are seldom explained in simple terms. No scientific background needed—book is easy enough that any intelligent adult or youngster can understand it. Unabridged. 32pp. of photos; 57 figures. xii + 232pp. 5⅜ x 8.
T31 Paperbound $1.35

*THE RISE OF THE NEW PHYSICS (formerly THE DECLINE OF MECHANISM), A. d'Abro. This authoritative and comprehensive 2 volume exposition is unique in scientific publishing. Written for intelligent readers not familiar with higher mathematics, it is the only thorough explanation in non-technical language of modern mathematical-physical theory. Combining both history and exposition, it ranges from classical Newtonian concepts up through the electronic theories of Dirac and Heisenberg, the statistical mechanics of Fermi, and Einstein's relativity theories. "A must for anyone doing serious study in the physical sciences," J. OF FRANKLIN INST. 97 illustrations. 991pp. 2 volumes.
T3 Vol. 1, Paperbound $2.00
T4 Vol. 2, Paperbound $2.00

CATALOGUE OF DOVER BOOKS

SCIENCE AND HYPOTHESIS, Henri Poincaré. Creative psychology in science. How such concepts as number, magnitude, space, force, classical mechanics were developed and how the modern scientist uses them in his thought. Hypothesis in physics, theories of modern physics. Introduction by Sir James Larmor. "Few mathematicians have had the breadth of vision of Poincaré, and none is his superior in the gift of clear exposition," E. T. Bell. Index. 272pp. 5⅜ x 8.
S221 Paperbound **$1.35**

THE VALUE OF SCIENCE, Henri Poincaré. Many of the most mature ideas of the "last scientific universalist" conveyed with charm and vigor for both the beginning student and the advanced worker. Discusses the nature of scientific truth, whether order is innate in the universe or imposed upon it by man, logical thought versus intuition (relating to mathematics through the works of Weierstrass, Lie, Klein, Riemann), time and space (relativity, psychological time, simultaneity), Hertz's concept of force, interrelationship of mathematical physics to pure math, values within disciplines of Maxwell, Carnot, Mayer, Newton, Lorentz, etc. Index. iii + 147pp. 5⅜ x 8.
S469 Paperbound **$1.35**

THE SKY AND ITS MYSTERIES, E. A. Beet. One of the most lucid books on the mysteries of the universe; covers history of astronomy from earliest observations to modern theories of expanding universe, source of stellar energy, birth of planets, origin of moon craters, possibilities of life on other planets. Discusses effects of sunspots on weather; distance, age of stars; methods and tools of astronomers; much more. Expert and fascinating. "Eminently readable book," London Times. Bibliography. Over 50 diagrams, 12 full-page plates. Fold-out star map. Introduction. Index. 238pp. 5¼ x 7½.
T627 Clothbound **$3.50**

OUT OF THE SKY: AN INTRODUCTION TO METEORITICS, H. H. Nininger. A non-technical yet comprehensive introduction to the young science of meteoritics: all aspects of the arrival of cosmic matter on our planet from outer space and the reaction and alteration of this matter in the terrestrial environment. Essential facts and major theories presented by one of the world's leading experts. Covers ancient reports of meteors; modern systematic investigations; fireball clusters; meteorite showers; tektites; planetoidal encounters; etc. 52 full-page plates with over 175 photographs. 22 figures. Bibliography and references. Index. viii + 336pp. 5⅜ x 8.
T519 Paperbound **$1.85**

THE REALM OF THE NEBULAE, E. Hubble. One of great astronomers of our day records his formulation of concept of "island universes." Covers velocity-distance relationship; classification, nature, distances, general types of nebulae; cosmological theories. A fine introduction to modern theories for layman. No math needed. New introduction by A. Sandage. 55 illustrations, photos. Index. iv + 201pp. 5⅜ x 8.
S455 Paperbound **$1.50**

AN ELEMENTARY SURVEY OF CELESTIAL MECHANICS, Y. Ryabov. Elementary exposition of gravitational theory and celestial mechanics. Historical introduction and coverage of basic principles, including: the ecliptic, the orbital plane, the 2- and 3-body problems, the discovery of Neptune, planetary rotation, the length of the day, the shapes of galaxies, satellites (detailed treatment of Sputnik I), etc. First American reprinting of successful Russian popular exposition. Follow actual methods of astrophysicists with only high school math! Appendix. 58 figures. 165pp. 5⅜ x 8.
T756 Paperbound **$1.25**

GREAT IDEAS AND THEORIES OF MODERN COSMOLOGY, Jagjit Singh. Companion volume to author's popular "Great Ideas of Modern Mathematics" (Dover, $1.55). The best non-technical survey of post-Einstein attempts to answer perhaps unanswerable questions of origin, age of Universe, possibility of life on other worlds, etc. Fundamental theories of cosmology and cosmogony recounted, explained, evaluated in light of most recent data: Einstein's concepts of relativity, space-time; Milne's a priori world-system; astrophysical theories of Jeans, Eddington; Hoyle's "continuous creation;" contributions of dozens more scientists. A faithful, comprehensive critical summary of complex material presented in an extremely well-written text intended for laymen. Original publication. Index. xii + 276pp. 5⅜ x 8½.
T925 Paperbound **$1.85**

BASIC ELECTRICITY, Bureau of Naval Personnel. Very thorough, easily followed course in basic electricity for beginner, layman, or intermediate student. Begins with simplest definitions, presents coordinated, systematic coverage of basic theory and application: conductors, insulators, static electricity, magnetism, production of voltage, Ohm's law, direct current series and parallel circuits, wiring techniques, electromagnetism, alternating current, capacitance and inductance, measuring instruments, etc.; application to electrical machines such as alternating and direct current generators, motors, transformers, magnetic magnifiers, etc. Each chapter contains problems to test progress; answers at rear. No math needed beyond algebra. Appendices on signs, formulas, etc. 345 illustrations. 448pp. 7½ x 10.
S973 Paperbound **$2.95**

ELEMENTARY METALLURGY AND METALLOGRAPHY, A. M. Shrager. An introduction to common metals and alloys; stress is upon steel and iron, but other metals and alloys also covered. All aspects of production, processing, working of metals. Designed for student who wishes to enter metallurgy, for bright high school or college beginner, layman who wants background on extremely important industry. Questions, at ends of chapters, many microphotographs, glossary. Greatly revised 1961 edition. 195 illustrations, tables. ix + 389pp. 5⅜ x 8.
S138 Paperbound **$2.25**

CATALOGUE OF DOVER BOOKS

BRIDGES AND THEIR BUILDERS, D. B. Steinman & S. R. Watson. Engineers, historians, and every person who has ever been fascinated by great spans will find this book an endless source of information and interest. Greek and Roman structures, Medieval bridges, modern classics such as the Brooklyn Bridge, and the latest developments in the science are retold by one of the world's leading authorities on bridge design and construction. BRIDGES AND THEIR BUILDERS is the only comprehensive and accurate semi-popular history of these important measures of progress in print. New, greatly revised, enlarged edition. 23 photos; 26 line-drawings. Index. xvii + 401pp. 5⅜ x 8. **T431 Paperbound $2.00**

FAMOUS BRIDGES OF THE WORLD, D. B. Steinman. An up-to-the-minute new edition of a book that explains the fascinating drama of how the world's great bridges came to be built. The author, designer of the famed Mackinac bridge, discusses bridges from all periods and all parts of the world, explaining their various types of construction, and describing the problems their builders faced. Although primarily for youngsters, this cannot fail to interest readers of all ages. 48 illustrations in the text. 23 photographs. 99pp. 6⅛ x 9¼. **T161 Paperbound $1.00**

HOW DO YOU USE A SLIDE RULE? by A. A. Merrill. A step-by-step explanation of the slide rule that presents the fundamental rules clearly enough for the non-mathematician to understand. Unlike most instruction manuals, this work concentrates on the two most important operations: multiplication and division. 10 easy lessons, each with a clear drawing, for the reader who has difficulty following other expositions. 1st publication. Index. 2 Appendices. 10 illustrations. 78 problems, all with answers. vi + 36 pp. 6⅛ x 9¼. **T62 Paperbound 60¢**

HOW TO CALCULATE QUICKLY, H. Sticker. A tried and true method for increasing your "number sense" — the ability to see relationships between numbers and groups of numbers. Addition, subtraction, multiplication, division, fractions, and other topics are treated through techniques not generally taught in schools: left to right multiplication, division by inspection, etc. This is not a collection of tricks which work only on special numbers, but a detailed well-planned course, consisting of over 9,000 problems that you can work in spare moments. It is excellent for anyone who is inconvenienced by slow computational skills. 5 or 10 minutes of this book daily will double or triple your calculation speed. 9,000 problems, answers. 256pp. 5⅜ x 8. **T295 Paperbound $1.00**

MATHEMATICAL FUN, GAMES AND PUZZLES, Jack Frohlichstein. A valuable service for parents of children who have trouble with math, for teachers in need of a supplement to regular upper elementary and junior high math texts (each section is graded—easy, average, difficult —for ready adaptation to different levels of ability), and for just anyone who would like to develop basic skills in an informal and entertaining manner. The author combines ten years of experience as a junior high school math teacher with a method that uses puzzles and games to introduce the basic ideas and operations of arithmetic. Stress on everyday uses of math: banking, stock market, personal budgets, insurance, taxes. Intellectually stimulating and practical, too. 418 problems and diversions with answers. Bibliography. 120 illustrations. xix + 306pp. 5⅝ x 8½. **T789 Paperbound $1.75**

GREAT IDEAS OF MODERN MATHEMATICS: THEIR NATURE AND USE, Jagjit Singh. Reader with only high school math will understand main mathematical ideas of modern physics, astronomy, genetics, psychology, evolution, etc. better than many who use them as tools, but comprehend little of their basic structure. Author uses his wide knowledge of non-mathematical fields in brilliant exposition of differential equations, matrices, group theory, logic, statistics, problems of mathematical foundations, imaginary numbers, vectors, etc. Original publication. 2 appendixes. 2 indexes. 65 illustr. 322pp. 5⅜ x 8. **S587 Paperbound $1.75**

*MATHEMATICS IN ACTION, O. G. Sutton. Everyone with a command of high school algebra will find this book one of the finest possible introductions to the application of mathematics to physical theory. Ballistics, numerical analysis, waves and wavelike phenomena, Fourier series, group concepts, fluid flow and aerodynamics, statistical measures, and meteorology are discussed with unusual clarity. Some calculus and differential equations theory is developed by the author for the reader's help in the more difficult sections. 88 figures. Index. viii + 236pp. 5⅜ x 8. **T440 Clothbound $3.50**

*INTRODUCTION TO SYMBOLIC LOGIC AND ITS APPLICATIONS, Rudolph Carnap. One of the clearest, most comprehensive, and rigorous introductions to modern symbolic logic, by perhaps its greatest living master. Not merely elementary theory, but demonstrated applications in mathematics, physics, and biology. Symbolic languages of various degrees of complexity are analyzed, and one constructed. "A creation of the rank of a masterpiece," Zentralblatt für Mathematik und Ihre Grenzgebiete. Over 300 exercises. 5 figures. Bibliography. Index. xvi + 241pp. 5⅜ x 8. **S453 Paperbound $1.85**

*HIGHER MATHEMATICS FOR STUDENTS OF CHEMISTRY AND PHYSICS, J. W. Mellor. Not abstract, but practical, drawing its problems from familiar laboratory material, this book covers theory and application of differential calculus, analytic geometry, functions with singularities, integral calculus, infinite series, solution of numerical equations, differential equations, Fourier's theorem and extensions, probability and the theory of errors, calculus of variations, determinants, etc. "If the reader is not familiar with this book, it will repay him to examine it," CHEM. & ENGINEERING NEWS. 800 problems. 189 figures. 2 appendices; 30 tables of integrals, probability functions, etc. Bibliography. xxi + 641pp. 5⅜ x 8. **S193 Paperbound $2.25**

CATALOGUE OF DOVER BOOKS

THE FOURTH DIMENSION SIMPLY EXPLAINED, edited by Henry P. Manning. Originally written as entries in contest sponsored by "Scientific American," then published in book form, these 22 essays present easily understood explanations of how the fourth dimension may be studied, the relationship of non-Euclidean geometry to the fourth dimension, analogies to three-dimensional space, some fourth-dimensional absurdities and curiosities, possible measurements and forms in the fourth dimension. In general, a thorough coverage of many of the simpler properties of fourth-dimensional space. Multi-points of view on many of the most important aspects are valuable aid to comprehension. Introduction by Dr. Henry P. Manning gives proper emphasis to points in essays, more advanced account of fourth-dimensional geometry. 82 figures. 251pp. 5⅜ x 8. T711 Paperbound $1.35

TRIGONOMETRY REFRESHER FOR TECHNICAL MEN, A. A. Klaf. A modern question and answer text on plane and spherical trigonometry. Part I covers plane trigonometry: angles, quadrants, trigonometrical functions, graphical representation, interpolation, equations, logarithms, solution of triangles, slide rules, etc. Part II discusses applications to navigation, surveying, elasticity, architecture, and engineering. Small angles, periodic functions, vectors, polar coordinates, De Moivre's theorem, fully covered. Part III is devoted to spherical trigonometry and the solution of spherical triangles, with applications to terrestrial and astronomical problems. Special time-savers for numerical calculation. 913 questions answered for you! 1738 problems; answers to odd numbers. 494 figures. 14 pages of functions, formulae. Index. x + 629pp. 5⅜ x 8. T371 Paperbound $2.00

CALCULUS REFRESHER FOR TECHNICAL MEN. A. A. Klaf. Not an ordinary textbook but a unique refresher for engineers, technicians, and students. An examination of the most important aspects of differential and integral calculus by means of 756 key questions. Part I covers simple differential calculus: constants, variables, functions, increments, derivatives, logarithms, curvature, etc. Part II treats fundamental concepts of integration: inspection, substitution, transformation, reduction, areas and volumes, mean value, successive and partial integration, double and triple integration. Stresses practical aspects! A 50 page section gives applications to civil and nautical engineering, electricity, stress and strain, elasticity, industrial engineering, and similar fields. 756 questions answered. 556 problems; solutions to odd numbers. 36 pages of constants, formulae. Index. v + 431pp. 5⅜ x 8. T370 Paperbound $2.00

PROBABILITIES AND LIFE, Emile Borel. One of the leading French mathematicians of the last 100 years makes use of certain results of mathematics of probabilities and explains a number of problems that for the most part, are related to everyday living or to illness and death: computation of life expectancy tables, chances of recovery from various diseases, probabilities of job accidents, weather predictions, games of chance, and so on. Emphasis on results not processes, though some indication is made of mathematical proofs. Simple in style, free of technical terminology, limited in scope to everyday situations, it is comprehensible to laymen, fine reading for beginning students of probability. New English translation. Index. Appendix. vi + 87pp. 5⅜ x 8½. T121 Paperbound $1.00

POPULAR SCIENTIFIC LECTURES, Hermann von Helmholtz. 7 lucid expositions by a pre-eminent scientific mind: "The Physiological Causes of Harmony in Music," "On the Relation of Optics to Painting," "On the Conservation of Force," "On the Interaction of Natural Forces," "On Goethe's Scientific Researches" into theory of color, "On the Origin and Significance of Geometric Axioms," "On Recent Progress in the Theory of Vision." Written with simplicity of expression, stripped of technicalities, these are easy to understand and delightful reading for anyone interested in science or looking for an introduction to serious study of acoustics or optics. Introduction by Professor Morris Kline, Director, Division of Electromagnetic Research, New York University, contains astute, impartial evaluations. Selected from "Popular Lectures on Scientific Subjects," 1st and 2nd series. xii + 286pp. 5⅜ x 8½. T799 Paperbound $1.45

SCIENCE AND METHOD, Henri Poincaré. Procedure of scientific discovery, methodology, experiment, idea-germination—the intellectual processes by which discoveries come into being. Most significant and most interesting aspects of development, application of ideas. Chapters cover selection of facts, chance, mathematical reasoning, mathematics, and logic; Whitehead, Russell, Cantor; the new mechanics, etc. 288pp. 5⅜ x 8. S222 Paperbound $1.35

HEAT AND ITS WORKINGS, Morton Mott-Smith, Ph.D. An unusual book; to our knowledge the only middle-level survey of this important area of science. Explains clearly such important concepts as physiological sensation of heat and Weber's law, measurement of heat, evolution of thermometer, nature of heat, expansion and contraction of solids, Boyle's law, specific heat. BTU's and calories, evaporation, Andrews's isothermals, radiation, the relation of heat to light, many more topics inseparable from other aspects of physics. A wide, non-mathematical yet thorough explanation of basic ideas, theories, phenomena for laymen and beginning scientists illustrated by experiences of daily life. Bibliography. 50 illustrations. x + 165pp. 5⅜ x 8½. T978 Paperbound $1.00

History of Science and Mathematics

THE STUDY OF THE HISTORY OF MATHEMATICS, THE STUDY OF THE HISTORY OF SCIENCE, G. Sarton. Two books bound as one. Each volume contains a long introduction to the methods and philosophy of each of these historical fields, covering the skills and sympathies of the historian, concepts of history of science, psychology of idea-creation, and the purpose of history of science. Prof. Sarton also provides more than 80 pages of classified bibliography. Complete and unabridged. Indexed. 10 illustrations. 188pp. 5⅜ x 8. T240 Paperbound **$1.25**

A HISTORY OF PHYSICS, Florian Cajori, Ph.D. First written in 1899, thoroughly revised in 1929, this is still best entry into antecedents of modern theories. Precise non-mathematical discussion of ideas, theories, techniques, apparatus of each period from Greeks to 1920's, analyzing within each period basic topics of matter, mechanics, light, electricity and magnetism, sound, atomic theory, etc. Stress on modern developments, from early 19th century to present. Written with critical eye on historical development, significance. Provides most of needed historical background for student of physics. Reprint of second (1929) edition. Index. Bibliography in footnotes. 16 figures. xv + 424pp. 5⅜ x 8. T970 Paperbound **$2.00**

A HISTORY OF ASTRONOMY FROM THALES TO KEPLER, J. L. E. Dreyer. Formerly titled A HISTORY OF PLANETARY SYSTEMS FROM THALES TO KEPLER. This is the only work in English which provides a detailed history of man's cosmological views from prehistoric times up through the Renaissance. It covers Egypt, Babylonia, early Greece, Alexandria, the Middle Ages, Copernicus, Tycho Brahe, Kepler, and many others. Epicycles and other complex theories of positional astronomy are explained in terms nearly everyone will find clear and easy to understand. "Standard reference on Greek astronomy and the Copernican revolution," SKY AND TELE-SCOPE. Bibliography. 21 diagrams. Index. xvii + 430pp. 5⅜ x 8. S79 Paperbound **$1.98**

A SHORT HISTORY OF ASTRONOMY, A. Berry. A popular standard work for over 50 years, this thorough and accurate volume covers the science from primitive times to the end of the 19th century. After the Greeks and Middle Ages, individual chapters analyze Copernicus, Brahe, Galileo, Kepler, and Newton, and the mixed reception of their startling discoveries. Post-Newtonian achievements are then discussed in unusual detail: Halley, Bradley, Lagrange, Laplace, Herschel, Bessel, etc. 2 indexes. 104 illustrations, 9 portraits. xxxi + 440pp. 5⅜ x 8. T210 Paperbound **$2.00**

PIONEERS OF SCIENCE, Sir Oliver Lodge. An authoritative, yet elementary history of science by a leading scientist and expositor. Concentrating on individuals—Copernicus, Brahe, Kepler, Galileo, Descartes, Newton, Laplace, Herschel, Lord Kelvin, and other scientists—the author presents their discoveries in historical order, adding biographical material on each man and full, specific explanations of their achievements. The full, clear discussions of the accomplishments of post-Newtonian astronomers are features seldom found in other books on the subject. Index. 120 illustrations. xv + 404pp. 5⅜ x 8. T716 Paperbound **$1.65**

THE BIRTH AND DEVELOPMENT OF THE GEOLOGICAL SCIENCES, F. D. Adams. The most complete and thorough history of the earth sciences in print. Geological thought from earliest recorded times to the end of the 19th century—covers over 300 early thinkers and systems: fossils and hypothetical explanations of them, vulcanists vs. neptunists, figured stones and paleontology, generation of stones, and similar topics. 91 illustrations, including medieval, renaissance woodcuts, etc. 632 footnotes and bibliographic notes. Index. 511pp. 5⅜ x 8. T5 Paperbound **$2.25**

THE STORY OF ALCHEMY AND EARLY CHEMISTRY, J. M. Stillman. "Add the blood of a red-haired man"—a recipe typical of the many quoted in this authoritative and readable history of the strange beliefs and practices of the alchemists. Concise studies of every leading figure in alchemy and early chemistry through Lavoisier, in this curious epic of superstition and true science, constructed from scores of rare and difficult Greek, Latin, German, and French texts. Foreword by S. W. Young. 246-item bibliography. Index. xiii + 566pp. 5⅜ x 8. S628 Paperbound **$2.45**

HISTORY OF MATHEMATICS, D. E. Smith. Most comprehensive non-technical history of math in English. Discusses the lives and works of over a thousand major and minor figures, from Euclid to Descartes, Gauss, and Riemann. Vol. I: A chronological examination, from primitive concepts through Egypt, Babylonia, Greece, the Orient, Rome, the Middle Ages, the Renaissance, and up to 1900. Vol. 2: The development of ideas in specific fields and problems, up through elementary calculus. Two volumes, total of 510 illustrations, 1355pp. 5⅜ x 8. Set boxed in attractive container. T429,430 Paperbound the set **$5.00**

Nature

AN INTRODUCTION TO BIRD LIFE FOR BIRD WATCHERS, Aretas A. Saunders. Fine, readable introduction to birdwatching. Includes a great deal of basic information on about 160 different varieties of wild birds—elementary facts not easily found elsewhere. Complete guide to identification procedures, methods of observation, important habits of birds, finding nests, food, etc. "Could make bird watchers of readers who never suspected they were vulnerable to that particular virus," CHICAGO SUNDAY TRIBUNE. Unabridged, corrected edition. Bibliography. Index. 22 line drawings by D. D'Ostilio. Formerly "The Lives of Wild Birds." 256pp. 5⅜ x 8½. **T1139 Paperbound $1.00**

LIFE HISTORIES OF NORTH AMERICAN BIRDS, Arthur Cleveland Bent. Bent's historic, all-encompassing series on North American birds, originally produced under the auspices of the Smithsonian Institution, now being republished in its entirety by Dover Publications. The twenty-volume collection forms the most comprehensive, most complete, most-used source of information in existence. Each study describes in detail the characteristics, range, distribution, habits, migratory patterns, courtship procedures, plumage, eggs, voice, enemies, etc. of the different species and subspecies of the birds that inhabit our continent, utilizing reports of hundreds of contemporary observers as well as the writings of the great naturalists of the past. Invaluable to the ornithologist, conservationist, amateur naturalist, and birdwatcher. All books in the series contain numerous photographs to provide handy guides for identification and study.

LIFE HISTORIES OF NORTH AMERICAN BIRDS OF PREY. Including hawks, eagles, falcons, buzzards, condors, owls, etc. Index. Bibliographies of 923 items. 197 full-page plates containing close to 400 photographs. Total of 907pp. 5⅜ x 8½.
Vol. I: T931 Paperbound **$2.50**
Vol. II: T932 Paperbound **$2.50**
The set Paperbound **$5.00**

LIFE HISTORIES OF NORTH AMERICAN SHORE BIRDS. Including 81 varieties of such birds as sandpipers, woodcocks, snipes, phalaropes, oyster catchers, and many others. Index for each volume. Bibliographies of 449 entries. 121 full-page plates including over 200 photographs. Total of 860 pp. 5⅜ x 8½.
Vol. I: T933 Paperbound **$2.35**
Vol. II: T934 Paperbound **$2.35**
The set Paperbound **$4.70**

LIFE HISTORIES OF NORTH AMERICAN WILD FOWL. Including 73 varieties of ducks, geese, mergansers, swans, etc. Index for each volume. Bibliographies of 268 items. 106 full-page plates containing close to 200 photographs. Total of 685pp. 5⅜ x 8½.
Vol. I: T285 Paperbound **$2.50**
Vol. II: T286 Paperbound **$2.50**
The set Paperbound **$5.00**

LIFE HISTORIES OF NORTH AMERICAN GULLS AND TERNS. 50 different varieties of gulls and terns. Index. Bibliography. 93 plates including 149 photographs. xii + 337pp. 5⅜ x 8½.
T1029 Paperbound **$2.75**

LIFE HISTORIES OF NORTH AMERICAN GALLINACEOUS BIRDS. Including partridge, quail, grouse, pheasant, pigeons, doves, and others. Index. Bibliography. 93 full-page plates including 170 photographs. xiii + 490pp. 5⅜ x 8½. **T1028 Paperbound $2.75**

THE MALAY ARCHIPELAGO, Alfred Russel Wallace. The record of the explorations (8 years, 14,000 miles) of the Malay Archipelago by a great scientific observer. A contemporary of Darwin, Wallace independently arrived at the concept of evolution by natural selection, applied the new theories of evolution to later genetic discoveries, and made significant contributions to biology, zoology, and botany. This work is still one of the classics of natural history and travel. It contains the author's reports of the different native peoples of the islands, descriptions of the island groupings, his accounts of the animals, birds, and insects that flourished in this area. The reader is carried through strange lands, alien cultures, and new theories, and will share in an exciting, unrivalled travel experience. Unabridged reprint of the 1922 edition, with 62 drawings and maps. 3 appendices, one on cranial measurements. xvii + 515pp. 5⅜ x 8. **T187 Paperbound $2.00**

THE TRAVELS OF WILLIAM BARTRAM, edited by Mark Van Doren. This famous source-book of American anthropology, natural history, geography is the record kept by Bartram in the 1770's, on travels through the wilderness of Florida, Georgia, the Carolinas. Containing accurate and beautiful descriptions of Indians, settlers, fauna, flora, it is one of the finest pieces of Americana ever written. Introduction by Mark Van Doren. 13 original illustrations. Index. 448pp. 5⅜ x 8. **T13 Paperbound $2.00**

COMMON SPIDERS OF THE UNITED STATES, J. H. Emerton. Only non-technical, but thorough, reliable guide to spiders for the layman. Over 200 spiders from all parts of the country, arranged by scientific classification, are identified by shape and color, number of eyes, habitat and range, habits, etc. Full text, 501 line drawings and photographs, and valuable introduction explain webs, poisons, threads, capturing and preserving spiders, etc. Index. New synoptic key by S. W. Frost. xxiv + 225pp. 5⅜ x 8. **T223 Paperbound $1.45**

CATALOGUE OF DOVER BOOKS

LIFE HISTORIES OF NORTH AMERICAN MARSH BIRDS. A wealth of data on 54 different kinds of marsh bird (flamingo, ibis, bittern, heron, egret, crane, crake, rail, coot, etc.). Index. Bibliography. 98 full-page plates containing 179 black-and-white photographs. xiv + 392pp. 5⅜ x 8½. **T1082 Paperbound $2.75**

LIFE HISTORIES OF NORTH AMERICAN DIVING BIRDS. Thirty-six different diving birds including grebe, loon, auk, murre, puffin, and the like. Index. Bibliography. 55 full-page plates (92 photographs). xiv + 239pp. 5⅜ x 8½. **T1091 Paperbound $2.75**

LIFE HISTORIES OF NORTH AMERICAN WOOD WARBLERS. Covers about 58 types. Index. Bibliography. 83 full-page plates containing 125 black-and-white photographs. xi + 734pp. of text. 5⅜ x 8½.
Vol. I: **T1153 Paperbound $2.50**
Vol. II: **T1154 Paperbound $2.50**
The set Paperbound **$5.00**

LIFE HISTORIES OF NORTH AMERICAN FLYCATCHERS, LARKS, SWALLOWS, AND THEIR ALLIES. Complete information on about 78 different varieties. Index. Bibliography. 70 full-page plates (117 photographs). xi + 555pp. of text. 5⅜ x 8½. **T1090 Paperbound $2.75**

AMERICAN WILDLIFE, AND PLANTS: A GUIDE TO WILDLIFE FOOD HABITS, A. C. Martin, H. S. Zim, A. L. Nelson. Result of 75 years of research by U. S. Fish and Wildlife Service into food and feeding habits of more than 1,000 species of birds and mammals, their distribution in America, migratory habits, and the most important plant-animal relationships. Treats over 300 common species of birds, fur and game animals, small mammals, hoofed browsers, fish, amphibians, reptiles by group, giving data on their food, ranges, habits and economies. Also focuses on the different genera of plants that furnish food for our wildlife, animals that use them, and their value. Only thorough study of its kind in existence. "Of immense value to sportsmen, naturalists, bird students, foresters, landscape architects, botanists," NATURE. "Undoubtedly an essential handbook," SCIENTIFIC MONTHLY. Unabridged republication of 1951 edition. Over 600 illustrations, maps, etc. Classified bibliography. Index. x + 500pp. 5⅜ x 8. **T793 Paperbound $2.25**

HOW TO KNOW THE WILD FLOWERS, Mrs. Wm. Starr Dana. A Guide to the names, haunts, and habits of wild flowers. Well-known classic of nature lore. Informative and delightful. Plants classified by color and season of their typical flowers for easy identification. Thorough coverage of more than 1,000 important flowering, berry-bearing and foliage plants of Eastern and Central United States and Canada. Complete botanical information about each important plant. Also history, uses, folklore, habitat, etc. Nomenclature modernized by C. J. Hylander. 174 full-page illustrations by Marion Satterlee. xii + 481pp. 5⅜ x 8½.
T332 Paperbound $1.85

HOW PLANTS GET THEIR NAMES, L. H. Bailey. Introduction to botanical nomenclature for the horticulturist and garden-lover. Discussions of Carl Linnaeus, "father of botany," and analysis of his definitions of genus and species, a brief history of the science before Linnaean systematization, a chapter on plant identification, a mine of information on the rules of nomenclature and Latin stems and word-endings used in botanical nomenclature, with pronunciation guides. An important section contains a full list of generic terms of horticultural literature and common Latin words and their English botanical applications and meanings. "Written with knowledge and authority, charm and eloquence and poetic imagination on the varied aspects of the author's specialty," New York Times. 11 illustrations. vi + 181pp. 5⅜ x 8½. **T796 Paperbound $1.25**

THE CACTACEAE: DESCRIPTIONS AND ILLUSTRATIONS OF PLANTS OF THE CACTUS FAMILY, N. L. Britton and J. N. Rose. Definitive study of plants of the Cactus Family. The authors devoted more than 15 years of research to this monumental task and produced an exhaustive, rigorously scientific account never likely to be superseded. 3 major classifications, or tribes, are recognized, under which they arrange and describe in full detail 124 genera and 1,235 species of cactus from all over the world. Complete data on each species: leaves, flowers, seeds, fruit, distribution, growth, spines, stem structure, economic uses, etc. In addition, 125 keys facilitate identification of genera and species. For teachers and students of botany and forestry, naturalists, conservationists, and nature lovers, this is an indispensable work. Unabridged republication of second (1937) edition. First edition originally published under the auspices of the Carnegie Institution, Washington, D.C. 4 vols. bound as 2. 1279 illustrations, photographs, sketches, etc. 137 plates. Total of xxvii + 1039pp. 8 x 10¼. **T771 Clothbound, 2-volume set $20.00**

GUIDE TO SOUTHERN TREES, Elwood S. and J. George Harrar. A handy, comprehensive 700-page manual with numerous illustrations and information on more than 350 different kinds of trees, covering the entire area south of the Mason-Dixon line from the Atlantic Ocean to the Florida Keys and western Texas. Descriptions range from the common pine, cypress, walnut, beech, and elm to such rare species as Franklinia, etc. A mine of information on leaves, flowers, twigs, bark, fruit, distribution etc. of each kind of tree. Eminently readable, written in non-technical language, it is an indispensable handbook for all lovers of the outdoors. Revised edition. Index. 81-item bibliography. Glossary. 200 full-page illustrations. ix + 709pp. 4⅝ x 6⅜. **T945 Paperbound $2.25**

CATALOGUE OF DOVER BOOKS

WESTERN FOREST TREES, James B. Berry. For years a standard guide to the trees of the Western United States. Covers over 70 different subspecies, ranging from the Pacific shores to western South Dakota, New Mexico, etc. Much information on range and distribution, growth habits, appearance, leaves, bark, fruit, twigs, etc. for each tree discussed, plus material on wood of the trees and its uses. Basic division (Trees with needle-like leaves, scale-like leaves, and compound, lobed or divided, and simple broadleaf trees), along with almost 100 illustrations (mostly full-size) of buds, leaves, etc., aids in easy identification of just about any tree of the area. Many subsidiary keys. Revised edition. Introduction. 12 photos. 85 illustrations by Mary E. Eaton. Index. xii + 212pp. 5⅜ x 8.
T1138 Paperbound **$1.35**

MANUAL OF THE TREES OF NORTH AMERICA (EXCLUSIVE OF MEXICO), Charles Sprague Sargent. The magnum opus of the greatest American dendrologist. Based on 44 years of original research, this monumental work is still the most comprehensive and reliable sourcebook on the subject. Includes 185 genera and 717 species of trees (and many shrubs) found in the U.S., Canada, and Alaska. 783 illustrative drawings by C. E. Faxon and Mary W. Gill. An all-encompassing lifetime reference book for students, teachers of botany and forestry, naturalists, conservationists, and all nature lovers. Includes an 11-page analytical key to genera to help the beginner locate any tree by its leaf characteristics. Within the text over 100 further keys aid in easy identification. Synopsis of families. Glossary. Index. 783 illustrations, 1 map. Total of 1 + 891pp. 5⅜ x 8.
T277 Vol. I Paperbound **$2.25**
T278 Vol. II Paperbound **$2.25**
The set **$4.50**

TREES OF THE EASTERN AND CENTRAL UNITED STATES AND CANADA, W. M. Harlow, Professor of Wood Technology, College of Forestry, State University of N. Y., Syracuse, N. Y. This middle-level text is a serious work covering more than 140 native trees and important escapes, with information on general appearance, growth habit, leaf forms, flowers, fruit, bark, and other features. Commercial use, distribution, habitat, and woodlore are also given. Keys within the text enable you to locate various species with ease. With this book you can identify at sight almost any tree you are likely to encounter; you will know which trees have edible fruit, which are suitable for house planting, and much other useful and interesting information. More than 600 photographs and figures. xiii + 288pp. 4⅝ x 6½.
T395 Paperbound **$1.35**

FRUIT KEY AND TWIG KEY TO TREES AND SHRUBS (FRUIT KEY TO NORTHEASTERN TREES, TWIG TREE TO DECIDUOUS WOODY PLANTS OF EASTERN NORTH AMERICA), W. M. Harlow. The only guides with photographs of every twig and fruit described—especially valuable to the novice. The fruit key (both deciduous trees and evergreens) has an introduction explaining seeding, organs involved, fruit types and habits. The twig key introduction treats growth and morphology. In the keys proper, identification is easy and almost automatic. This exceptional work, widely used in university courses, is especially useful for identification in winter, or from the fruit or seed only. Over 350 photos, up to 3 times natural size. Bibliography, glossary, index of common and scientific names, in each key. xvii + 125pp. 5⅝ x 8⅜.
T511 Paperbound **$1.25**

HOW TO KNOW THE FERNS, F. T. Parsons. Ferns, among our most lovely native plants, are all too little known. This modern classic of nature lore will enable the layman to identify any American fern he is likely to come across. After an introduction on the structure and life of ferns, the 57 most important ferns are fully pictured and described (arranged upon a simple identification key). Index of Latin and English names. 61 illustrations and 42 full-page plates. xiv + 215pp. 5⅜ x 8.
T740 Paperbound **$1.35**

OUR SMALL NATIVE ANIMALS: THEIR HABITS AND CARE, R. Snedigar, Curator of Reptiles, Chicago Zoological Park. An unusual nature handbook containing all the vital facts of habitat, distribution, foods, and special habits in brief life histories of 114 different species of squirrels, chipmunks, rodents, larger mammals, birds, amphibians, lizards and snakes. Liberally sprinkled with first-hand anecdotes. A wealth of information on capturing and caring for these animals: proper pens and cages, correct diet, curing diseases, special equipment required, etc. Addressed to the teacher interested in classroom demonstrations, the camp director, and to anyone who ever wanted a small animal for a pet. Revised edition, New preface. Index. 62 halftones. 14 line drawings. xviii + 296pp. 5⅜ x 8⅛.
T1022 Paperbound **$1.75**

INSECT LIFE AND INSECT NATURAL HISTORY, S. W. Frost. Unusual for emphasizing habits, social life, and ecological relations of insects, rather than more academic aspects of classification and morphology. Prof. Frost's enthusiasm and knowledge are everywhere evident as he discusses insect associations, and specialized habits like leaf-mining, leaf-rolling, and case-making, the gall insects, the boring insects, aquatic insects, etc. He examines all sorts of matters not usually covered in general works, such as: insects as human food; insect music and musicians; insect response to electric and radio waves; use of insects in art and literature. The admirably executed purpose of this book, which covers the middle ground between elementary treatment and scholarly monographs, is to excite the reader to observe for himself. Over 700 illustrations. Extensive bibliography. x + 524pp. 5⅜ x 8.
T517 Paperbound **$2.25**

Philosophy, Religion

GUIDE TO PHILOSOPHY, C. E. M. Joad. A modern classic which examines many crucial problems which man has pondered through the ages: Does free will exist? Is there plan in the universe? How do we know and validate our knowledge? Such opposed solutions as subjective Idealism and realism, chance and teleology, vitalism and logical positivism, are evaluated and the contributions of the great philosophers from the Greeks to moderns like Russell, Whitehead, and others, are considered in the context of each problem. "The finest introduction," BOSTON TRANSCRIPT. Index. Classified bibliography. 592pp. 5⅜ x 8.
T297 Paperbound **$2.00**

HISTORY OF ANCIENT PHILOSOPHY, W. Windelband. One of the clearest, most accurate comprehensive surveys of Greek and Roman philosophy. Discusses ancient philosophy in general, intellectual life in Greece in the 7th and 6th centuries B.C., Thales, Anaximander, Anaximenes, Heraclitus, the Eleatics, Empedocles, Anaxagoras, Leucippus, the Pythagoreans, the Sophists, Socrates, Democritus (20 pages), Plato (50 pages), Aristotle (70 pages), the Peripatetics, Stoics, Epicureans, Sceptics, Neo-platonists, Christian Apologists, etc. 2nd German edition translated by H. E. Cushman. xv + 393pp. 5⅜ x 8.
T357 Paperbound **$1.85**

ILLUSTRATIONS OF THE HISTORY OF MEDIEVAL THOUGHT AND LEARNING, R. L. Poole. Basic analysis of the thought and lives of the leading philosophers and ecclesiastics from the 8th to the 14th century—Abailard, Ockham, Wycliffe, Marsiglio of Padua, and many other great thinkers who carried the torch of Western culture and learning through the "Dark Ages": political, religious, and metaphysical views. Long a standard work for scholars and one of the best introductions to medieval thought for beginners. Index. 10 Appendices. xiii + 327pp. 5⅜ x 8.
T674 Paperbound **$1.85**

PHILOSOPHY AND CIVILIZATION IN THE MIDDLE AGES, M. de Wulf. This semi-popular survey covers aspects of medieval intellectual life such as religion, philosophy, science, the arts, etc. It also covers feudalism vs. Catholicism, rise of the universities, mendicant orders, monastic centers, and similar topics. Unabridged. Bibliography. Index. viii + 320pp. 5⅜ x 8.
T284 Paperbound **$1.85**

AN INTRODUCTION TO SCHOLASTIC PHILOSOPHY, Prof. M. de Wulf. Formerly entitled SCHOLASTICISM OLD AND NEW, this volume examines the central scholastic tradition from St. Anselm, Albertus Magnus, Thomas Aquinas, up to Suarez in the 17th century. The relation of scholasticism to ancient and medieval philosophy and science in general is clear and easily followed. The second part of the book considers the modern revival of scholasticism, the Louvain position, relations with Kantianism and Positivism. Unabridged. xvi + 271pp. 5⅜ x 8.
T296 Clothbound **$3.50**
T283 Paperbound **$1.75**

A HISTORY OF MODERN PHILOSOPHY, H. Höffding. An exceptionally clear and detailed coverage of western philosophy from the Renaissance to the end of the 19th century. Major and minor men such as Pomponazzi, Bodin, Boehme, Telesius, Bruno, Copernicus, da Vinci, Kepler, Galileo, Bacon, Descartes, Hobbes, Spinoza, Leibniz, Wolff, Locke, Newton, Berkeley, Hume, Erasmus, Montesquieu, Voltaire, Diderot, Rousseau, Lessing, Kant, Herder, Fichte, Schelling, Hegel, Schopenhauer, Comte, Mill, Darwin, Spencer, Hartmann, Lange, and many others, are discussed in terms of theory of knowledge, logic, cosmology, and psychology. Index. 2 volumes, total of 1159pp. 5⅜ x 8.
T117 Vol. 1, Paperbound **$2.25**
T118 Vol. 2, Paperbound **$2.25**

ARISTOTLE, A. E. Taylor. A brilliant, searching non-technical account of Aristotle and his thought written by a foremost Platonist. It covers the life and works of Aristotle; classification of the sciences; logic; first philosophy; matter and form; causes; motion and eternity; God; physics; metaphysics; and similar topics. Bibliography. New Index compiled for this edition. 128pp. 5⅜ x 8.
T280 Paperbound **$1.00**

THE SYSTEM OF THOMAS AQUINAS, M. de Wulf. Leading Neo-Thomist, one of founders of University of Louvain, gives concise exposition to central doctrines of Aquinas, as a means toward determining his value to modern philosophy, religion. Formerly "Medieval Philosophy Illustrated from the System of Thomas Aquinas." Trans. by E. Messenger. Introduction. 151pp. 5⅜ x 8.
T568 Paperbound **$1.25**

LEIBNIZ, H. W. Carr. Most stimulating middle-level coverage of basic philosophical thought of Leibniz. Easily understood discussion, analysis of major works: "Theodicy," "Principles of Nature and Grace," "Monadology"; Leibniz's influence; intellectual growth; correspondence; disputes with Bayle, Malebranche, Newton; importance of his thought today, with reinterpretation in modern terminology. "Power and mastery," London Times. Bibliography. Index. 226pp. 5⅜ x 8.
T624 Paperbound **$1.35**

CATALOGUE OF DOVER BOOKS

THE SENSE OF BEAUTY, G. Santayana. A revelation of the beauty of language as well as an important philosophic treatise, this work studies the "why, when, and how beauty appears, what conditions an object must fulfill to be beautiful, what elements of our nature make us sensible of beauty, and what the relation is between the constitution of the object and the excitement of our susceptibility." "It is doubtful if a better treatment of the subject has since been published," PEABODY JOURNAL. Index. ix + 275pp. 5⅜ x 8.
T238 Paperbound **$1.00**

PROBLEMS OF ETHICS, Moritz Schlick. The renowned leader of the "Vienna Circle" applies the logical positivist approach to a wide variety of ethical problems: the source and means of attaining knowledge, the formal and material characteristics of the good, moral norms and principles, absolute vs. relative values, free will and responsibility, comparative importance of pleasure and suffering as ethical values, etc. Disarmingly simple and straightforward despite complexity of subject. First English translation, authorized by author before his death, of a thirty-year old classic. Translated and with an introduction by David Rynin. Index. Foreword by Prof. George P. Adams. xxi + 209pp. 5⅜ x 8. T946 Paperbound **$1.45**

AN INTRODUCTION TO EXISTENTIALISM, Robert G. Olson. A new and indispensable guide to one of the major thought systems of our century, the movement that is central to the thinking of some of the most creative figures of the past hundred years. Stresses Heidegger and Sartre, with careful and objective examination of the existentialist position, values—freedom of choice, individual dignity, personal love, creative effort—and answers to the eternal questions of the human condition. Scholarly, unbiased, analytic, unlike most studies of this difficult subject, Prof. Olson's book is aimed at the student of philosophy as well as at the reader with no formal training who is looking for an absorbing, accessible, and thorough introduction to the basic texts. Index. xv + 221pp. 5⅜ x 8½. T55 Paperbound **$1.50**

SYMBOLIC LOGIC, C. I. Lewis and C. H. Langford. Since first publication in 1932, this has been among most frequently cited works on symbolic logic. Still one of the best introductions both for beginners and for mathematicians, philosophers. First part covers basic topics which easily lend themselves to beginning study. Second part is rigorous, thorough development of logistic method, examination of some of most difficult and abstract aspects of symbolic logic, including modal logic, logical paradoxes, many-valued logic, with Prof. Lewis' own contributions. 2nd revised (corrected) edition. 3 appendixes, one new to this edition. 524pp. 5⅜ x 8. S170 Paperbound **$2.00**

WHITEHEAD'S PHILOSOPHY OF CIVILIZATION, A. H. Johnson. A leading authority on Alfred North Whitehead synthesizes the great philosopher's thought on civilization, scattered throughout various writings, into unified whole. Analysis of Whitehead's general definition of civilization, his reflections on history and influences on its development, his religion, including his analysis of Christianity, concept of solitariness as first requirement of personal religion, and so on. Other chapters cover views on minority groups, society, civil liberties, education. Also critical comments on Whitehead's philosophy. Written with general reader in mind. A perceptive introduction to important area of the thought of a leading philosopher of our century. Revised index and bibliography. xii + 211pp. 5⅜ x 8½.
T996 Paperbound **$1.50**

WHITEHEAD'S THEORY OF REALITY, A. H. Johnson. Introductory outline of Whitehead's theory of actual entities, the heart of his philosophy of reality, followed by his views on nature of God, philosophy of mind, theory of value (truth, beauty, goodness and their opposites), analyses of other philosophers, attitude toward science. A perspicacious lucid introduction by author of dissertation on Whitehead, written under the subject's supervision at Harvard. Good basic view for beginning students of philosophy and for those who are simply interested in important contemporary ideas. Revised index and bibliography. xiii + 267pp. 5⅜ x 8½.
T989 Paperbound **$1.50**

MIND AND THE WORLD-ORDER, C. I. Lewis. Building upon the work of Peirce, James, and Dewey, Professor Lewis outlines a theory of knowledge in terms of "conceptual pragmatism." Dividing truth into abstract mathematical certainty and empirical truth, the author demonstrates that the traditional understanding of the a priori must be abandoned. Detailed analyses of philosophy, metaphysics, method, the "given" in experience, knowledge of objects, nature of the a priori, experience and order, and many others. Appendices. xiv + 446pp. 5⅜ x 8. T359 Paperbound **$2.25**

SCEPTICISM AND ANIMAL FAITH, G. Santayana. To eliminate difficulties in the traditional theory of knowledge, Santayana distinguishes between the independent existence of objects and the essence our mind attributes to them. Scepticism is thereby established as a form of belief, and animal faith is shown to be a necessary condition of knowledge. Belief, classical idealism, intuition, memory, symbols, literary psychology, and much more, discussed with unusual clarity and depth. Index. xii + 314pp. 5⅜ x 8. T235 Clothbound **$3.50**
T236 Paperbound **$1.50**

LANGUAGE AND MYTH, E. Cassirer. Analyzing the non-rational thought processes which go to make up culture, Cassirer demonstrates that beneath both language and myth there lies a dominant unconscious "grammar" of experience whose categories and canons are not those of logical thought. His analyses of seemingly diverse phenomena such as Indian metaphysics, the Melanesian "mana," the Naturphilosophie of Schelling, modern poetry, etc., are profound without being pedantic. Introduction and translation by Susanne Langer. Index. x + 103pp. 5⅜ x 8. T51 Paperbound **$1.25**

CATALOGUE OF DOVER BOOKS

THE ANALYSIS OF MATTER, Bertrand Russell. A classic which has retained its importance in understanding the relation between modern physical theory and human perception. Logical analysis of physics, prerelativity physics, causality, scientific inference, Weyl's theory, tensors, invariants and physical interpretations, periodicity, and much more is treated with Russell's usual brilliance. "Masterly piece of clear thinking and clear writing," NATION AND ATHENAEUM. "Most thorough treatment of the subject," THE NATION. Introduction. Index. 8 figures. viii + 408pp. 5⅜ x 8. S231 Paperbound **$1.95**

CONCEPTUAL THINKING (A LOGICAL INQUIRY), S. Körner. Discusses origin, use of general concepts on which language is based, and the light they shed on basic philosophical questions. Rigorously examines how different concepts are related; how they are linked to experience; problems in the field of contact between exact logical, mathematical, and scientific concepts, and the inexactness of everyday experience (studied at length). This work elaborates many new approaches to the traditional problems of philosophy—epistemology, value theories, metaphysics, aesthetics, morality. "Rare originality . . . brings a new rigour into philosophical argument," Philosophical Quarterly. New corrected second edition. Index. viii + 301pp. 5⅜ x 8 T516 Paperbound **$1.75**

INTRODUCTION TO SYMBOLIC LOGIC, S. Langer. No special knowledge of math required — probably the clearest book ever written on symbolic logic, suitable for the layman, general scientist, and philosopher. You start with simple symbols and advance to a knowledge of the Boole-Schroeder and Russell-Whitehead systems. Forms, logical structure, classes, the calculus of propositions, logic of the syllogism, etc., are all covered. "One of the clearest and simplest introductions," MATHEMATICS GAZETTE. Second enlarged, revised edition. 368pp. 5⅜ x 8. S164 Paperbound **$1.75**

LANGUAGE, TRUTH AND LOGIC, A. J. Ayer. A clear, careful analysis of the basic ideas of Logical Positivism. Building on the work of Schlick, Russell, Carnap, and the Viennese School, Mr. Ayer develops a detailed exposition of the nature of philosophy, science, and metaphysics; the Self and the World; logic and common sense, and other philosophic concepts. An aid to clarity of thought as well as the first full-length development of Logical Positivism in English. Introduction by Bertrand Russell. Index. 160pp. 5⅜ x 8. T10 Paperbound **$1.25**

ESSAYS IN EXPERIMENTAL LOGIC, J. Dewey. Based upon the theory that knowledge implies a judgment which in turn implies an inquiry, these papers consider the inquiry stage in terms of: the relationship of thought and subject matter, antecedents of thought, data and meanings. 3 papers examine Bertrand Russell's thought, while 2 others discuss pragmatism and a final essay presents a new theory of the logic of values. Index. viii + 444pp. 5⅜ x 8. T73 Paperbound **$1.95**

TRAGIC SENSE OF LIFE, M. de Unamuno. The acknowledged masterpiece of one of Spain's most influential thinkers. Between the despair at the inevitable death of man and all his works and the desire for something better, Unamuno finds that "saving incertitude" that alone can console us. This dynamic appraisal of man's faith in God and in himself has been called "a masterpiece" by the ENCYCLOPAEDIA BRITANNICA. xxx + 332pp. 5⅜ x 8. T257 Paperbound **$2.00**

HISTORY OF DOGMA, A. Harnack. Adolph Harnack, who died in 1930, was perhaps the greatest Church historian of all time. In this epoch-making history, which has never been surpassed in comprehensiveness and wealth of learning, he traces the development of the authoritative Christian doctrinal system from its first crystallization in the 4th century down through the Reformation, including also a brief survey of the later developments through the Infallibility decree of 1870. He reveals the enormous influence of Greek thought on the early Fathers, and discusses such topics as the Apologists, the great councils, Manichaeism, the historical position of Augustine, the medieval opposition to indulgences, the rise of Protestantism, the relations of Luther's doctrines with modern tendencies of thought, and much more. "Monumental work; still the most valuable history of dogma . . . luminous analysis of the problems . . . abounds in suggestion and stimulus and can be neglected by no one who desires to understand the history of thought in this most important field," Dutcher's Guide to Historical Literature. Translated by Neil Buchanan. Index. Unabridged reprint in 4 volumes. Vol I: Beginnings to the Gnostics and Marcion. Vol II & III: 2nd century to the 4th century Fathers. Vol IV & V: 4th century Councils to the Carlovingian Renaissance. Vol VI & VII: Period of Clugny (c. 1000) to the Reformation, and after. Total of cii + 2407pp. 5⅜ x 8.

T904 Vol I	Paperbound **$2.50**
T905 Vol II & III	Paperbound **$2.50**
T906 Vol IV & V	Paperbound **$2.50**
T907 Vol VI & VII	Paperbound **$2.50**
	The set **$10.00**

THE GUIDE FOR THE PERPLEXED, Maimonides. One of the great philosophical works of all time and a necessity for everyone interested in the philosophy of the Middle Ages in the Jewish, Christian, and Moslem traditions. Maimonides develops a common meeting-point for the Old Testament and the Aristotelian thought which pervaded the medieval world. His ideas and methods predate such scholastics as Aquinas and Scotus and throw light on the entire problem of philosophy or science vs. religion. 2nd revised edition. Complete unabridged Friedländer translation. 55 page introduction to Maimonides's life, period, etc., with an important summary of the GUIDE. Index. lix + 414pp. 5⅜ x 8. T351 Paperbound **$2.00**

Orientalia

ORIENTAL RELIGIONS IN ROMAN PAGANISM, F. Cumont. A study of the cultural meeting of east and west in the Early Roman Empire. It covers the most important eastern religions of the time from their first appearance in Rome, 204 B.C., when the Great Mother of the Gods was first brought over from Syria. The ecstatic cults of Syria and Phrygia — Cybele, Attis, Adonis, their orgies and mutilatory rites; the mysteries of Egypt — Serapis, Isis, Osiris, the dualism of Persia, the elevation of cosmic evil to equal stature with the deity, Mithra; worship of Hermes Trismegistus; Ishtar, Astarte; the magic of the ancient Near East, etc. Introduction. 55pp. of notes; extensive bibliography. Index. xxiv + 298pp. 5⅜ x 8.
T321 Paperbound $1.75

THE MYSTERIES OF MITHRA, F. Cumont. The definitive coverage of a great ideological struggle between the west and the orient in the first centuries of the Christian era. The origin of Mithraism, a Persian mystery religion, and its association with the Roman army is discussed in detail. Then utilizing fragmentary monuments and texts, in one of the greatest feats of scholarly detection, Dr. Cumont reconstructs the mystery teachings and secret doctrines, the hidden organization and cult of Mithra. Mithraic art is discussed, analyzed, and depicted in 70 illustrations. 239pp. 5⅜ x 8.
T323 Paperbound $1.85

CHRISTIAN AND ORIENTAL PHILOSOPHY OF ART, A. K. Coomaraswamy. A unique fusion of philosopher, orientalist, art historian, and linguist, the author discusses such matters as: the true function of aesthetics in art, the importance of symbolism, intellectual and philosophic backgrounds, the role of traditional culture in enriching art, common factors in all great art, the nature of medieval art, the nature of folklore, the beauty of mathematics, and similar topics. 2 illustrations. Bibliography. 148pp. 5⅜ x 8.
T378 Paperbound $1.25

TRANSFORMATION OF NATURE IN ART, A. K. Coomaraswamy. Unabridged reissue of a basic work upon Asiatic religious art and philosophy of religion. The theory of religious art in Asia and Medieval Europe (exemplified by Meister Eckhart) is analyzed and developed. Detailed consideration is given to Indian medieval aesthetic manuals, symbolic language in philosophy, the origin and use of images in India, and many other fascinating and little known topics. Glossaries of Sanskrit and Chinese terms. Bibliography. 41pp. of notes. 245pp. 5⅜ x 8.
T368 Paperbound $1.75

BUDDHIST LOGIC, F.Th. Stcherbatsky. A study of an important part of Buddhism usually ignored by other books on the subject: the Mahayana buddhistic logic of the school of Dignaga and his followers. First vol. devoted to history of Indian logic with Central Asian continuations, detailed exposition of Dignaga system, including theory of knowledge, the sensible world (causation, perception, ultimate reality) and mental world (judgment, inference, logical fallacies, the syllogism), reality of external world, and negation (law of contradiction, universals, dialectic). Vol. II contains translation of Dharmakirti's Nyayabindu with Dharmamottara's commentary. Appendices cover translations of Tibetan treatises on logic, Hindu attacks on Buddhist logic, etc. The basic work, one of the products of the great St. Petersburg school of Indian studies. Written clearly and with an awareness of Western philosophy and logic; meant for the Asian specialist and for the general reader with only a minimum of background. Vol. I, xli + 559pp. Vol. II, viii + 468pp. 5⅜ x 8½.
T955 Vol. I Paperbound $2.35
T956 Vol. II Paperbound $2.35
The set $4.70

THE TEXTS OF TAOISM. The first inexpensive edition of the complete James Legge translations of the Tao Te King and the writings of Chinese mystic Chuang Tse. Also contains several shorter treatises: the T'ai Shang Tractate of Actions and Their Retributions; the King Kang King, or Classic of Purity; the Yin Fu King, or Classic of the Harmony of the Seen and Unseen; the Yu Shu King, or Classic of the Pivot of Jade; and the Hsia Yung King, or Classic of the Directory for a Day. While there are other translations of the Tao Te King, this is the only translation of Chuang Tse and much of other material. Extensive introduction discusses differences between Taoism, Buddhism, Confucianism; authenticity and arrangement of Tao Te King and writings of Chuang Tse; the meaning of the Tao and basic tenets of Taoism; historical accounts of Lao-tse and followers; other pertinent matters. Clarifying notes incorporated into text. Originally published as Volumes 39, 40 of SACRED BOOKS OF THE EAST series, this has long been recognized as an indispensible collection. Sinologists, philosophers, historians of religion will of course be interested and anyone with an elementary course in Oriental religion or philosophy will understand and profit from these writings. Index. Appendix analyzing thought of Chuang Tse. Vol. I, xxiii + 396pp. Vol. II, viii + 340pp. 5⅜ x 8½.
T990 Vol. I Paperbound $2.00
T991 Vol. II Paperbound $2.00

CATALOGUE OF DOVER BOOKS

EPOCHS OF CHINESE AND JAPANESE ART, Ernest T. Fenollosa. Although this classic of art history was written before the archeological discovery of Shang and Chou civilizations, it is still in many respects the finest detailed study of Chinese and Japanese art available in English. It is very wide in range, covering sculpture, carving, painting, metal work, ceramics, textiles, graphic arts and other areas, and it considers both religious and secular art, including the Japanese woodcut. Its greatest strength, however, lies in its extremely full, detailed, insight-laden discussion of historical and cultural background, and in its analysis of the religious and philosophical implications of art works. It is also a brilliant stylistic achievement, written with enthusiasm and verve, which can be enjoyed and read with profit by both the Orientalist and the general reader who is interested in art. Index. Glossary of proper names. 242 illustrations. Total of 704 pages. 5⅜ x 8½.

T364-5 Two vol. set, paperbound **$5.00**

THE VEDANTA SUTRAS OF BADARAYANA WITH COMMENTARY BY SANKARACHARYA. The definitive translation of the consummation, foremost interpretation of Upanishads. Originally part of SACRED BOOKS OF THE EAST, this two-volume translation includes exhaustive commentary and exegesis by Sankara; 128-page introduction by translator, Prof. Thibaut, that discusses background, scope and purpose of the sutras, value and importance of Sankara's interpretation; copious footnotes providing further explanations. Every serious student of Indian religion or thought, philosophers, historians of religion should read these clear, accurate translations of documents central to development of important thought systems in the East. Unabridged republication of Volumes 34, 38 of the Sacred Books of the East. Translated by George Thibaut. General index, index of quotations and of Sanskrit. Vol. I, cxxv + 448pp. Vol. II, iv + 506pp. 5⅜ x 8½.   T994 Vol. I Paperbound **$2.00**
T995 Vol. II Paperbound **$2.00**

THE UPANISHADS. The Max Müller translation of the twelve classical Upanishads available for the first time in an inexpensive format: Chandogya, Kena, Aitareya aranyaka and upanishad, Kaushitaki, Isa, Katha, Mundaka, Taittiriyaka Brhadaranyaka, Svetarasvatara. Prasna — all of the classical Upanishads of the Vedanta school—and the Maitriyana Upanishad. Originally volumes 1, 15 of SACRED BOOKS OF THE EAST series, this is still the most scholarly translation. Prof. Müller, probably most important Sanskritologist of nineteenth century, provided invaluable introduction that acquaints readers with history of Upanishad translations, age and chronology of texts. and a preface that discusses their value to Western readers. Heavily annotated. Stimulating reading for anyone with even only a basic course background in Oriental philosophy, religion, necessary to all Indologists, philosophers, religious historians. Transliteration and pronunciation guide. Vol. I, ciii + 320pp. Vol. II, liii + 350pp.

T992 Vol. I Paperbound **$2.00**
T993 Vol. II Paperbound **$2.00**
The set **$4.00**

Dover publishes books on art, music, philosophy, literature, languages, history, social sciences, psychology, handcrafts, orientalia, puzzles and entertainments, chess, pets and gardens, books explaining science, intermediate and higher mathematics mathematical physics, engineering, biological sciences, earth sciences, classics of science, etc. Write to:

Dept. catrr.
Dover Publications, Inc.
180 Varick Street, N. Y. 14, N. Y.

5J0125